In My Remaining Years

Jean Grae

In My Remaining Years

FLATIRON
BOOKS
NEW YORK

www.flatironbooks.com

Skull emoji © Eugene B-sov / Shutterstock
Post-it note art © Lyudmyla Kharlamova, AVS-Images,
Avocado_studio / Shutterstock

Designed by Donna Sinisgalli Noetzel

Library of Congress Cataloging-in-Publication Data

Names: Grae, Jean, author.
Title: In my remaining years / Jean Grae.
Description: First edition. | New York : Flatiron Books, 2025.
Identifiers: LCCN 2024042550 | ISBN 9781250857538
    (hardcover) | ISBN 9781250857552 (ebook)
Subjects: LCSH: Grae, Jean. | Rap musicians—United
    States—Biography. | LCGFT: Autobiographies.
Classification: LCC ML420.G7855 A3 2025 | DDC
    782.421649092 [B]—dc23/eng/20240916
LC record available at https://lccn.loc.gov/2024042550

Our books may be purchased in bulk for promotional,
educational, or business use. Please contact your local
bookseller or the Macmillan Corporate and Premium Sales
Department at 1-800-221-7945, extension 5442, or by email at
MacmillanSpecialMarkets@macmillan.com.

First Edition: 2025

10 9 8 7 6 5 4 3 2 1

For Tsidi and Sathima.

Nadxieli and Sylvia. Patsy and Edina. Littles and Grace Jones.

Contents

In My Remaining Years

Introduction

When I began dating my second husband, in the summer of 2014, I was in a deep depression. My mother had died just a few months before. I had lost my really nice apartment and was living in a terrible "garden level" apartment that had neither a garden, nor was there anything "level" about it. There was, however, a family of raccoons, rats, or both residing in my ceiling. It was the worst apartment I had ever lived in, even though I was working the hardest I had ever worked in my life. I was making whole albums within twenty-four-hour spans, all by myself, and then trying to sell them on the internet. Just to survive. I was determined to never go back on rap tours with any abusive people. Through tears and choked words, I had pled my case, given ultimatums, and they had not chosen my protection. So I was doing the only thing I could, making do with what I had left. But choosing my own physical and mental safety felt like a punishment.

I had been in this cycle for months, and all I wanted was to stop working for a millisecond. Just a millisecond! An early, unfair, and annoying death seemed very inevitable, or whatever is more inevitable than inevitable. I considered doing it by my own hand, but I'd tried that when I was younger and it just felt like I would be letting the unfair death win. So I kept going and waited for better circumstances to kick in. There was no way for me to maintain any semblance of a healthy lifestyle, so I drank to cope. I hardly slept and couldn't see an end to the incredibly destructive loop. I was so mad that my choices were: burn out in poverty, endure physical and mental abuse, kill myself, or wait to die in a few years. I just wanted to have a regular life and not die from hustling independent albums on social media. Killed by crafting comedic Christmas music? How embarrassing. I wished I could tell people how I felt.

It was 2014, so "speaking out" wasn't going to get me anywhere, except for further isolation. Risking not being able to sell even the small amount of work I was selling was a no. Setting myself up to be constantly berated in public and asked to talk about only abuse—another no. I was barely, rarely, ever allowed to talk about being anything other than being "female." Ooh, a "female" rapper! And never being able to discuss your craft—whatever it may be—that you love and take such painstaking measures to create, is such a slow killer. A waning degradation of will, motivation, and creativity. Not to mention, it really makes you hate what you once loved, including yourself. Also a hard "no" to being publicly honest and speaking out about being poor. These days, on social media, I still watch so many independent artists struggle through poverty silently. Doing their best to present their art and themselves in the best light possible. Most people don't notice. I know the signs.

One night, during one of our many drunken late-night conversations in our burgeoning relationship, I expressed repeatedly that I didn't have much time left. That if I was lucky, I would die sometime in my early forties and that made me *so sad*, because my plan had never been to die young from capitalism and misogyny. I had so many people left to be! Things to do! When I was little, I very intentionally and carefully planned out my future lives.

I set dates, decades, ages at which I would accomplish milestones and switch careers. Most of them involved some form of entertainment or a creative field. In my elementary school yearbook picture, when everyone had to pick a future career, I just chose ENTERTAINER. They had provided too small a box for me to list all the things I would become. And by 2014, I had done the things I was supposed to do so far—on time, which was a crazy achievement in the face of such oppressive adversity and literal violent opposition. To not only do them, but do them masterfully? Sheiiiit. Even if the lives had lasted shorter than I thought they would, I had done them. But I had finally reached a wall that was closing in on me. I was devastated at missing out on plans because people were stupid. I would never do my one-person show. I would never write my book at the age of forty-five. I would never . . . learn how to play tennis.

That night I had drawn a picture of myself in a very cute tennis outfit and shown it to my boyfriend, crying. In true Jean fashion, my chagrin at missing out on tennis was not about failing to learn the actual sport. It was about missing the opportunity to wear super cute outfits. And to carry the coolest-looking racquets. "Look," I said, through heavy droplets of vodka tears, pointing at my drawing. "Look how cute I look. It's so sad that I have to die." A tear plunked itself right onto my penned tank top, dissolving my art torso instantly. "Ohhh nooo!" I cried out, drunkenly. "I can't even live on paper?" I grabbed the bottle of New Amsterdam Vodka and chugged it. "Ahhhh," I cried out in the pain of poor-children-quality vodka.

I had already come to know *good* vodka, and my life was Benjamin Buttoning in quality on all fronts. "I can't even have good vodka to die with!" I sobbed all over the drawing and ruined the rest of it. This despair was completely new. I wasn't afraid of death, just an untimely death brought about by *systemic circumstances*. I understood that death comes for everyone, and that eventually my plans would be cut short. I was fine with that. It made sense. I've been surrounded by death and casual death references for as long as I can remember. I grew up with a mother who would casually say things in her very distinct brand of innocence and surprising dark humor like, "Oh, it doesn't matter. I could step out into the street and get hit by a bus." Often, there was no segue to a comment like this. I could have just asked for orange juice.

"What? You're not going to get hit by a bus, Mummy." I would shake my head at her morose quips. She would sigh and look into the distance wistfully. "I could just get hit . . . by a bus." She would laugh. I started to wonder if she *wanted* to get hit by a bus. She could have done it easily and not even left our block. Twenty-Third Street between Seventh and Eighth Avenues had multiple bus lines running all day and night. So many chances! And, it was Chelsea, Manhattan, in New York City in the 1980s. There was a multitude of death options all around us! And I don't even mean the ones you're thinking of, given the time period and location. I don't mean like crack addiction, or being murked by a serial killer wearing amber-tinted aviator glasses and a flannel shirt. No one in my family was gonna do crack, and 1980s serial killers, for the most part, left non-White people alone. I mean that regular NYC shit had fewer safety regulations than today. Personally, I always thought I might get crushed by a falling construction crane. There were so many of them around the city all the time. And when the letter Z fell off the Discovery Zone Child Entertainment Center across the street, I thought, "That coulda been it for me."

Seemed like a very reasonable way to die, since the Wicked Witch in the *The Wiz*° was crushed by the flying Z that plummeted to the ground when Dorothy crashed through the giant OZ sign after she'd been swept up by a snowstorm from her block in Harlem. And *The Wiz* is so NYC-based that it has always been more of a murder documentary/musical for me. I guess I could have gotten murdered by a serial killer with tinted aviator glasses who was feeling froggy, but I wasn't scared of dying that way. In New York City, you grow up being less afraid of strangers, "dangerous situations," and more afraid of inanimate objects. And Gen Xers, we've been trained to embrace death all along.

"*Death is everywheeeeeeere,*" I sang loudly.

I danced, slowly waved around my bright yellow Sony Sports Walkman. Depeche Mode's "Fly on the Windscreen" blaring into my eleven-year-old ears. It was 1988 and I was in my bedroom, belting out a tune that described intimate urgency in the inevitable face of mortality.

"*Come here. Kiss me. Noooooow.*"

I slunk my hand into the air with a "come hither motion." I was practicing my vocals and moves in order to seduce Andrew Oh, my sixth-grade art class crush. I had just learned that he also loved Depeche Mode, and this meant that we needed to be together! I never got up the nerve to slither out from behind the acrylic paints corner

---

° The 1978 Sidney Lumet directed film, an adaptation of the 1974 Broadway musical (same name). If you don't enjoy *The Wiz*, don't talk to me. I've seen it nine million times and will see it nine million times more.

and serenade him with my best Dave Gahan impression, but I did solidify my mortality salience with that *Black Celebration* album. At eleven, I didn't know that my death embracin' would serve me so well in the next few years. But it was amazing prep work, because I was about to be a feral New York City teen.

You know what? Forget teen, we were feral *preteens* before the rest of puberty even hit us. Proficient in guzzling whole 40s° for self, for dolo, down to the monkey piss backwash, by the age of twelve. Chain-smoking Newports and stealing Ralph Lauren Polo from Macy's by "throwing it up the back"† of our backpacks. We didn't hang out until the streetlights came on, because that doesn't signal any change of action in NYC. We hung out until the sun came up and then we hung out some more after that. We smoked so much terrible weed that we should have been sponsored by tiny plastic baggies. And we didn't even have to leave our headquarters in Washington Square Park to get the shitty nickel‡ or dime bags of shake that we were smoking. We just rolled up blunts and smoked right there in the broad daylight. Children, getting fucked-up in the park.

Drinking our 40s wrapped in paper bags, forming little cliques within larger cliques. Doing our walk up West Fourth and Sixth to Eighth Street, making a right and continuing to Broadway, another right and maybe a stop at the massive store UNIQUE, but probably hanging the next right at Tower Records to head to the park. Along the way, there were friends to see. Those who worked in stores, or sold stuff on the street. Crushes we were trying to shoot our shots at. Maybe there would be a stop at McDonald's or the Waverly Diner, if we had money, to get a Cheeseburger Deluxe. If we didn't, to share a

---

° A disgusting malt liquor that for some reason was/is sold in many sizes, including cans, forty-ounce (hence the name) and sixty-four-ounce bottles. Teenagers like me drank them like juice. °*throws up in mouth*° Like juice. The preferred brand of NYC kids was Olde English.

† When stealing Polo clothes from the department store, we would hide the items either between our backs and large backpacks, or under our shirts, still covered by the backpacks. Kleptomaniac children. But fashionable!

‡ A nickel bag of weed is a tiny baggie of terrible quality weed that costs $5. Dime bags, $10.

plate of fries among the four of us as we made our little "lemonades" from lemon slices and packets of sugar. So many friends and stories of adventures, laughs, and good times. And most of those friends are dead now.

It was normal for there to be a shootout in a club. Normal. We were in those clubs as early as twelve—and shit, we had weapons too! Box cutters hidden in our sneakers and Aqua Netted buns. Razor blades under tongues and tiny axes hooked into our Carhartt work-wear hammer loops. Switchblades and hunting knives and yes, guns. It was normal to have to duck and run when, just a moment before, you had been dancing your face off in a club like the Octagon, Home Bass, the Tunnel, or Sound Factory. It was normal to scramble off the rink at the sound of gunshots piercing the air, whizzing by your head at a roller rink like Empire or Skate Key. It was normal to hear that your close friend had been shot and died in a fight. By a wayward or intentional bullet. Stabbed. Bludgeoned with a hammer. Violence was . . . normal.

Our train ads, at the time, were about getting your ripped earlobes repaired because it was expected that someone would yank the cheap gold door knockers° right off your ears. I was held at gunpoint on the D train for my door knocker earrings, but I gave 'em up calmly and quickly. Our train ads also held the comic strip tales of Julio y Marisol, a couple dealing with the effect of HIV and AIDS on their lives. Be-cause it was still normal for someone to die from AIDS-related com-plications. One of my teen boyfriends met his fate that way. It was normal to hear that someone had overdosed. We were surrounded by death, so being afraid of it would have been *ab*normal. At a certain point, you couldn't keep up with the funerals. We just lived thinking, "Of course I'm not gonna die tonight. That's not how my story ends." And some of us were wrong.

I say this to give you some context before you dive into this book that holds my penchant for so comfortably and jokingly "getting deathy

---

° Large gold earrings that have the traditional shape of a door knocker. Some have a bamboo-like appearance, called Bamboo earrings. I still wear many varieties of these.

with it." I have been forced to embrace the idea of impermanence and had to trust my intuition and my heart in saying "this is not how my story ends" thousands of times. I've clawed my way out of dangerous situations, of deep suicidal depressions, abusive relationships, and moments where hope felt absolutely nonexistent. I don't think that I'm lucky. I don't think that I'm better than anyone else who didn't make it. I don't know how to properly explain it to you. I just know that I won't be done with this life anytime soon. And that the lives I planned and imagined along the way with partners didn't make it to this place with me. And I'm all right with that because *I did*. I fucking made it.

I made it to do my one person show. I made it to start writing this book at the age of forty-five. And in the future, when you see me on Instagram wearing a cute little tennis outfit and carrying a cool racquet, you'll know why it's such a big deal. I have a lot of plans to get to. I have a lot of lives to live. And death will come for me, as it will for all of us. But until then, I will Keep Living real fucking hard, in my remaining years.

In my remaining years,
I will not be trapped on a set
of my own design.

1.

The Puppet Show

Did you know there are no support groups for people who are trapped living on the set of their own puppet show in the middle of a global pandemic lockdown?"

When I posed this question to my new online therapist, she replied, "I'm sorry?" I nodded in agreement and said quietly, "Me too, Jennifer. Me too."

"No, no." She shook her head slightly, inching closer to the screen. "I was asking you—what kind of support—I don't think I heard you correctly—I'm sorry." Her forehead furrowed. I repeated my word salad factoid again. I knew it wasn't a normal sentence. That was the issue. But, unfortunately, it was *my* normal. I'd been searching for help on Google for a few months, sometimes while screaming each word out loud and pressing the keys with maximum intensity. The **P** on my laptop keyboard was notably loose.

Jennifer and I stared at each other in silence. Her eyes narrowed. Her mouth formed the shape of potential expressions a couple of times, but nothing came out. I did list "comedian" as one of my occupations when applying for the service, so it was plausible that she thought I was making a ha-ha.

At her third inhale and frown, I thought it would be best to offer a more relatable problem. "I think I want a divorce," I said firmly. Jennifer's face relaxed immediately. "Oh. Okay, great!" Her shoulders softened as she attempted to rein in her happiness. "Not, *great*, but that's—"

"It was exacerbated by the puppets," I interrupted and chugged the Negroni I'd made a carafe of in preparation for the session. I wanted to be more relatable, but I also needed to talk about my actual situation with a professional and not keep unloading my puppet life issues onto my friends, none of whom had any experience being trapped on the set of their own puppet show in the middle of a global pandemic lockdown. This was my third attempt at an online therapist in a month, and I was well versed in the confusion I'd encounter while relaying my problems. I really wasn't confused about the divorce. I was spiraling about the puppets and the pandemic. To Jennifer's credit, it is an absolutely bonkers situation to unpack. To my credit, again, that's why I was looking for professional assistance.

To be clear: you shouldn't be trapped on the set of your own elaborate puppet show in a pandemic. You definitely shouldn't move three times during a global pandemic. The initial move was out of Brooklyn, the night of the first protests after the murder of George Floyd. The protestors reached our house on the eve of our move. We wanted to be outside with them because, of course, Fuck The Police.

We lived right next to a large police precinct. A shoddy wire fence separated us from their parking lot, which was also home to three gasoline pumps. That afternoon there had been a heavy series of knocks on the door. Ones that jolted our very anxious cat up out of his slumber on a moving box and sent him sprinting up the stairs to hide. I wanted to do the same, as the knocks were unmistakable for anything else other than "the cops." The only other knock it could have been, *maybe*, was a friend pretending to knock *like* the cops. The kind where you yell "why're you knocking like the fucking cops" as you walk to the door and then open it, adding "what's wrong with you?"

But the city was still in lockdown and our friends had only come by in the past few days to say tearful goodbyes through our screened backyard window. Sliding the mesh aside briefly, to exchange sanitized gift packages between our latex-gloved hands. Our masked faces were unable to properly relay how deeply terrified we were of the multiple apocalypses in play. So it couldn't be a friend at the door, for these reasons, and also because I could feel the electric and menacing tension in the air. My heart pounded in my chest with the same intensity as the knocks, and my first thought was, "We're going to die today." A completely valid thought as a person in this body, in that moment, and in light of all the surrounding moments. My brain also simultaneously went into New Yorker mode, which is "Aye, stop knocking on my door like that! Fuck is wrong with you?" I know it's the most stereotypical thing you could do in New York Speak to say, "Aye, I'm walkin' here!" I didn't say any of this out *loud*, because—cops. I opened the door, attempting to breathe normally.

The cop asked me if we "had any cameras on the property." I said, "No." He leaned back and glanced around the front of the house and left without another word, stomping down the steps and out of sight. I closed the door quickly, blood pounding in my head, and wished that we had packed our giant U-Haul, which was parked right outside, the night before, instead of planning to both finish packing and leave the city in the morning.

It had been over a year of this kind of heart racing, panic-induced existence by the time I started looking for an online therapist. We had finally landed in our house in Baltimore, after two other moves: a nightmare of a time in North Carolina and a short, anxiety-riddled stay at another Baltimore location. I wished I'd turned down the job I was on, but we had no other options for working income. My husband couldn't tour, for obvious reasons, even though his album had just been released. And my fully staffed puppet show, which was supposed to start shooting in April 2020, had, of course, been canceled—also for obvious reasons.

So, sure . . . I could do that show at home if the company paid me! Sure, my husband could *learn how to make puppets from scratch, make seven of them in a couple of months, and yeah, I could rewrite all six episodes of the show, find a new home, and then build an entire set to film the show in our home and figure out how to shoot it alone. Mmmhmm. Sure! *cries in the fetal position* Sure.*

Why didn't we dip into our savings to get by during—*hahahahaha,* independent artists don't have any *savings*. *Most people* don't have savings. How do you pronounce that? "*Sah-veens?*" We didn't even have health insurance (still don't). "*Inshurahnce?*" Must be nice. The fear of a doctor's bill made us extra careful and extra panicked about making contact with any other living (deadly?) being during our moves. An added isolation apocalypse layer, firmly stacked in what was becoming an infinitely layered apocalypse lasagna, a drippy dish no one had fucking ordered. How unfortunate. I used to love lasagna.

It is difficult to drive many hours through many states with your partner, your giant U-Haul truck, all of your belongings, and your anxious (but team player) cat in the middle of a global pandemic and countrywide civil protests. Especially when only one of you drives (not me and not the cat). As I mentioned before, I am a New Yorker. You may or may not know that many New Yorkers do not know how to drive for various reasons. Mostly because we grew up in a big city with a vast public transportation system. But also, owning a car is expensive. Parking a car where I grew up, in the middle of Manhattan, would have been damn near impossible, and neither of my parents owned a car. I don't think my mother ever knew how to drive, but I know my stupid father did. I'm pretty sure that when they lived elsewhere— Cape Town, Europe—he drove. But never in New York. Whenever I meet people who live in New York that drive, I assume they are transplants, or grew up in other boroughs of the city. Potentially, just farther uptown in Manhattan. But not in Chelsea, or really, anywhere downtown. The Rarity of Driving rule might be broken if the non-transplant city person in question comes from a rich family that has another house elsewhere. There, they might learn how to drive near a lake, or something. I don't know how rich people learn how to drive. We did not have another house in America. We did not have a lake.

Not being able to drive had never been an issue for me. I'd traveled globally my whole life, but my home base had always been NYC. I do consider "driving" to be a very American skill to have. It's necessary in a country where most cities are nonwalkable. You either know how to drive, or—don't live there. This is partially why I had never lived in another state. I had considered only Miami. I like Miami. It's a twenty-four-hour, hot, walkable town with beaches, cigarette smoking, and great food. It feels like Cape Town and New York had a spicy baby, and it's just a three-hour flight from NYC. I don't "get" a lot of America, but I "get" Miami—it's a cool city. Cool, minus the flying critters I do not like to manifest, so I won't type the name. They are actually my main aversion for moving there. That and, well, *Florida* . . . what is you doing, baby?

You may or may not know that New Yorkers (including me) generally don't lead with calling ourselves "Americans" for many reasons. Overseas, we don't identify ourselves by stating, "I'm an American." Because the treatment you'll receive after sharing that information will be very different from saying, "I'm a New Yorker." We don't say it for the upgraded treatment though. We say it because we've had a very different experience than the rest of the country. A *lot* of it involves growing up in a walkable city. A lot of it involves being immersed in so many diverse cultures all the time. A lot of it involves the fast pace and intentional (mistaken as chaotic) energy we are used to. And even more of it involves our general nature. I'm not saying that all native (and *almost* native like me) New Yorkers have had the same experience, but there are similarities, and I don't mean the stereotypical "Aye, I'm walkin' here" accent. The sentiment of it though . . . yes, definitely. We also introduce ourselves this way because we immediately want people to know that we do not take any responsibility for the rest of the country's feelings and views, please, and thank you so much. That's why most plastic bags and coffee cups from NYC say THANK YOU on them. I know that people like to say "Ugh, you make being from New York your whole personality." I don't disagree, but it's not a choice. Our city is inside of us for as long as we live, wherever we are. Thank You.

I think that when I tell people I don't drive, the shocked response mainly comes from the fact that I have a *lot* of skills, so it's assumed that I would also have one so commonplace. I know that this sounds like I'm giving a speech from *Taken*, but it's not that far off. Some of my skills are innate and some I have spent decades honing and perfecting. I have told many people that I meet and keep in my friend group why we should stay a community. It is for our collection of varied apocalypse skills. I don't know how to drive, but in an apocalypse, I am a *very* good leader who will make sure that none of us get killed, because I will also be making the decisions on who needs to get the fuck out of the group. They are a liability, a wild card, a charlatan. My traumatic experiences with terrible people have led me to read terrible people very quickly. As an Old School New Yorker, I'm sussing out every environment in one point three seconds. I smell things you don't smell, because of my hyperosmia (super smelling). I see the colors you can't—I'm a tetrachromat. I am an excellent planner and I am very particular. I am hyper-*hyper* sensitive to changes in the air and sounds. And my experience in artist poverty has led me to be an amazing cook who can make meals for ten people out of *nothing*. You see nothing in that ransacked zombie supermarket. I see a three-course meal.

I have other skills, but most importantly, I have led large groups of people and not had the calling to turn evil. And in case you're wondering, because of the things I have listed, yes, I have been clinically tested for ADHD and autism a few times (I had to make sure). I don't understand how I'm not, but until further testing proves otherwise—I am simply composed of many singular heightened experiences. This is a recurring theme for my existence. All this to say, when I met my then-husband I clocked that he possessed a team-needed driving apocalypse skill. "You're in!" I'd yelled at him.

I assumed that one day we would have to use his driving skill in an apocalypse-like situation, because I am a dark motherfucker like that. But you're never really prepared for what it's going to feel like when you're in it and the apocalypse is apocalypsing. I guess that also applies to being middle-aged, but we have so much time to get to that, hold tight.

It's not like we didn't know what our apocalypse skills were, but the real-life version is very different from the pillow talk version. It was physically and mentally very difficult on my husband, because besides my lack of driving knowledge, my body had started to be (for three years) in confusing, excruciating chronic pain. And it had become almost impossible for me to lift any heavy objects. Unfortunately, *lifting heavy objects* is the bulk of activities that happen during moving, and he was forced to do so much. No one wants to overwork their partner in a terrible situation, and also, no one wants to feel so . . . fucking . . .

useless. Being physically strong was on my apocalypse skill list and it had dropped off at such an inconvenient time. I fulfilled all of my team leader jobs. My planning, timing, and executing but . . . I couldn't do all of the things that needed to get done by two human bodies, and I felt so fucked-up for "letting the team down."

I was used to being *unusually* strong. Some of that comes from "moving a couch up twelve flights of stairs, twenty different times, by yourself" single living in New York shit and some is just that I'm a freak of nature who used to close-distance-punch-open fully locked doors. A mash-up of hyperindependence and innate strength, if you will. Having to learn to do things myself after being let down, being put on hold, and being unwavering in achieving my goals on time. Also, from growing up in a very punk and jazz sort of way, which always involves having to improvise to survive. It's one thing to learn how to work around your constantly screaming perfectionism in your scrappy DIY-arranged life in order to get things done. It is another mental skill set to deal with the fact that your body will no longer let you be as strong as you are in your mind, in order for you and your most beloved to be safe. I didn't know what had happened to me, so I assumed that it was age. I was in my forties and, of course, my body was losing strength, right? I cried and apologized to my husband so many times during the moves.

"I'm sorry I can't help! I wish I was younger! You should have married someone younger, so you wouldn't have to do this alone." Of course he said, "It's okay and don't say that" and, of course, I kept thinking it. *Why couldn't this pandemic have happened ten years ago?* I was so strong in my thirties. I could have done so much more. So much more.

Something had been happening to me over a few years, and the pain was scary. But I hadn't attended to it because—*Inshuuuuurahnce?* Those of us who have never had *Inshuuuuurahnce* know only its rhyming sibling *ENDURANCE!* Once, I broke my foot on tour in

---

* *Za Gaman*, which translates as *The Endurance*, is a Japanese television show from the 1980s. It's like *Fear Factor*, or the many other game shows now, where contestants attempt to outdo each other by withstanding unpleasant experiences.

Australia and I continued the rest of the tour with my fully broken, swollen, and dangling foot that I could not (but did) put weight on. For five more shows. Hobbling onstage and on international flights. Capitalism. *ENDURANCE!*

In Baltimore, the *ENDURANCE* of the physical tasks passed, but as the months went by, the *ENDURANCE* of isolation was the mental feat that I don't believe anyone was fully prepared for. Not even the self-proclaimed introverts who had made it through the first few months of quarantine in pretty good shape. The apocalypse just kept giving. Shit, we really needed to see some other human beings. But again, if one of us got sick . . . how would we do anything? I wasn't even scared about the illness. I was scared about not being able to work. So we remained isolated.

"What do you mean you have a bubble and you guys hang out? We haven't seen anyone else in a fucking year and a half. A bubble? You must have *Inshuuuuurahnce*."

I was gobsmacked at friends of ours who were having get-togethers. We, on the other hand, had started playing YouTube videos of "restaurant ambience" quietly as we ate dinner, so we could feel like people who were around other people. The tiny clanks of utensils and light chatter of fake meals playing from a laptop on our dining table while we ate real food. If a person didn't listen too closely, they wouldn't notice that all of the talking in the ambience was just gibberish on a loop. But we are both music producers, so there was no way for us to unhear it. I'm not saying that we turned it off. We kept doing it. I'm saying that it definitely made us more insane. I never brought up "pretend restaurant" to any of the therapists that I spoke to. I figured that "puppets are killing me" was doing a lot of heavy lifting in the issues department. Plus, one of my therapists told me about a bubble that she and her husband were in, so I figured that people with *Inshuuuuurahnce*, or without autoimmune issues, probably wouldn't understand.

I have made a living from my imagination, for all of my professional life, in so many different ways. And I have felt isolation, for all of my professional and personal life, in so many different ways. But at no moment before the pandemic had I ever felt like I was literally going full-fledged bonkers from isolation. Falling fully over the edge, with a nonstop cacophony of internal screaming every single second of every single day.

I don't know if you know how hard it is to build a home during a global pandemic, maybe you do. A lot of us did it. And I would like to offer my congratulations on the mind-melting and body-breaking processes that you had to go through. I understand. I don't know if you have ever tried to build a pretend home life space, disguised as a real home life space because it is a literal television set built for the use of puppets, and then had to live in it. But on the very small off chance that you did, please contact me. We are not well.

It is one thing to not be able to order any furniture or household items online because everything is on back order. It is another level of hell to have to make sure that nothing you order for your home will be a copyright infringement. Not a curtain. Not a pattern on a hand towel. Not a book. Not anything. If a person looked too closely, they could notice that all the art on the walls was done by the people who lived there. They might spot the overly symmetrical position of the couches in the living room. Perhaps they'd move one of the couch cushions and reveal a giant hole cut into its side for the operation of puppets. I turned every book around to hide the spine, ripped the labels off our kitchen items. A cabinet in the kitchen had a removable top and was the exact size for one of us to climb into and operate a puppet. It may not have been evident to the passing eye, but it was all mise-en-scène. I was never just "sitting on the couch and watching television." I was in a shot for Episode Two, Scene Three. And yes, this also definitely made me *more* insane.

After I explained this through a stream of tears to my first online therapist, she sat quietly and exhaled hard. "That sounds really messed up and I'm sorry. I don't know what I can tell you." This was very sad news to me, as I was definitely hoping that someone could tell me something. Before I had searched for an online therapist, I'd tried to solve the problem myself by searching "severe work and mental burn-out solutions." All of the answers were relatively the same, sometimes in different orders:

1. Don't take your work home with you/create a work-life balance.
2. Consider a vacation.
3. Shift your perspective/change of scenery.
4. Seek out healthy friendships and connections.
5. Take a break.

"Well, fuck me, I guess!" I laughcriedscreamed as I leaned into the couch and pushed my hands away against the air. My right arm lodged into the puppet hole and came out the other side, which prompted the cat to attack it. I laughed and cried harder as his tiny teeth gripped my wrist. "Fuck me," I cried weakly.

You might want to respond to this with, "Kim, there were people dying," which is absolutely true.

I know that the main concern for the world was not "puppets." I was *also* having a very fucking hard time concentrating on the fucking puppets. I know how absolutely petrified the majority of the world was during this time. I was *also* absolutely petrified. I was afraid of losing my mind. I was afraid I was in the process of losing my partner. I was afraid of getting Covid and ruining our lives. I was afraid of whatever the fuck Trump's next move was gonna be, lest we all forget that panicked part of EVERY DAY.

I was afraid for the election. I was afraid of a civil war, which seemed very realistic (and still does). I was afraid for the protesters, the kids, the—I was afraid for our future yes, because what were we going to do after a fucking puppet show? Was this the end of the world? The end of the fucking world and I'm making PUPPETS!?! I was afraid for all of it and all of us. All. Of. Us.

The trucks full of dead Covid patients in NYC. The replaying of George Floyd being murdered, over and over again, thousands of times. Watching the Covid death toll mount on the CNN DEATH COUNTER that we all stared at all day every day. All of these were real, real bad activities to keep engaging in. As someone who needs all the information all the time, they were unavoidable. As someone who does "okay" in deathy situations, it was too much. Too fucking much.

"Must be nice!" I seethed at one of the puppets. "Must be fucking nice to not have to feel or see anything!" I was spitting through my clenched teeth at it and poking it in the eye. I wanted to make a joke about if it "felt" that, but I was too angry. As the sentient puppet who was being controlled by capitalism, I was jealous of the ones who were only controlled by me. I was angry that I hadn't been more specific to the universe when I put my dream plans into the ether so many decades ago: "I want to be just like Jim Henson and Mr. Rogers and I will make my own puppet show that will help adults, just like the other puppets help children."

How was I supposed to know to add "not in a global pandemic, potential race war, under various forms of duress, and in a very unreasonable time schedule. Oh and—" I could add so many things. But the more I thought about it, the more I just felt like an asshole for complaining. Don't people overcome the worst odds and go on to be glorious? Weren't there so many more people going through far worse things than I was? Who was I to fucking complain about any of my—

You know the guy that Will Smith played in The Pursuit of Happyness *wrote that book when he was homeless and living in his car.*

My inner monologue interrupts my complaints and says this to me *all the time.* I don't know why my brain has picked this example as my "shame of choice." I have seen the movie *The Pursuit of Happyness* exactly *one time*, in 2007. I don't know if that dude wrote the book while he was homeless and living in his car. Real talk, I don't even fuck with Will Smith like that. I have nothing against him, but I did a couple songs with Jazzy Jeff once, that was cool—what I'm saying is, our brains pick fucked-up things from our subconscious vaults of life's expectations to make us feel guilty for feeling burned out and crazy. For feeling like we need to take a break and get our health together, even in AN APOCALYPSE. For not being ecstatic about productivity even when it's killing us. For not being more grateful that we at least have a home to complain about.

The guy Will Smith played didn't have a home and he still found time to write a book maybe. And, he didn't complain.

Again, I don't know if that's true! But he should have complained. He had a lot of things to complain about! I guess that's really jumping the gun, because bottom line, he shouldn't have been homeless. And I shouldn't have had to make a fucking puppet show in the middle of a deadly global pandemic. But I did, because I didn't want to be homeless. Both can be true and worthy of complaints.

| | |

I separated from my husband and moved back to New York City, by myself. During my time there, I had some incredibly trying months. That's a nice way of saying, "I wished for an asteroid to hit the earth." I'd moved back to Bushwick, Brooklyn, where I had lived many times in my young adult years, and I was feeling like I'd massively back-tracked. This is not who I was supposed to be at this age. This is not the neighborhood I'd wanted to make my big NYC return to. Even if it *was* a loft. This *was not* my beautiful life.

In the early 2000s, I'd moved to Brooklyn from Manhattan knowing full well I was the fourth horseman of gentrification, while also accepting the subpar living conditions that people in their twenties accept as "just fine." Now, walking around the neighborhood, I saw the same kinds of people I used to be. Just happy to have their first apartment and very nonchalant about everything. As people in their twenties are and should be—minus the very important gentrification part. I felt like everyone's puppet mom. My body being placed in positions forcibly. My reactions to everyone, not the dialogue I had written for this part of my life, for this age. I hated these changes to the script. Hated.

"It's a big change," everyone said to me. "But it will be good because you'll be back home and we're all here! We're so glad you're home!" I was tired, lonely, and to be honest, quite sick of change.

All right with the fucking changes already. I just wanted to be *home*. And rest. Not to make *yet another home* by myself and *not* rest. I looked at a puppet arm sticking out of a moving box. "Fucking asshole," I said from across the room and went to go smoke a cigarette out the window. As I gazed out on the parking lot below, it hit me. Everything was changing in the absolute wrong way.

Once, at my 2002 Bushwick railroad apartment, I'd heard two kids playing in the backyard two floors under my open window. "Let's play superheroes!" the little girl said with quiet excitement. "Okay!" There was a pause and then, "Ohh, oooooh." The girl's low lament grew louder. Which superhero was she—I was interrupted by her announcement—"Ohhh nooo!" She quietly, slowly, wailed: "Everything's chaaaanging!"

I've heard this refrain in my head ever since. It was, for some reason, shocking. I had played "superheroes" as a child, but in all of my superhero-playing experience, I, nor anyone else in the game, had ever thought about *leading with our character's origin story.* Certainly not by diving into actual play by *reenacting the physical and mental response* to it. We just started playing superheroes, midjourney superheroes. I've carried that kid's view on "changing" with me all these years. And it always had felt like such a comforting way to embrace the uncertainty of life. I would mutter "everything's chaaaanging" under my breath, or say it loudly, in the midst of big changes. But in my backtracking apartment, it didn't fucking work.

Everything didn't feel like it was just "changing," at that point. It felt like it was falling the fuck apart. Maybe if that kid had said "everything's faaaallling apaaaart," I would have navigated my years after very differently. *Change* is welcomed. I always initiate big moves and shifts. Progress happens with change, for all of us. I understand that the transitions in between are more than likely going to be places of great discomfort in various ways. And I know that it's important to know it's gonna be scary and difficult, but to do it anyway. But . . . there is a difference between "change" and "repeatedly being punched in the face while you're already lying on the floor in a pool of your own blood." My situation was much more . . . the latter. And not just my situation, but the collective situations of the peoples on the planet.

That was what I wanted to scream at everyone who was refusing to talk about mid/post-pandemic things with me. Everyone on Earth hadn't just been through a *lil change* that was *kinda hard and needed in order to progress.* Most of us are *still* being repeatedly punched in the face by so many things that happened during that time period. And we still aren't talking to each other about it. We're not sharing our experiences, and sharing experiences really helps people feel *less isolated.* Fuck. I really needed to talk to *everyone* about this. I really needed to talk to *someone* about this. I guess—goddammit! Not again!

| | |

"But how does that make you feel?" I wanted to ask, leaning back in my comfortable chair, lighting a cigarette. "Let's talk more about *you.*"

I was talking to my new therapist and trying to shove down the urge to therapy them right back. I had warned them that I might do this, and if I did, they should stop me. I didn't say it though. I was getting used to squelching my feelings, and that didn't feel like an accomplishment. It felt gross.

My therapist was nice, queer, nonbinary, mixed race, a very intentional choice, and I dug their energy a lot. I dug their energy so much that I wanted to stop the session and say, "So do you just wanna hang out and be friends, or what?" Because that's what I wanted. I wanted to talk and kiki with a friend. Some friends. To take a trip. Or to check into an oldey-timey sanitarium by the seaside somewhere together. Someplace where a caretaker would wheel us out onto a dock, right before sunset, and maybe brush our hair while we sipped tea, or wine, or both. And we would stay there for a month. Just getting ourselves the fuck together, crying, swimming, being fed good food. But a *modern* oldey-timey sanitarium because they didn't let the coloreds in the real old ones. I wanted *that.* Not psychotherapy, which just felt like paying for a "friend escort." Again, it felt gross, even though she was so nice. I didn't say any of that either. I didn't tell them that I still wanted my husband to just take his fucking meds and keep his promises, so that we didn't have to go it alone.

I also didn't even try bringing up puppets in my session, but I did make sure that the ones in my home were out of sight of my computer camera. I'd forgotten that there was a puppet hand visible in a Zoom meeting the week prior and everyone had stopped to say, "Ooh! Is that a puppet!" "No!" I'd responded angrily, kicking the box away with my foot. People love to talk about puppets. I used to love talking about puppets, and now I have very severe puppet-related trauma. Which I guess is my one very weird and unique experience that I took from our shared human experience. Even my husband has no puppet-related trauma. But it's a big world, I'm sure someone out there's got it too.

Like me, you also may have gotten separated or divorced during the pandemic. You may have been wondering what was happening to your body, your thoughts, and your feelings as they were reacting to the apocalypses around us, and then the gift of perimenopause opened right in your fucking face and you didn't even know it until later—or maybe, until right now. You, like me, may have come to understand so many things about yourself that would have taken years without the isolation of pandemic quarantines and lockdowns. What an expedited microwave of a personal fucking journey that was. What an unexpectedly forced microscope, held to our own bodies and thoughts, our personal and intimate relationships. Our productivity, ambitions, and work. We came out with so much more and so much less. Figuring out our needs for the spaces we live in, since we didn't know that was all we might have. I know so many people who are absolutely unwilling to live without an outdoor space now. It is a dealbreaker. My dealbreaker turned out to be—my whole life. I did not want it. I could not do it.

Even though you may not know the exact drama of literally *living on the set of your own puppet show in a global pandemic*, it does not escape me that *everything* was so surreal that you may have *felt* (pun intended) like you were living on the set of your own hellish puppet show, where everything was just pretend. And maybe you also tried telehealth therapy during this and thought, *"This . . . this is not enough fucking help for where I'm at."* Perhaps you offered up "homeschooling is hard" in your session instead of saying what you wanted to say, as you sipped a Negroni from a large carafe: "I would like to murder my partner and then use their body as a means to lift weight and get in shape, because all of the free weights on Amazon have been out of stock for months and quite frankly, these biceps aren't gonna build themselves, Denise."

I don't think that psychotherapy is for everyone. The same way I wouldn't tell anyone to "journal" or to "take a relaxing bath." I'll smack that journal out of your hand and pee in your bathwater. Somatic therapy, music, cooking, a hot Karen Silkwood–level pummeling water pressure shower, traveling, adventuring, and yes, talking to friends works for me. I haven't been able to do any of those things in the way that I need to feel good again. To be able to think, sort out my feelings, so that I don't feel like a capitalism puppet. Or a middle-aged hormones puppet. Or a backtracking-on-my-life puppet. But I will.

Now that we know an apocalypse can happen at any time, more than anything, what I want to work on—is joy. Not productivity, but joy, so when the next apocalypse horseman rides up with fucking puppets on its hands, I am far more able to deal with it. Which may seem like a crazy and pretend ambition to a lot of people. Sure! But I have lived in a pretend house. With pretend sounds and feelings. And the worst part of it all is that I built it *myself*. What a fucking metaphor for this country.

In my remaining years,
I may still bend over backward,
but I will not BREAK

2.

I Sing the Body . . . Elastic?

I lay on our new mattress. Me and my four new pillows, all of them strategically tucked under and around various parts of my body. My mouthguard in, my wrist brace on, my night glasses not falling down my face, I waved my legs around the new crispy sheets. Waved them just enough to feel the coolness, but not enough to dislodge the pillow squished between my thighs. If my thigh pillow became dislodged, I would be in an excruciating amount of pain. If my thigh pillow became dislodged, my hip would sublux, which means it would partially dislocate. Actually, if any of the pillows dislodged from their current positions, I would be in danger of suffering multiple dislocations. The thought crossed my mind, and I stopped moving my legs completely. They do have pillows that strap onto your body, thus preventing your joints from dislodging, but I'd already spent so much money on non-strappy, great-quality-for-adults-who-know-things pillows. Perhaps I'd get all of the strappy ones in the next round of bedding purchases. Until then, practicing being more still, at least until I fell asleep, was the way to go.

I sighed and pushed my head down into my *first* pillow. It conformed to my neck, which felt great. I was sure I wouldn't fling it across the room in the middle of the night, in utter frustration and discomfort. I had been doing that move for as long as I could remember. But this pillow had removable pieces of memory foam so I could adjust the filling to my own preference. I had made it thin and carved out a small nook for neck support. It was so much better than the strictly "made for neck" pillows I'd tried. My very thin neck and very small head didn't like those. They were way too fluffy.

"More like pill*high*," I'm sure I dad-joked too many times to the cat, Littles. Or my husband. Or the air. There had been a time when we'd had more bed pillows, but those had been mostly decorative. They played minor roles such as "watching a bed movie propping pillow #1." They made the bed look nice during the day, and it had felt like an accomplishment to have them (hate that for me). Over time, it became increasingly clear that they were simply there as set decoration to help us perform the "real adults in a relationship" scene we've all been watching forever. In movies, in film, maybe in our own families:

The couple makes small talk as they remove many, many pillows from the bed. Maybe the dialogue is something that drives the plot forward, but the act of pillow removal establishes their relationship dynamic. Perhaps the husband makes a joke like, "Why do we even have so many pillows?!" The wife shakes her head. "Sheesh. This guy! He doesn't understand anything about making a home! What a man thing to man man man!"

The audience nods in respective agreement to the scene. "So true, so true," they nod. "Only woman make pillow fuss." They grunt softly as the couple continues to place an unimaginable number of decorative pillows on other useless furniture in the bedroom. The End of Bed Bench. The Chair. Sometimes a Window Seat. I'm not mad at the fact that I had forced us to perform *Pillows: The Play*, for years. I was only trying to build a successful home and relationship with the tools I had. My aspirational relationship goals, ripped from depictions of happy marriages on various-size screens.

These new pillows, however, were for comfort and body issues and did not get removed from the bed every night. One was to thwart homicide: my husband's wedge pillow that sort of made me less murdery about his sleep apnea. Sort of. Do you know how much great pillows cost? A lot, but less than murders and hospitals. I'd also bought a few new sets of sheets, and those were unbelievably cheap. I am kidding, they were all very expensive. Do you know how much great sheet sets cost? Have you just found out? Call me! I wanna scream about it! I bought cotton percale sheets, because those are the ones that feel best to me and I don't wake up hot, or just generally upset by sheets. What, was I not going to buy the expensive sheets? After all that sheet research I did to find them, what was I going to do? Keep being uncomfortable, and uncrisp?

"We're all gonna die, maybe even tomorrow. So, what, I'm not gonna have fucking nice sheets? Fuck that!" I declared without anyone arguing this purchase at all. I closed my laptop like I had changed the world. It was a change, if maybe not an earth-shattering one. I was proud of myself for buying a few high-priced things at one time. You never know when your brain is gonna let you spend the money, ya know?

"Do it while the thought is there and regret it later on," said absolutely no accountant or financial advisor ever. Whatever. I didn't care anymore. I wanted nice things on and around my body. Was I not old enough to have nice things? Did I not deserve good bedding after all of my service to the planet? Hmm, my bones did feel like they were loose and rattling around inside of me. My bones probably needed more stuff than the things that went *on* the bed.

"You don't feel that? I don't understand how you're not in an overwhelming amount of pain all the time from this shitty mattress because *my* body feels like a bone salad. Do you *not* feel like a bone salad?" I asked my husband this question many times during what would become the last era of Shitty Mattress.

"I can sleep on anything." He shrugged.

"Well just because you *can* doesn't mean you *should.*"

I squinted my eyes in both annoyance at his uncaring about the quality of our mattress being a priority and in understanding that he is eight years younger than me. "He doesn't feel like old bones inside. Got them goddamn young bones," I whispered as I stood up and my knees sounded like a car crashing into a Bubble Wrap factory.

There had been a time in my life too when mattress quality had not been a priority. Remember your young body? The one that could sleep on a collage of shrapnel? Well, those times were over for me. I was now like "The Princess and the Pea." I felt all parts of bedding, couches, or chairs. I felt every undesirable centimeter beneath my body, all the tiny imperfections. I felt every part of my body that wasn't supported and desperately needed support. "Hahaha, this is like relationships," I thought about mattresses but did not say to anyone out loud. I assumed that my increased body awareness and product quality awareness were due to three things:

1. KNOWLEDGE

I was now older and knew some shit about the quality of products. It has become important to look at fabrics, cushioning, warranties, sustainability, and comfort. You can feel when something is poorly made, because you have had more experience. The way that I am repulsed by all the material used to make clothing that they sell in every store I used to love. How could I not see the shitty seams? The plastique wrinkles, the way it clung to my skin. The unbreathable junk of it all. Once you know, you can never go back.

2. OLD

"Ahhhhh" and "Hghhhheeh" and "HeMP-ahhh—oof," says everyone at a certain age when doing anything physical. I had started to do this too, because that's . . . that's the old thing, right? You turn thirtysomething and start complaining about your back and knees. You make the "ooh my aching bones" sounds, because oldey Bones B' Hurtin' obviously. Of course, old hurtin' bones are gonna need more comfort.

3. DANCE

I was under the assumption that my particular brand of old pain included decades-old dance injuries. I had spent so many years of my young life in a number of intense dance classes, and everyone knows that dancers sustain lots of joint damage, which tends to worsen later in life. Every time my knees popped, I said, "ballet." My hips, "years of turnout." ° My wrists, my high arches, achy—"lack of movement, they got used to being used for dance so much." Not just old. Old dancer. Old dancer need better support for loose limbs and sore joints. Old dancer get good mattress.

Do you know how much good mattresses cost? Yeah, you probably do. Do you know how long it takes to choose a fucking mattress? I rarely get overwhelmed in my quest for knowledge. But there should be a support group for mattress researchers. We are not okay.

"I just want a fucking mattress! Just tell me which one! Just tell me—ahhhh!"

Twenty tabs, fifteen windows, and tens of pages of notes were open on my laptop screen at all times. I had bookmarked innumerable sites with mattress pictures and mattress information. I watched endless YouTube mattress reviews. I watched third party reviews with no stake in the "beds" game, but it was hard to tell who wasn't being sponsored by Big Mattress. I slapped on my Hercule Poirot mustache and re-searched all those individuals as well. Thrice over, I weighed myself, my husband, the cat, to confirm that our combined weight wouldn't be a factor. Did I need a mattress that could ensure a full glass of wine would go undisturbed if my husband plopped down on it? The ads kept showing that. Hmmm. I did have a full glass of wine . . . a lot. Edge support? I do sit on the edge of the bed a lot. The number of contributing factors to research was mounting. My search history was getting weird.

Best hybrid mattress for side sleepers with hip problems
Diet trends for this year
Best mattress in the world
Best mattress in the world on a budget

° The rotation of the leg (from the hip) which causes the feet to turn outward. Over time, this can be very damaging to a dancer's lower back and general lower body. In my years of ballet, I was always praised for my excessively wide turnout. Sigh.

Why is horsehair in expensive mattresses
Where do they source horsehair for mattresses from horse
    which horses
Why am I like this
Edge support mattress best
Which hybrid mattress sagging
Face sagging fixes
SAG AFTRA
Saatva

I had started to type in: MATTRESS WHY.

| | |

It took a month of mind-numbing research before I chose our new bed. Then it took another month for it to arrive. This was in part because of not only COVID delays and back orders but also that's how Big Mattress works. Deliveries can take months. During the wait, I managed my pain with the knowledge that it would be better *soon*. That *soon* had a delivery date, and sometimes it can be really helpful to get through shit if you know exactly when it will end. Not all the time, but sometimes. I wonder if death might also work that way? Hmm. I twirled my mustache.

I was terrified that I had made the wrong mattress decision and that my better "soon" might not come. But the mattress ended up being fantastic. I flopped down on it the day it arrived and exuded many "Huuuuuhhhhhhhs" of contentment. I got up and didn't even "HeMP-ahhh—oof!" That night, I slept so well. I didn't feel like a bone salad. I didn't weep softly and accept pain relief pills at 3:00 a.m. I just went to sleep at night and then woke up in the morning. Wow! What a concept! This glorious contentment lasted about three weeks.

"HeMP-ahhh—oof! Ehhhhhh fuck ehhh fuck." I was once again performing "Sighs of Pain," the song of my people. Frustrated for myself, my husband, for Littles (the cat), who really loved sleeping on my legs but could never stay there due to my constant shifting. "Huuuh map!" Littles would say, getting up and shooting me a disappointed look. "I know, I know, I'm sorry," I'd say softly as he hopped off the bed and walked to the door, serving me one last glance and an angry, "Maap!" before disappearing around the corner. I knew it wasn't the mattress this time. I sat up in bed and pulled my laptop onto my achy legs. "Ow!" I had barely turned my left knee to the side and I felt it completely dislocate. This wasn't the first time that had happened. It was more anxiety inducing and uncomfortable than painful. Every time it occurred I felt a rush of panic: "What if it never goes back into place?" This time was no different, and I talked myself down, silently.

"It's gonna be okay. Just calm down. It'll go back." And it always did at some point. But those moments of feeling like a broken doll were so scary. I had to do something about this. I had to find some sort of physical therapist. I couldn't find one near us that specialized in rehabilitating dancers, but there were PTs and chiropractors at a sports facility. That seemed like the closest fit and I was down to try anything. I wished I had "*Inshuuuuurahnce*," but I was far past the "Enduuuraaance" portion of this pain. Out of pocket it was, as per usual. Goddammit.

"You're really flexible! Wow!"

The chiropractor was pushing my entire leg slowly toward my body. I was face-up on the drop table with my knee hovering over my chest. "Wow!" he exclaimed, pushing my leg farther. My whole leg lay flat against my torso. "Wooow!" he said slower. "Are you a dancer?" He returned my leg to the table gently and stepped back, hands on his hips.

"I was, when I was a kid." I paused for dramatic purposes. "Until my ballet teacher broke my foot."

He nodded. "Oh, I'm sorry that happened to you."

I speak of my broken-foot tale in the way that many men talk about a college football injury, but without the deep-seated resentment and loss. "I learned very early on that you can live many lives. Fulfill a lot of dreams and move on to do other things. It's okay." I deliver this (very true) speech that no one asks for and sit up. "But I'm still really flexible."

"Yeah! Yeah, I can see that. And that's a really good way of looking at things too." He is kind and impressed, but my body still fucking hurts.

"I was just hoping that I could get some decompression, or some release today, and then I'm sure it's part of a longer program, which is great. I just don't want to feel like a bone salad anymore." I finish and we both nod at each other.

"Bone salad, that's a first," he says. We continue nodding.

He tested me at various stations with different equipment. My problem wasn't balance or a need to improve mobility. It wasn't flexibility or lack of exercise. I was frustrated and left feeling like an unexplained misfit, yet again. I arrived home dejected and very much still in pain. "Hghhhheeh," I shouted as I sat down on the couch. What was wrong with me? I was running out of ideas. I spent the next month in deep online searches.

"I have a Beighton score of seven!" I rushed into the kitchen to proclaim my discovery.

"Se-ven," I said, hitting the syllables and dotting the air with my thumb and index finger pressed together, stressing the importance of the statement.

"Okay," my husband responded. "Is that a high score—also, I don't know what the Brighton—"

"Beighton," I corrected him.

"I don't know what the Beighton test is," he said, correctly.

"Hypermobility!" I yell. "It's a test for hypermobility!" I was yelling with the fervor of Nicolas Cage in any movie where he has deciphered a code that explains how anything in the universe works. Specifically, in the movie *Knowing*.

"I'm hypermobile, don't you see! This explains everything!" I rushed out of the room, in my way of rushing, which has never been particularly fast.

"Everything!" I yelled while looking straight ahead and still "rushing" and immediately realizing why I've never been able to rush. Realizing why I wouldn't have looked over my shoulder to yell my remaining word. I reached the stairs, grabbing the banister, and definitely did not ascend the steps quickly. I have never gone up, or down, any steps quickly. "Fucking everything!" I yelled at the stairs, because I have always had to stare at stairs in order to be able to use them.

I have always known I was very flexible. I've even referred to myself as being hypermobile. I had *not* known that it was an *actual disorder* that had so many other symptoms, issues, and side effects. We, as a generation of people, did not think that anyone who could move and bend the way I could had a *problem*. Anyone who could move and bend like me had a *talent* and was sent to dance class. Or gymnastics. And we were praised for the things we could do. Over the next few weeks, I would burst into many rooms in the house with new information about my hypermobility spectrum disorders (HSDs) issues.

"This is why I've never been able to ride a bike! This is why I don't want to learn how to drive, even though it could open up so many new worlds for me! This is why I'm so nervous on stairs!" I was Nic Cage again, wildly waving my hands around, but in small circles, so as not to hurt my disorder bones.

"I have a lack of spatial awareness! I have"—I checked my phone's notes, where I kept a list of my recent discoveries—"ahh! I have decreased proprioception! That means that I can't tell where my fucking body is in space because my joints are all"—I motioned slightly more wildly—"they're so disconnected!"

Suddenly, my mouth dropped and I sat down slowly.

"Oh my god. Oh my god. This is why I couldn't get off the *floor* in gymnastics. This is—grand jetés. This is why I couldn't leap in ballet." I leaned back on the couch and started to cry. "It wasn't my fault."

I said softly, "It wasn't my fault." I cried so deeply that afternoon, because for the things I was praised to do in the places I was put, there were all the things I could never do. And up until that moment, I had felt like such a failure.

Perhaps you have been able to put a name to the thing inside of you that prevents you from doing something you so desperately want to do. Or perhaps you have been privileged with never experiencing that kind of block. Brain betrayal. Body betrayal. I hope that it hasn't been that way for you, but I understand so very much if it has. The gift of being able to know myself and the sadness that it provided all arrived at the same time. It was overwhelming. I thought about every moment in my past when I hadn't been able to be "completely successful."

Eight-year-old me, in gymnastics summer camp at the McBurney

YMCA,* across the street from our apartment. I could do a million splits all over the place, no problem! Legs behind my head? I sit like that for *funsies*. Cartwheel, now hold on. Wait . . . wait a minute. I could not get my body to kick my legs off the floor and have my full weight suspended solely by my arms, for any amount of time. The anxiety surrounding the thought of not being grounded was crippling. And don't even *think* about saying "flip" to me. A flip? Where no part of my body would be touching the floor? Why, I would land right on my neck and break my entire spine. How dare you even suggest such a thing?

At the end of our summer camp, our class did a gymnastics demo for our families and friends. I claimed the "floor performance" portion of the program and chose "The Love Theme (Instrumental)" from the movie *St. Elmo's Fire* as my music, because it was 1985. I felt accomplished, proud, and successful, with complete confidence when I finished. But that lasted only a moment before the dread set in because there was still one obstacle to complete. The goddamn pommel horse.

Over the weeks of camp, I had feigned stomach sicknesses and a variety of sprains to avoid interacting with the pommel horse. I also used this technique through all my years in public school, whenever— *sports*. But today, every student had to pommel horse it up. Unfortunately, I was positioned to go first. I glared at the Horse of Evil. But it wasn't solely the pommel horse itself that was the threat, it was all the factors surrounding the pommel horse. The running to reach it. The springboard I'd land on that would launch me (omg, omg, omg) in the air and onto the Horse of Doom. The metal handles I'd have to balance myself on while somehow pulling my legs through without breaking my wrists, knees, and ankles. The dismount pose at the end was the only thing I knew I could perform.

Okay. Okay. I breathed deeply. Okay? Okay! I could do this? I could do this! Everyone would clap and cheer so hard and I would *not* shatter my body into a million pieces. I glanced up at the crowd

---

* *The* YMCA from the song, also very aptly titled "YMCA." Like there are many, but this *is the* one.

before closing my eyes and focusing on my self–pep talk. "Break my wrists—no! I am not going to break my wrists!" I opened my eyes, locked the pommel horse in my sights, and started to (kind of) run.

Ten minutes later I was at home, lying on my stomach on my bed, pretending to read one of my favorite books, *Charlotte's Web*. I was probably holding the book upside down. My mother entered the room. "Tsidi . . ." She sounded concerned. I turned around very casually.

"Hi! I love you," I said, breathing hard. She blinked in silence, before leaving the room without offering a response. I don't know what *I* would have said to my child who I had just watched run up to a pommel horse, karate chop it, walk around to the side, and salute invisible judges. My child who had jogged directly out of the gymnasium doors, the demonstration still going. Mmmhmm. I had jogged right out of the YMCA, across the street, into the Chelsea Hotel, into the elevator, and into our apartment. I was still dressed in my unitard when my mom walked in, decompressing, and out of breath from all the jogging.

"I wasn't clumsy." I turned to my husband, my eyes still full of tears. "I wasn't clumsy at all."

I thought about how mad I would get when everyone in the world would say: "It's like riding a bike! You never forget!" Shut up. "Well, I kind of used to be able to ride a bike in my hallway and this is not like that at all!" So many boyfriends were convinced that they would be the one who could teach me how to ride a bike. They didn't understand how I could have forgotten. I would throw up my hands. "It's probably because I learned in a hallway?"

White-knuckled and internally screaming, I tried to bike outside. I failed. I unwisely took *bike* to a new level with "moped" but crashed one into some tables at a street café while on tour in Amsterdam. I remember, vividly, watching the people at the tables jump up, scream, and run with their belongings as my moped (without me on it; I had already slid off and was lying on the street, watching from a distance) careened into the seating area, hit the wall of the café. Thankfully no humans were harmed. I hadn't wanted to get on a moped—had not wanted to with every fiber of my being—but everyone else on tour had gotten one. It was either get left behind or inevitably crash.

I remember arriving in Paris after taking the train from London.

Our tour van was parked across the street from the train station. Everyone else had run across the busy road, dodging speeding cars effortlessly while dragging their suitcases behind them. I stood frozen, unable to determine a safe-enough break in the flow of traffic. Though I will jaywalk any street in New York City, with my eyes closed, the French drive like crazy people. This sort of unfamiliar speed and its danger have given me absolute nightmarish anxiety attacks for my whole existence. I can gauge neither how my body will react, nor how the cars will react to my body, and I don't have enough points of reference, or information, to Frogger my way across roads like this. Maybe after spending some months in Paris, I'd be able to navigate busy intersections, but . . . after five minutes of eye darting and heart-racing panic, I turned around, went back into the train station, and got a drink. They pulled the van around later.

Almost everything I could think of in my life had been affected by hypermobility and everything it came with. It had been a bonus in activities like dance, gymnastics, and sex. It had been the source of fun parlor tricks. At several parties I have been wheeled out in a tiny suitcase from which I slowly, creepily emerged. I sit with my legs folded up to my chest on long flights. I would sometimes (all the time) wrap my fingers around each other, bending them all the way down and say "See?" as a fun trick to do, everywhere. I would fall into splits in nightclubs and do all of Willi Ninja's° moves while watching Madonna's *Vogue* video. No one ever thought that I should "go see a doctor" because I was just—bendy. End of story.

"Oh, that's just how Bernice is. She reads slow," someone might say about a little girl who probably needs to get checked out for dyslexia, or a list of other learning disabilities. "Oh, you know your auntie Sarah. She doesn't like to leave the house, leave her be." Maybe Auntie Sarah has agoraphobia? Someone please help. "Oh that Tsidi, you know she just grinds her teeth so much. She loves to chew!" That's bruxism, you

---

° The Grandfather of Vogue—an iconic self-taught dancer and choreographer who rose to prominence in the Harlem Ballroom scene of the early 1980s and took the form of dancing known as "voguing" global. Also, Mother of the House of Ninja.

guys. Please help all of us. So many people didn't (and still don't) go to doctors for a lot of reasons. Normalizing medical issues as personality traits. Money. Rightful distrust of the government and health professionals. Money. No access to health care. Lack of information and access to information. Time. Money. Religion. Time. Money. Money. Time. *Inshuuuuurahnce.*

A week after my breakthrough, I was sure I was also suffering from a friend of hypermobility: postural orthostatic tachycardia syndrome (POTS). Many of the symptoms rang very true to me. I finally felt as if I had enough information to find a doctor and make an appointment. And also had some more out-of-pocket payment money. Now, if you are a person wondering why I did all this research *before* just going to see a doctor, it's because I know that I have to be overprepared for everything, because I'm not going to be believed, taken seriously, or get the treatment I deserve, unless I walk into a room with an equal or a greater amount of information than the person I am going to talk to who is an actual professional at that job. If that sounds unreasonable and exhausting, you are correct. If you also have to do this, I am sorry. We are very tired. We also have so many acquired self-research degrees that we cannot use in any professional setting, but for fuck's sake we should be able to.

I knew that this doctor visit wouldn't answer all my questions, but I hoped it would be a good jump-off point with an actual professional and I could get some bloodwork done. After a frustratingly short general examination, the doctor handed me a box of weight-loss medication. I was livid. I immediately told him how racist that was. Get that BMI out of my face! Was it not reasonable that I might be heavier than my normal weight at the moment? Now in Baltimore, I was adjusting to living in a mostly unwalkable section of the city, and we *were still in a global pandemic.* He then tried to explain how nutrition worked, at which point I lost it and went on a five-minute-long rant about anti-inflammatory foods, probiotics, complex carbs, and listed every single spice, vegetable, fruit, grain, and morsel of edible items I put in my body.

"I cook ninety-nine percent of all my meals, every day, from scratch, with fresh produce and no processed foods. Do you?" I was reaching New York City levels of anger. I could hear my accent shift and I had leaned in sideways when I said "do you," which meant that clapping my hands in between words would be next. When that happens, no one is safe. The appointment ended with him continuing to suggest that I had rheumatoid arthritis, which I highly doubted. "Yeah fine. Test for all the things! You don't have to convince me to take tests, I want all of the information! I am an information person!"

Just take the fucking tests, clown.

A week later, I sat in a video meeting with that dumbass doctor.

"What do you mean that the lab *lost half of my blood*? What does that mean? How does that happen? My BLOOD?" I am definitely yelling. I am fuming. Because, what? All he said was "yeah."

I immediately thought about Henrietta Lacks[*] before I kept going off.

"You're being *very* casual about this. Do they lose people's blood *all the time*?" I felt light-headed, and I couldn't tell if it was the POTS, or me envisioning my missing blood. "Just gimme the test results, man," I said, exhausted with life.

Surprise, surprise! I tested positive for NOTHING. The rheumatoid arthritis was the one thing on the list that I shouted, "Yeah, I know!" to, since he had been so adamant about it. He then suggested, unironically, that I find a specialist who could help me figure out my hypermobile issue. He also said that he didn't know anyone he could recommend, since it was more common in children.

"No it's fucking not," I responded and promptly ended the video. Did I mention that I had gone to this doctor because it said "Hypermobile Specialist" on his website? Cool. Cool, cool, cool.

A week later, I was deep into researching actual specialists and also buying supplies to help myself. Braces, all kinds of pillows to help my

---

[*] In 1951, Henrietta Lacks (an African American woman) was being treated for cervical cancer at Johns Hopkins University, and those motherfucking doctors removed cells from her tumors without her knowledge or consent. Her cells, now known as HeLa cells, could amazingly, endlessly, reproduce and have been used for many scientific breakthroughs, including the development of the COVID-19 vaccine.

body's subluxation issues. Straps to hold my joints in place. So many bands, to make her . . . not dance.*

My husband had gotten me on the waitlist for a telehealth consultation with a great HSD/EDS specialist. But they were in such high demand that my appointment was a whole year away. If I was going to make it in one piece to that appointment, I would have to have a lifestyle overhaul. Not just braces, pillows, and mattresses. Everything about how I lived every day. I was relieved. Great, change this whole life. So that's how I did my best to approach it. I changed *e v e r y t h i n g*.

Turns out, I didn't have just hypermobility. I have Ehlers-Danlos syndrome (EDS).

very small, cheap confetti cannon

Ehlers-Danlos comes with a bunch of fun things that, upon being laid out, didn't make me feel sad. This had been the most drawn-out whodunnit, and I was just glad to know that the killer was Mr. Ehlers, with the disconnected tissues, in the library. In all instances, I don't care *what* the answers are, I would always rather have a shitty answer than no answer. I mean this for my own physical and mental issues and any situation outside of my body. I have always been like this, but in my forties my tolerance for not getting straightforward answers, in order to do my best, man . . . it really decreased. The chronic pain and the feeling of becoming useless were tough, but not knowing why had been far more damaging.

Now, yelling "yes, give me the tests, I want the information!" at any doctor would be a useless act, if I then had received the information, done nothing with it, and continued with my life, like . . . "aww man . . . I wish I could feel better. If only I knew what to do!" I have a very difficult time dealing with people who get the answers and solutions to their biggest problems and then do not do everything they possibly can, utilizing the knowledge they have just acquired, to fix

---

* The rap tune "Bandz a Make Her Dance" by Juicy J is not about hypermobility aids, but it is about rubber bands wrapped around stacks of money being used to make women dance.

the problems. It doesn't have to be a thing that gets fixed overnight, come on. I am *grown*, grown. I understand that things take time and take trials and errors. But it does require a consistent effort. Not a sometimey, casual bit of application. Just saying "I'm going to fix it, or work on it, or address it" does not mean that you have actually done it. Discussing how to make something less painful is not the same thing as actually doing the work to make it less painful. And, yes, I am talking about how I dealt with my diagnosis *and* what happened in my marriage. At a certain point, my flexibility became only a weakness. And just because it appeared that I could bend quite far, it did not mean that I would never break.

A whole lifestyle change means that I can no longer work jobs that demand sitting for an extended time. Some of my jobs, like scoring and composing, can yield seventy-two-hour workdays and deadlines that are detrimental to my mind and my body. I can't do it anymore. In the middle of my diagnosis, I was (this is going to sound like a fever dream) scoring, composing, and vocal coaching for an animated Christmas special with Steve Urkel—yes, with real life Jaleel White. While working on this, I was in the worst pain I have ever been in, but invisible disabilities are so hard to explain to people. Like marriage, from the outside, things can look perfectly fine. But my body was on fire at all times.

I began missing deadlines, not sleeping at all to make up for having to stand up and move my aching body in between playing through scenes. I would wander around my neighborhood in ten-minute breaks, every sixteen hours or so, bawling my face off and blasting "Cornfield Chase" from the *Interstellar* soundtrack because I needed to hear something that sounded bigger than my pain. I tried to keep pushing the deadlines they had, and I just couldn't make it. "Maybe I'll die," I thought, super angry that it would be a Steve Urkel Christmas special that took me out. That sounded worse than—oh no! Was I being threatened by death with yet another comedy Christmas album!

Delusional, I dramatically yelled through tears, "Fuck you, Jesus!" at the sky above the elevated M train on Broadway and Myrtle over the sound of my therapeutic Hans Zimmer. If you've ever been to the intersection of Broadway and Myrtle, you know that my behavior was the least of the noise and delusional activities that take place in that portal to hell of a corner.

I got fired from that job three days after my Jesus sky screaming and it was the best news I have ever received in my life. It was the WORST for my finances, but you know what? It fucking changed me as a person. I will never, ever work for a large corporation again. I don't give a fuck how whimsical the job sounds; it is not. I will never ever do any job that breaks me again. Not mentally and not physically. It's not even a choice I have to make. It's just not possible if I want to live. And the same goes for my views on marriage. Never, ever again . . . if I want to live.

I've come to think of EDS as my hero. My saving grace and the very strange jokester that lives within me. It's a rare group of disorders, and in that way, we're much alike. Doctors have a hard time identifying it. I vibe with that. Chronic pain? Yes, it's terrible, but I also get to look young for a really long time, because that's a side jam of Mr. Ehlers: little to no wrinkles and velvety skin. But—extreme exhaustion! Let's see what else: the dislocations and the joint noise—ooh! I'm a variant, like redheads, and I have extreme resistance to many drugs. I wish that I'd had that super important tidbit of information to relay to my anesthesiologist prior to my major surgery, because people with EDS have *woken up during surgery.* You read that right! But knowing this finally explained why I can drink the extreme levels of caffeine I do. Even better, it explained the two times I tried my best to do cocaine but it just didn't work! I had told my friend that her cocaine was broken, and she rightfully said, "No. Jean, it is not." I've been asking random people for *years* about my cocaine experience. Hoping someone might have the insight to solve this banned episode of *Scooby-Doo*-esque mystery. Ahh. To have the answers so you now know how to move forward in life is truly wonderful.

I am more selfish now. I don't think that's a bad thing. My selfishness doesn't harm others, and it doesn't harm me. It does exactly the opposite. It would be different if my disorders and conditions were curable, or even ones that had a definitive timeline for ravaging. Instead, I have things that are manageable. They require care, rest, peace, and attention. They demand I take care of myself. They demand that I say no to harmful things. I can't be mad at that. They are very reasonable demands we should all have for our lives, with or without rare genetic disorders. They give me superpowers. They want good quality items. Honestly, slay, EDS. You deserve, Queen. Not as a treat, just as a standard of living.

If I hadn't felt the physical effects of EDS, I wonder how long it would have taken me to stop bending until I was totally broken. Chalking it all up to how we're "supposed to feel at certain ages." What compromises we are expected to, or supposed to, make in order to be in relationships, especially with men. And most of all, I wonder how long it would have taken me to order this *fucking amazing mattress.*

In my remaining years,
I will reclaim my own echoes.

3.

You Can't Go Home,
but You Can Stay Here

W hat do you think this is? A hotel?"

This may be a fairly normal thing to yell at your teenage child when they start coming home at all hours of the night, but it was not, it turns out, an accurate or effective thing to yell at me. "But this *is*"—I paused, lowering the volume of my rebuttal—"a hotel," I muttered under my breath, stomping lightly back to my room. For one, we *did* in fact live in a hotel, but I knew what she meant. This hotel was our *home*.

My parents moved us into the Chelsea Hotel in 1977.° I was around eight months old at the time and still stick to the joke I enjoy telling: "I was in the building when Sid Vicious allegedly killed Nancy.† I say

---

° Technically, it is named the Hotel Chelsea. But only tourists, posers, or Laszlo Cravensworth call it that. It is colloquially known as the Chelsea Hotel. Or simply, the Chelsea.

† In 1978, Nancy Spungen (the girlfriend of Sid Vicious, the bassist of the Sex Pistols) was found dead in the bathroom of the couple's room at the Chelsea Hotel from a single stab wound to her abdomen. Vicious was charged with second-

allegedly, because anyone could have been the killer. It could have been me!" Before you say "a baby couldn't kill a whole adult," hold on now. I was an Est. 1977 Chelsea Hotel baby.

In 1978, I was a Chelsea Hotel baby that wore a lot of OshKosh B'Gosh rompers. The rompers with pockets on the front. Pockets just the right size for housing a switchblade. Where would I get that switchblade? I dunno, like anywhere? It was 1978 in New York City! I could have bought a house and two tons of heroin with seven dollars that I made from selling a finger painting. Also, before my depth issues kicked in, I was apparently a very agile baby and could have tackled the three flights of elaborate staircases between our lofted studio apartment on the fourth floor (room 410) and Sid and Nancy's (room 100). No one would have stopped me. They'd have seen a baby splattered in blood and said "cool baby." Maybe Andy Warhol would have said "cool baby." Then he would have leaned down and asked me—in his creepy-ass voice—if I wanted to be a part of The Factory. I would hold a tiny, bloody baby thumbs-up of approval. There I'd be, that night, a baby at Studio 54. A baby covered in blood, sitting atop a mountain of coke on a glass table and clapping my tiny hands together gleefully at the sight of an orgy. Marveling and gurgling at Grace Jones's skin. Asking her to teach me some French.

"Goo-goo, ga-ga! *Cette fête est vraiment super!*" I'd blurt out and giggle, waving my switchblade in the air and having a blast. "Who is that fabulously cool and bloodied baby with the knife, atop the cocaine?" People would go wild with admiration and have no concern for my safety because, again, it was 1978 in New York City. Besides, my mom was friends with Viva, a muse of Warhol's who was also raising her kids at the Chelsea and who, I'm assuming, was at Studio 54. So, I'd have adult supervision . . . of sorts. None of this party outing happened, but it could have. Sure!

But it was my baby agility (not murder or disco orgies) that prompted my parents to change apartments. "Mummy! She's up here

---

degree murder but died of a heroin overdose while out on bail in 1979, before the case went to trial. There is much speculation that Vicious did not kill Nancy, but the case remains unsolved.

again!" my brother, six years older than me, would cry out. He had
been very much enjoying the solace of his lofted bed area until I had
learned to climb its steep ladder and ruin his entire life. I don't remember any of this, but my mom relayed the stories to me many
times. "I don't even know how you got up there so fast, I would just
turn around for one second and"—she would shake her head and look
into the distant past with confusion—"you were so fast." I would nod,
also confused at how I'd been able to so speedily traverse a steep
object. "Anyways, that's when we knew we had to get a bigger place."

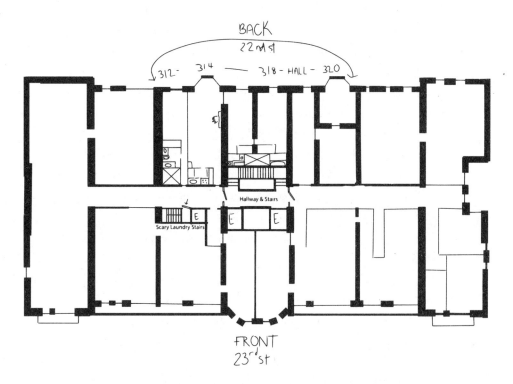

Our new home, on the third floor, was a two-bedroom, two-
bathroom space. A suite, made of two rooms. There was no loft for
me to scramble up and ruin lives, but for the years that my brother
and I shared a room, before he reached his teen years, we also shared
a bunk bed. I suppose the time he spent trying to kill me in my sleep
by doing things like stuffing M&Ms in my nose was a long-form spin-
off of his original "life ruining" show. Ya know. Great older-brother
stuff. Sure!

This new spacious apartment faced the rear of the building, away from the hustle, bustle, and constant noise of Twenty-Third Street. The windows in all the rooms were huge and looked out onto the respective rears of the buildings on Twenty-Second Street. Sitting on the wide ledges of the bay windows in our living room, ledges big enough to sit criss-cross applesauce, leaning forward on my elbows and resting my chin in my hands, I imagined what it would be like to step outside of your home into a private outdoor space. I watched from up high as people below hosted barbecues and dinner parties. As they tanned in the summertime. I watched kids exit their indoor spaces and play outdoors. Privately! They kicked balls around and giggled. They rode bikes and ran around with what, at the time, seemed like limitless space.

"What a dream," I thought and pushed my face against the window to the outdoor-privacy-play candy store. They were doing what I saw people do outside in the movies, on the television, and in books! And they didn't even live in the suburbs!

When my brother and I wanted outdoor play space, we would have to be taken to parks—Washington Square, Abingdon, Central. And my mother did take us to play and enjoy actual grass, outdoor space, and playgrounds quite a lot. But like most New York City kids who grew up in apartment buildings, it was and remains a rarity (even though I could see kids doing it) to have direct access to "go play outside." I have to remind many a nostalgic American Gen Xer who talks about "playing outside until the streetlamps came on," or "drinking from the water hose," that I did not have that experience. Running outside to play on Twenty-Third Street between Seventh and Eighth Avenues would be insane. And drink from what hose? We didn't even live on a street where you could open a fire hydrant during the summertime and play in that classic imagery of a New York gutter beach environment that I know people always imagine me doing, after I tell them where I grew up. But, no. I only envied that experience. And also only watched it in the movies, on the television, and read about it in books. You see, NYC apartment building kids are not a monolith, and we are built different. In all parts of the city, we are built different. Downtown Manhattan kids are built different. And Chelsea Hotel kids, although there are only a handful of us . . . well . . . we're real fucking different.

If you want to learn how to ride a bike, a good place to not do it is in a six-foot-wide hallway, on the third floor of a hundred-year-old historic building with slippery marble floors. This is *partially* why I do not know how to ride a bike. Propping the swinging doors at each end of the elevator bank open, by jamming folded chunks of cardboard ripped from my mom's record shipping boxes—I did try. I would attempt to ride to the ends of the hallways, all the way through, but the obstacles were always perilous. Falling off the bike onto beautiful, smooth marble would look extremely elegant, but it would really hurt. Fabulously falling into anyone's front door would also suck. Also, you can't really catch much speed in a 150-foot hallway. If you did, and didn't panic-brake fast enough, you could also crash headfirst through the window at the north end of the corridor. And don't forget the moving obstacles of random people, either exiting the elevators, their apartments, rooms, or going up and down the heart of the building's expansive staircase. So many factors to consider, and I didn't even toss in my general anxiety about sensing how my body moved through space.

I did my best to play in the hallway like the kids in the movies, on the television, in books, and outside my window. I would reluctantly kick an echoing ball around (loudly, since sound absorption is not a quality of marble) and sometimes play color tag with friends. I even tried super-panicked roller skating—also not great on marble. It always felt as if I were an alien who had seen footage of children playing and was trying to do my best to prove that I, indeed, was a human child enjoying human child activities.

When my mom would open our door and sigh, saying, "All right, Tsidi, that's enough now. Too much noise." I'd superbly feign my "Aww, man! Aww shucks" as I grabbed my ball, or gripped the black glossy wall molding to steady my slow, knee-shaking, clunky, roller skate walk back to the promised land, the threshold of our door. But truly, I just wanted to go back inside and read a book, or play *Pitfall* or *Adventure* on our Atari 2600 video game system. I wanted to lie on my stomach, on a quilt placed in front of our working fireplace, as a Duraflame log crackled and burned all the colors. As my *It's the Great Pumpkin, Charlie Brown* vinyl played for the hundredth time on our big veneer laminate stereo system, I'd pick at the fraying edges of the old, thin emerald-green carpet that framed the cold black tiles of the fireplace and kick my legs as I recited all the parts of the record out loud. *"What a fool I was! Trick or treats come only once a year. And I miss it by sitting in a* pumpkin patch *with a blockhead. You owe me restitution!"* I'd say, along with Sally, over the soothing Vince Guaraldi soundtrack. Sally was rightfully angry. What a fucking waste of her time. I'm sure that *The Great Pumpkin* is also where I learned that men will fucking waste your goddamn time.

"Too much noise," out there, with all the playing, indeed. I began to understand that I didn't enjoy doing what the kids in movies, on television, and in books were doing. I just wanted to have the option to not enjoy it. I wanted to choose my own adventure, because isn't that what the books* said I could do?

If there was any type of play I could do around the building that thrilled me, it was going downstairs to the lobby pay phones. A friend and I squeezing ourselves into the narrow glass booth and closing the metal-framed bifold door for "privacy." Only one of us could sit on the cold, worn metal seat, and it was usually me. Sometimes we had the benefit of a page of phone numbers ripped from the row of flip-up phone books nearby, but that was only if we had enough change to make *real* prank phone calls. My repertoire during those phone calls was old dad jokes, like, "Is your refrigerator running? Well, you should go catch it." Followed by a quick hang-up and giggles galore. But my favorite prank calls were always free and always to the information number 411. I would ask the answering operator the most random questions.

"What is the biggest butterfly in the world?"
"Who is cuter? Trey Ames or River Phoenix?"
"How do they make the ice blocks that form igloos so
    perfectly square?"

When the operator expressed their annoyance instead of providing an answer, I would loudly say, "But I thought this was the number for

---

* Choose Your Own Adventure books. You know, wildly popular in the 1980s. Start a story, sometimes you die and have to start over. Great for kids! Many deaths!

information! Why don't you know?" I'd slam the phone down with success as we burst into wild guffaws and out the bifold doors. Running and laughing all the way across the lobby to the stairwell entrance that also housed the secret side door to enter El Quijote, the Spanish restaurant that is still part of the hotel.

When I got older, I used to slip into that door and get a pack of Winstons for my mom from the cigarette machine. And a pack for myself. Sometimes I would grab a takeout order that was sitting on the top of the bar, if the bag was large enough. A large bag meant that it was a whole broiled lobster, and I fucking loved their lobsters. I didn't *have* to steal lobsters; my mother took us down to eat at El Quijote a lot. But free delicious lobsters, I'm saying. I've had lobsters all over the world and nothing has ever beat theirs. I went to El Quijote when they reopened in 2022 and ordered the lobster, excited to kind of be "home." It was theoretically a good lobster, I guess. The same way that, for instance, when they replaced Aunt Viv on *The Fresh Prince of Bel-Air*, the new actress was a good actress. But those of us who had been watching since the beginning knew it was all wrong. The whole show felt, well, off. Not because of nostalgia. I know what nostalgia looks like. Feels like. Smells like. Tastes like. This felt like erasure. And erasure tastes different.

That same year, my friend Dave Hill (who also lived at the Chelsea for some time) invited me to Gene's Restaurant in the West Village for lunch. An old school NYC staple of a place, Gene's hit me with a very specific wave of nostalgia as soon as I stepped in the door. As we sat at the bar, drinking heavily poured glasses of heavy red wine, I whipped around, sniffing hard. "This smells . . . It smells and it feels exactly like El Quijote. It's so specific!" I said to Dave, who told me that the restaurant did, indeed, have the same owners as the OG El Quijote. I ran my hands over the heavy menu and the old bar top. "Of fucking course. I would know this anywhere. This feels like home." In a city like New York, where everything is constantly being replaced, evolving, and changing—sometimes for good, but mostly for evil—it is rare to experience "feeling home."

When I went to the new El Quijote, I wasn't necessarily looking for "home." I wanted to know if they understood what things to fix and improve on and what things to keep. They didn't. I wanted to know if it would feel off, because I know how they got there. It did. Not to anyone else who would stay there, because they couldn't know. But I did. I felt everything. And I wasn't just eating at the reopened restaurant. I had booked one of the rooms in the newly reopened hotel. It was a soft launch and only a limited number of rooms were available. The rest were still being renovated. I wasn't, as far as I knew, looking for "home" when I made my reservation. I hadn't been back at the Chelsea since being forcibly evicted after the building was bought in 2011.* I had walked past the building a few times, but generally made it my business to steer clear of the entire block because the trauma was still trauma-ing.

I could have stayed at my usual place, the Ace Hotel in Brooklyn, while I was in town looking for my new apartment. But I wanted to know if the Chelsea's hotel section understood what things to fix, improve on, and what things to keep. They didn't. I wanted to know if it would feel off, because I know how they got there. It did. Not to anyone else, because they couldn't know. But I did. I felt everything. In my small room, I ran my fingers over the cold black tiles of the nonworking fireplace. It wasn't the third floor, but the tiles were mine.

I touched the ornate door to my room, now covered with a slick new coat of black paint, and it was "mine" too. No longer white and peeling. Not chipped and holding an old shaky brass chain lock. The handle was bright and shiny gold, with a computerized lock that opened with a key card. My old key, on its old green key chain that said 314, wouldn't work here, even if I hadn't lost it so long ago. They had erased that space. But the carvings and curves and weight of the door were all still "mine." I thought about the email that another resident had sent me in 2011, when most of us were in court fighting to keep our apartments.

I'd left to go on tour in the midst of the evictions battle, and she

---

* In May 2011 real estate developer Joseph Chetrit announced that he bought the hotel for eighty million dollars. Many tenants who had been there for a long time, my family included, ended up in court fighting for our places. Many lost, or gave up, like me.

alerted me that they had padlocked the door to my apartment. I had finally decided to give up the fight. I'd already had to make the terrible decision to tell my mom she had to move back to South Africa for a little bit while I got the apartment in order and dealt with renovating it for her, after I found out about the building being sold. I had been watching her mental health decline for a couple of years and as that degraded, her hoarding escalated to alarming heights. There was no one else on the continent to deal with any of these new developments. No family support that wasn't thousands of miles away. There was only me.

For a very long time, I assumed it was undiagnosed dementia and the onset of Alzheimer's that led to the decline of my mother's cognitive issues and the deterioration of the apartment she once kept so beautifully. Perhaps it was partially those things. But, I've since read some of her interviews from that time, and they were all so sharp, witty, and full of passion. When she got to talk about music and creativity—she was fine. I think that otherwise, she was severely depressed. Depressed, as a still hopeless romantic who was served divorce papers in her seventies, by an abusive narcissist. From not being able to be independent. From still having to fight to be acknowledged as an artist, as a woman, as a Coloured person, a South African, and a New Yorker. From spending all those years building us a home and feeling like a fool for waiting in the pumpkin patch with no restitution. My mother always said, "I'm not an American, I'm a New Yorker," and she loved her city with all her heart. I'm still working on banishing the guilt of not being able to save our home, her home. Of telling her she had to leave, because I couldn't do any better for us at the time. Returning to the Chelsea to stay for a night was my way of trying to close our doors. To revisit the ghosts of ourselves. To let them go.

When I tell people that I grew up in the Chelsea Hotel, the reaction is always wide-eyed, and I know the reaction is based on a few things. "Oh wow, that must have been crazy!" is a common response.

I shrug. "Not really, it was just home." I keep shrugging as I dash their hopes of hearing that I crawled down the stairs to murder Nancy

Spungen. That is what they are thinking. They are thinking about scandals and suicides and rock star shit. Of Janis Joplin and Oscar Wilde and, of course, Andy Warhol. Echoes that still ring through the halls of Leonard Cohen composing a classic tune about the infamous building. They are not thinking of little me, being tucked in and falling asleep to *Fraggle Rock*, the sound and glow of electricity from an old television bathing my room. They don't care about the smell of my mom's lamb and cabbage bredie being made in "the big pot" wafting through our ever-growing apartment. At one point we had knocked down walls and combined all the rooms from 312 to 320. It was a massive space.

They don't think about my brother and me, seated in those classic chrome and cane dining chairs with the holes in them that grew over time from both sitting and the insistent prodding of our tiny fingers. People are not thinking about siblings, viciously kicking each other under the table. We kicked so much that we wore a hole in the thinning carpet from our feet repeatedly scuffing the floor. Over the years, the strategic yet beautiful rugs that my mom bought to hide the worn-down spots in the living room would change locations. And I know that those new owners, who had come to inspect the condition of the apartment on the day I was forced to vacate—those people who looked at everything, including me, with such disgust—I know they saw that worn-down scuffed spot that had been under our dining table and thought it was not representative of the cool and luxe place that the Chelsea Hotel was going to be. It was gross and poor and not "the right kind of memory."

When I say that I grew up in the Chelsea Hotel, people are not thinking about me being scared every time I was forced to wait by the dank freight elevator in the hallway when my mom would get the call from the head of housekeeping, Doris, or maybe one of the other housekeeping ladies in the basement, that they were sending our washed and folded laundry back upstairs. That's how our laundry got done. Bag it up, hope that my mother wouldn't ask me to go put it on the creepy, scary elevator after she had called Doris and said, "I'm sending the laundry down." They would wash it in the big industrial machines that also did the building's linens for the guests. Sometimes I would have to take that elevator down all the way into the basement to give Doris, or one of the other sweet women, an envelope filled with two twenty-dollar bills from my mother for the week's wash. That was the worst, since I couldn't just put the money envelope on the elevator by itself. I would hold my breath the whole time, not because of any smell, but to avoid screaming at the level of "kid scared" I was. I would hope that they would be busy downstairs and I wouldn't have to make conversation. They were so nice, but I wanted to jump out of my skin as I responded to their lovely chats through clenched teeth.

Waiting for the elevator *in* the basement was never an option. I would bolt up the freight stairs to the lobby and then try to regulate my breathing in the *real* elevators on the way back up to our apartment. I don't know if anyone else who lived in the building did their laundry this way, but we did. At least we did until management told us we couldn't, sometime in the 1990s. I, for one, didn't take into consideration at the time that this was a new major inconvenience for my mother. Only that it was a win for me. You, dear reader, may not know this, but it is very new for a "regular" apartment in NYC to have laundry in the building, let alone an in-unit washer and dryer. I have lived in two apartments in Brooklyn where I had both of these unicorn setups. And that is only in the last fifteen years. Life changing. But tourists and new people to the city don't think about this. Tourists reading my story wouldn't understand why my mom, wisely, still snuck the laundry down there for a few years.

People won't think about us having a "hotel phone," in addition to our other three phone lines. It was a brown old-school phone that sat on an old orange, rusted filing cabinet by the dining table. On it, you could press just one button to reach the front desk, or dial other rooms. You could contact the "scary" basement housekeeping and also dial out, if you wanted to for some reason. When my father was away on tour, he chose this phone to repeatedly call my mom when they were in the middle of an international fight. People are not thinking about that phone insistently ringing at three, four, five in the morning, because time zones will really exacerbate the annoyance of phone fight callbacks.

People can't fathom that so much homework was done inside of those Chelsea walls. That I lost my virginity in my mom's bed when she was away on tour. That I blew so much weed smoke into the bathroom vent, standing on the toilet, and that my friends and I giggled ourselves to sleep pining over our elementary school crushes and that I etched mine, ARI PATZ, into the wall by my bed with a pencil, so I could run my hands along it at night. Ari was my first crush and kind of my first date. He was "that boy." You know, *that boy* in school who everyone was in love with. The boy that you put in your MASH° origami, paper game of the future, and do your best to calculate placement so you'll end up with him.

My dream elementary school MASH lineup was always:

Marry: ARI
Car: IROC Z
Job: ARTIST
Money: MILLIONAIRE
Kids: 2
Where: NEW YORK CITY
Live in: LOFT

Kids in Manhattan playing MASH rarely used the actual "MASH." In New York it was MLSB: Mansion, Loft, Shack, Brownstone. Or MPSA: Mansion, Penthouse, Shack, Apartment. We couldn't even fathom living in a HOUSE! Who could fucking have a HOUSE in Manhattan or . . . anywhere? I don't know why "Mansion" seemed more reasonable than "House." I suppose because we saw mansions in person. Big Gilded Age mansions that take up whole blocks were/

° MASH is a children's game played by writing lists of categories and choices, with the hopes of predicting one's future. The acronym MASH stands for Mansion, Apartment, Shack, and House, followed by even more fun traditional values of "adult life goals." One player writes their list and draws a swirl until another player says STOP. The lines of the swirl are counted and the first player uses that number to work their way down the list and cross their written options off until they are left with their FUTURE ADULT LIFE! Well, that's how we played.

are normal to walk past. In any case, whenever I played this game and tragically ended up living in a Shack, with a pogo stick as my vehicle, working as Sewer Maintenance Person, if I got Ari as a husband who would take care of our fifteen kids, I would feign sadness to my friends. "Aww, man!" I would say, bubbling inside with fifth-grade crusherflies and glee. "Aww, shucks!" By the way, the loft I imagined living in was definitely hobbled together from many of my friends' parents' lofts, but specifically, from the Patzes' iconic SoHo loft. Even living in the Chelsea Hotel wasn't as fucking cool as living in a giant artist's loft in SoHo. Real talk, I still don't think it is. Been chasing that dream for years.

At my West Village, extremely progressive elementary school, PS3, Ari had dated my classmate and one of the "cool, popular, pretty girls," Taryn, for quite some time. They were "that couple." Until Taryn decided she wanted to break up with him and return the locket he had given her, in a style that contained all the fifth-grade drama that kids hold. I'ma be real with you, I *think* I was volunteered to be the person who handed the locket back to him, but it absolutely might have been someone much closer to Taryn in that friend group. Maybe Mara, or Haydee.

Much of that day is a blur. It was a *big deal.* A big deal, their breakup. And I was sort of friends with Taryn and the cool girls, but like . . . on the outskirts of the group, always unsure if I would get an invite to a hangout, or a sleepover. That riding-the-edge-of-a-clique feeling, where you're sure they're making fun of you behind your back. Always afraid that a sleepover might be the setup for an elaborate prank at your expense. I didn't feel pretty enough to not always be suspicious that any activity they included me in had malicious intent.

I would never have asked Ari to the dance if I'd thought in a million years that he would say yes. I didn't want the cool girls' wrath. I only did it because my best friend called and asked him to the dance and he said no. I made a follow-up phone call to him, as a weirdly put together BFF plan, to see if he was just gonna say no to everybody. I now wish I had not done that, but what was I supposed to do after his answer? Say, "Uhh, never mind, dream boy. 'Twas just a test!" If I tried real hard at a therapist's session, I could remember how that dance went. I know it was "not fun." I don't even think Ari liked me and I'm 100 percent unsure of how we got to an actual movie date.

Ari's mother, Julie, chaperoned us on this outing to the movie theater on West Fourth Street in Manhattan's West Village—for those who know, it's the one that is now an IFC movie theater. We saw *Adventures in Babysitting* and I don't think I paid attention to the movie at all. I was just in awe that I was there with him. Julie's chaperoning wasn't odd, since we were just fifth graders. But her very rightful level of a protective eye on her child was also because Ari's brother Etan had been kidnapped years before, in one of the most famous kidnapping cases in America.

Etan Patz had been on his way to PS3, years before I attended the same school. My brother was his age and a student there, but I'm unsure if they were ever in the same class. By the time Ari and I were classmates, in 1987, Julie had taken a job at PS3. When we both attended junior high together at the Clinton Program, a small school just a couple of blocks from the Chelsea, Julie also worked there. She was a really lovely woman, and I cannot imagine her level of concern for her child at all times. I think about it now and wish I could tell Julie that she was doing a great job, more than the best she could. When the contractors hired to revamp the Chelsea destroyed that wall with its etched memories, of course they wouldn't have known the deep New York City lore and fifth-grade drama contained in it. And even if they had only dry-walled and spackled, the current hotel guests would never consider that the wall behind an expensive new desk in their room held all the feelings of a little South African and her wishes to raise two children with a Jewish kid from SoHo.

Maybe closer to what people want is that the dent in the west wall of the living room was made by a mug my father threw at my mother, after he slapped her so hard that her blood splattered onto the same wall. They would probably understand that in the late 1980s, someone committed suicide by jumping from the eighth floor, into the well hole of the elaborate staircase. The body hit so many parts of the brass railing on the way down before it ultimately touched down that it cracked the first-floor landing. After that incident we sometimes forgot about the dents and would run our hands along them on the way down the stairs. Shuddering when our fingers dipped. Staring at the cracked landing, the broken black floor that held the shape of a mangled corpse and stayed that way far too long before being filled in and fixed.

Sure, there are some things they want to hear. But they don't know all the real echoes. The kindness and family of Jerry, Jerome, Charles, and Pete from the front desk. Or what it felt like in the early hours of the morning when a fire alarm would gather everyone in the lobby in their pajamas—long-term residents and guests alike—until it was safe to go back upstairs. They definitely don't think that the echoes ringing through the building are ten-year-old me, reluctantly taking piano lessons but being excited to follow the sheet music for "Maybe." My favorite song from my favorite movie musical, *Annie*. They don't know that since the late 1970s, the elevator on the left sometimes stopped at the first floor, even when you didn't press 1.

"Umm. Ethan Hawke moved in across the hall from us and he didn't respond to my mom saying hello to him once when they were in the elevator, so I was really fucking mean to him for a couple of years." I offer this as a Chelsea Hotel memory to starved strangers. "Oh, cool! Ethan Hawke!" they respond, grateful for this meh morsel.

I follow the Chelsea Hotel's Instagram account and let me tell you, it is always weird as fuck to see. Famous people throwing parties and getting ready in their rooms. I always wonder things like, Is that where I cried on the floor after that weird dude I met at Limelight dumped me? Lately, their posts have been touting how much the Chelsea is, and always has been, a "safe haven" for artists. And while this was true, in its heyday and especially when the icon himself, Stanley Bard, was the landlord of the building . . . let's be for fucking real. The same safe haven that padlocked my door? The same safe haven that swore it would let its long-term residents stay and then found loopholes to evict most of us?

Listen, maybe people who just started watching the show don't know that you've replaced Aunt Viv with a new Aunt Viv. But I know. I know what erasure tastes like. People write that I am from Brooklyn. Or, wildly, Philadelphia. Now, why is that? You know why. Like staying at the Chelsea for their soft open and like so much of my experience getting older, in this body, I am denied my own history and existence. Who decides who is worthy of claiming their lived experiences? Who is worthy of claiming their spaces and memories? And I don't mean just through the physical gentrification of spaces, I mean in the *idea* of existing.

"Lemme ask you a question, does this elevator still unexpectedly stop at the first floor sometimes?"

I am checking in for my two-night stay at the "new" Chelsea Hotel and asking the young woman at the front desk. "Yes!" she exclaims, perking up. "They've tried to fix it so many times and there's just nothing we can do." "Mmmhmm." I nod, smiling and looking over her head at the now open space in the staircase where the cracked corpse landing used to be. "Mmmhmm." I take my weird key card and walk to the other "Not Nancy" elevator. All of me is proud that at least there is still a loud ghost, but it's the ghost that they wanted anyway. The ghost that they will accept and not erase. Without a doubt, a ghost that they can sell, so I don't give them the information they want. Not until right now, with all of you as witnesses. Not until I can be a nonerased ghost too.

I can't go home to the Chelsea, or even just to New York City. The first, for obvious reasons, and the second, well, part of the issue is monetary and in direct correlation to my current standards and dealbreakers for living. Besides, even if I *could* find a place in NYC right now that met all of my living criteria—my heart, brain, and body couldn't deal with the scrambling, clawing-eyes-out process that is trying to get an apartment there. It is a fucking nightmare situation. One that affects anxiety and your feeling of value and worth. If you have seen an amazing NYC apartment on Zillow, StreetEasy, or even Craigslist, you are already too late. You would have had to contact that place in the past, using a time machine, to find out it was available before everyone else in the world. Every single apartment I have ever gotten in NYC has been from sheer luck, insane exhausting persistence, and dealing with a person who is willing to be reasonable—especially about the documents I can provide, given my decades of unconventional work. If you want to feel terrible about yourself on various subatomic levels, I suggest trying to get an apartment in New York City.

Now, in my older years, "home" has had to become a different concept. One that is heavily influenced by my Chelsea experience. And sadly, by my very Wizard of Oz "just trying to get home" experience. Because I and many like myself are the unrecognized ghosts, the actual factual, real representatives of the city. More specifically, a part of the representation of Manhattan. Even more specifically—of Chelsea as a neighborhood. Maybe they would let me be a representative if I had grown up in the LES or in Harlem. Maybe that would be more believable for someone like me. Because I am not Chloë Sevigny or Natasha Lyonne. I am not Carrie Bradshaw, Samantha, Charlotte, or Miranda. Those are the Manhattanites and New Yorkers that people accept. But Chloë moved to New York when she was nineteen, from Connecticut. Natasha Lyonne is from Great Neck, New York. All of the characters on *Sex and the City* are transplants. Mostly from Connecticut. And you can do whatever you want with that information and it's not anyone's fault that they're from where they're from. I am just serving you some facts about representation, perception, and who is allowed to be who. Whom? Dammit.

My cell phone number, very intentionally, has a 212 area code. People from New York correct me when I give them my phone number, saying, "No, I need your cell." Because 212 is known as *the* Manhattan landline area code from back in the day. In my childhood household, we had three 212 numbers. In my adulthood, those numbers were all too expensive for me to purchase back. This is a thing you can do if the number is still available and you have enough money. I did not and do not have fifteen thousand dollars to purchase any of them. I chose a new one instead.

"I am claiming my almost birthright," I said a lot when I told people my number had changed. "Ooooh, a two-one-two! The status!" they would reply. This, I know. People do not let a 212 phone call go unanswered. That call has to be about money, someone from another time, or a real fucking New Yorker is, for some reason, trying to get in touch with you. It was the best I could do to carry home with me. It is still all I can afford.

The other parts of NYC that I will always carry with me, are free: my insane levels of hypervigilance. Old New Yorkers, real New Yorkers, we are all like this. My speed walking. If Google Maps says my destination is fifteen minutes away, I will be there in eight minutes. My low tolerance for bullshit. I don't sound like what a stereotypical New Yorker sounds like. I've been too many places, so I don't sound like I'm really from anywhere specific. But if I am angry, you will know where I am from. The New York will jump right the fuck out of me. Maybe some Spanglish and definitely some hard claps that punctuate the severity of my words. If I am in a good mood, some Jewish bubbie talk. I don't make eye contact on public transportation anywhere in the world and I know who among the public is concealing their crazy. If I do make any eye contact, it's with the other hypervigilant people who have also sussed out the crazy and we are assuring each other that if the shits go down, we got it, as a community.

I am my home, for the rest of my life. It's in me. All of our homes have contributed to making us who we are, who we will be. By the time you get to middle age, you've probably had a few homes. Some of you are lucky enough to be able to go back and touch your etched wall, childhood memories, to hug all your childhood friends. But many of you are just like me. For whatever reason, there is no way to return home and you might, like me, relate better to older people, because most of their childhood friends are fucking dead too.

You might, like me, have grown up in a place that is so gentrified, people cannot even *imagine* that you are from there. But there are only a handful of children with this very specific child experience of home at the Chelsea Hotel. And out of that handful, only two of us are not White. And out of those two, only one of us still lives in America. It is quite unique and quite lonely.

So, I am the sum of all my parts, and those parts include my Chelsea and New York City homes forever. But I want my existence restitution. And no one should fuck around and take that lightly because I am, after all, a New Yorker. More specifically, I am an Est. 1977 NYC Chelsea Hotel baby.

I could do anything.*points to own eyes, points to Chelsea Hotel, pulls out switchblade*

During mine
residual epoch—

X _____

4.

Call Me by My Name

Say something in African," said many of my schoolmates to me, my whole life.

"Well, there's not one language in Africa, first off," I'd respond. "There are thousands of African languages. There's not like . . . Africanese," I'd say to their noticeably disappointed faces. "Maybe you mean Afrikaans?"

"Yeah!" They'd perk up at hearing something that sounded enough like "Africanese" to satisfy their exotic thirsts. I would sigh. "I know *some* words, but I don't speak it fluently. My mom said she didn't want to teach me the language of our oppressors."

"Oh," my African American and other peers would say. Rife with anger at my inability to "African it up" for them. "Well, you're not a real African. Your name is weird. And your hair isn't African." Then they'd maybe call me "Serafina." Sometimes they'd sing the Life Savers commercial featuring the popular South African group at the time, Ladysmith Black Mombazo, at me. And many times they asked if my family in South Africa had lions and monkeys in their houses, or what it was like to see tigers walking around. "Like at the mall?" I'd respond while gathering together the fucking

UNICEF* chocolates and cardboard money boxes we were all forced to take home and sell to our neighbors.

I hated the UNICEF sales time of year for multiple reasons. I did not want to go door-to-door in our building and hock candy. Children do not want to do this. Why couldn't UNICEF fucking sell the chocolates themselves? Why the child labor? The pervasive idea of Starving African Children was unstoppable in the 1980s. Ads, songs, fundraising festivals. And it wasn't just the images of kids with distended bellies and flies everywhere, it was the general, incorrect poverty porn marketing of "Africa." You know that country, Africa? Where they don't know it's Christmas,† no one wears clothes, and there's no water? As the only African/Not African kid in school, you can guess why I was not thrilled to be involved in this activity.

Once, when I was very reluctantly selling the chocolates door-to-door on the eighth floor of the Chelsea, a woman asked me if her money would go directly to *my African family*. After that incident, my mom bought my whole supply of chocolates every year. I was grateful, because we were starving Africans, and now, at least, we could eat a box of terrible chocolates. We'd hopefully figure out what to do about the flies. And the thirst.

The 1980s were also a very strange time to be a specifically *South* African kid, for political reasons. Apartheid, sanctions, and divestments were very much common topics of conversations, and maybe this all wouldn't have been a thing I had to navigate as much every day if I hadn't attended such an extremely liberal artsy elementary school. We called our teachers and our principal by their first names. John. Dan. Fredlyn. Lucy. Our graduation "walk out song" was "Let the Sunshine In" by the 5th Dimension. And we sang a lot of folksy songs.

---

* The United Nations Children's Fund is a "humanitarian aid organization." Sure.
† The 1984 global hit "Do They Know It's Christmas" by Band Aid (a charity supergroup of British and Irish recording artists) berates the whole continent of Africa for the duration of the song. Fave lyrics: "And the Christmas bells that ring there are the clanging chimes of doom. Well tonight, thank God it's them instead of you." Fuck your mother, wtf.

One of them was "Marching to Pretoria."° A song popular on both fighting sides of the South African Boer War. It was an uncomfortable song for me to sing, to say the least. But not as uncomfortable as visiting family in Cape Town living under apartheid and actually doing things like riding the COLOURED section of the train, then coming back to America and having to write a book report on Rosa Parks.

A teacher said to me, "So many brave people fought and protested in the civil rights movement so that we all don't have to experience segregation. I'd really love you to write about this." "Right. But, I just did this." I would point to the back of the bus on the "olden times" Rosa Parks picture. "I did the segregations last week. So that's fun." It was not fun.

I was in a time machine by myself and there was no one to relate to. No Coloured kid counselor. No internet references to pull up of people who looked like me. No restaurant of Cape Coloured foods to visit on a field trip. My brother is six years older than me and his assimilation was going very differently, mostly because of our hair texture. Although our facial features are very similar, his tightly coiled 4C pattern fro and my loose 3B curls† move through the world in very dissimilar ways. Here in America, my father could be considered unquestionably, phenotypically Black. Which meant he was having a different experience from my mother, who was always confused for a myriad of other races that people seemed to hastily snatch from a grab bag like Scrabble tiles. Persian? Puerto Rican? Native American? Egyptian? And of course, for those not very astute—

"Your mom is White!" said not only classmates all through my school years but also people on Instagram last year, when I posted a picture of my mother. "No, she is not White. She is Coloured and I am

---

° Recorded by groups like the Weavers and the Highway Men, "Marching to Pretoria" sounds like a song sung by White people. This feels like a good description to me.

† These are categories of curl patterns. They range from 2B to 4C, the lower numbers starting at looser waves, the higher being tight coils. My 3B falls in the large ringlet, size of a sharpie curl. We did not have this information growing up. I figured out my curl pattern in my early forties. Wild.

also Coloured," I said all through my school years and also to people on Instagram last year. "You can't say *colored*. That's an outdated, derogatory term," Americans have said to me all my life. "I am aware of the history of the word and what it means for Black people in America especially," I respond carefully. "And I am not calling myself *colored* in that way. It is also spelled differently, but that's—I have been here almost all my life. I do understand. But, I am also *not from here*, as many people are not from here. People around the earth have different cultures, ethnicities, and even other racial classifications. Yes, for shitty reasons, but still yes. Maybe if everyone were more familiar with more peoples from around the world, they wouldn't say I phenotypically look like only the people they currently know. Because I look exactly like the people I am and—"

I am interrupted. "So you're not Black? You're saying you're *not Black*?" They are angry at me now. The same way they are angry at the new global pop-star Tyla, a Coloured woman from Johannesburg. Apparently America now knows there are two of us.

"I am saying that I am not from here, but I am also Black . . . but I can't say that everywhere . . . in addition to . . . see, in America I'm . . . but in South Africa . . . but in me . . ." My heart is racing. They keep going. "But your mom is White, so you're biracial?" I want to rip my skin off. "My mother is Coloured. My father is Coloured. My whole family is Coloured, on both sides of my family. We are a whole people, with a whole culture. With food and dialects and music. We are the most genetically diverse people on the planet and we are multigenerationally mixed. Kinda like Creole people. But way more mixing. You understand that Creole people exist, right?"

"So you're not from Africa?"

In my mind, I throw eight hundred iron tables across the room. I am Jean's lifelong frustration.

| | |

"What are you?"

The year is 1990 and I am "teen unwisely" making out with a very cute boy who works at the D'Agostino's supermarket a block from my house. We're going at it in a small corner of the supermarket's front exterior, which is definitely where a lot of people pee. Claaaassy. He'd just started working at D'Agostino's a week prior, and I had aggressively stalked and staked my neighborhood claim on him. I was very proud of my win. His high-top fade was impeccable. The making out was . . . fine. As we disengaged from a kiss, he decided it would be a good time to ask about my ethnicity. Lucky for him, I had just figured out a great new way to answer this question, and he was going to be the first person I used it on. The setup was perfect!

"I'm Batman," I growled in a gravely impression of Michael Keaton as Batman in the 1989 version of the movie.

"What?" Light-Skinned Cutie asked me, pulling back. "You being mad weird."

I growled again. "I'm Batman." I smiled.

He shook his head. "Yo, I don't even know what you're saying right now. What are you, like half White? 'Cause you talk like you're White. And your mom looks White."

I sighed, defeated. "I'm Dominican." I stepped back. "And my mom's not White. And, I don't talk White. That's not a thing." I was going to defend at least some portion of my existence if I couldn't be fully honest. I had also been "Dominican" for quite some time at this point.

"I mean, you sound like a White girl though." He shrugged and we went back to making out.

Explaining what and who I am has always been a tiresome and isolating journey. An odd one. Because although I am an immigrant and a child of self-exiled immigrants, I wasn't yet a year old when we came to America. So when people ask where I'm from, I say, "New York . . . but Cape Town . . . but . . ." And then I have to decide if the situation warrants all of my information. Because I am not an African American person from New York City, but really technically I *am* an "*African-American*," just not in the sense they would understand, definitely not like Elon Musk, and do I have time to explain that? I can't say that I'm South African, full stop, no other information. South Africans love telling me that I am not South African. To them I am American.

I am Jean's lifelong failed attempts at belonging.

I can't say that I'm first generation, I'm an "almost native New Yorker." Saying I'm first gen would mean denying my mother's very intentional, dangerous, and difficult act of traveling back to South Africa to birth both of her children on the African continent. Then she really committed to that idea and gave us both African names, which, by the way, makes my existence more confusing, especially in the Cape Coloured community where African names are not the norm. Both my brother and myself are the only people in all of the known generations of our family that have "African" names. It is confusing to people all over the world, that my mother was doing what Black Americans in the 1970s were doing—giving their children traditional African names. My aunts, cousins, uncles, grandparents? Nope. Joan. Anthony. Boris. Evelyn. Edward. My parents birth names are respectively Adolf Johannes Brand and Beatrice Bertha Benjamin.

When my father decided to convert to Islam, the same decision was made for our whole immediate family. Our last name legally changed from Brand to Ibrahim when I was three years old. At the same time, my father legally changed his first name to Abdullah and my mother changed hers to Sathima. A few years later, we became United States citizens. At that point, I was used to lugging around a lot of identification and a collection of documents to validate my existence. I don't think that I will ever let go of the envy I have for people who just have a lil' driver's license as their only ID. Seems nice, fun, and carefree. Ooh boy, what about people who have a lil' license with a name like Sarah Jones? Or Jeff Johnson! Ooh, ooh! What if the lil' license also says that they're born in America—hold on. I actually don't know if driver's licenses have birth country information on them. And I know that Eurocentric names and American births don't stop bad shit from happening to people for so many reasons. *whispers* *But there are times I am still envious of the streamlined processes y'all have access to that I don't.*

"This French visa application is gonna fucking suuuuck!" I wished I could have said all of that in French, but at the time Duolingo had only provided me with enough instruction to say I was "eating the orange." Although *"je mange l'orange"* is fun to say and a great alias, but it was not helpful at the moment. *"Merde!"* I hung up the phone using the French expletive I did know. *Shit*, indeed. I was one day into researching a French talent visa and I was already exhausted.

I'd been trying to book an appointment with the South African Embassy to apply for a copy of my birth certificate, but none of the phone numbers to any of the United States locations worked, nor did the website. If you ask me how I lost my birth certificate, well, I've moved ten times in the past ten years. I've had about six new lives—I don't know! It's probably somewhere in the world with my naturalization papers. But in order to get new copies of those papers, I'd have to first obtain a copy of my birth certificate, which can take up to a year. Why? Because people are unorganized and because I was born in the 1970s in a hospital filled with people who didn't think that I was a human being. This is just a portion of all the things I need to even start the process of a foreign visa. I am jealous of people who can simply ask their parents to look in the garage, or something, for their old things. I saw on the TV that's where families keep their children's old things. I don't know if that's true. I have never had any family here.

I have a completely unreliable "American experience."

It's such an extra othering feeling whenever I have to gather all my "identification" papers. Always a reminder that I am "other." Always extra work and more proof that I exist, still, in a constellation of legal identifiers I never agreed to. I wondered if, when it came time to renew my passport, I should change my name. Not to my father's original last name, no thanks. Not to my mom's maiden name—that would just be another man's name. Or my grandmother's last name—*merde!* There was no way to go back far enough to find a non-man's name! Stunning work, patriarchy.

I have since begun to think of what new name I would really love. It hasn't come to me yet. I love what my mother chose for me, but it also has ties to her desire to claim her connection to Africa. As a person who lived her life internationally, refusing to pass, and being loud about it— very big deal. I don't feel as if that's something I need to do, and as a person who chose and changed her own name, I think she'd understand. I'm not and have never been Muslim, so my last name has never made any sense for me. I never took the last names of either of my husbands and it was never really an option, not interested. Jean Grae has served me well, but I never intended for it to live so far outside of my rap career. Plus, in France I would be "jhahn," and that's totally different.

I am looking for something that speaks to all of who I really am. Who I have been and see myself being. It might still be a name that prompts "the silence." If you too are the child of immigrant parents, went through the American school system, and continue to exist in America as a person with a non-American name, you know the silence I'm talking about. That pause after so many other names have been rattled off with ease. That panic we've had the whole week before and on the first day in a new school, or with a new teacher, when all we wanna do is be normal. All we wanna do is blend the fuck in, but an adult with authority stands with furrowed brow and pauses. That person holds the power to dictate how our socialization will play out, and every second they don't call our name, our "othering" level elevates. "Ssss . . ." Furrow. "Tissd-" Squint. "Tah-cye." Can't take it anymore. "Tsidi," I yell.

"So the *T* is silent?" Kids are giggling. Most are turned around to stare. I gulp to swallow the guilt of the lie I'm about to tell. "Yeah. Like Cee-dee." Nodding and wanting to disappear. Just go to the next name, oh my God. "Like a compact disc player! Cool." Everyone laughs. That is not how you say it. Say the *T*, like *tsunami*. Once, I said it correctly, and the teacher said, "Like the tsetse fly!" And there I was, the starving African kid with flies all over my eyelids again. Kids made buzzing noises around me that year, the whole year. I learned to be vigilant and anticipate when my name would be called and get a jump on the teacher by just screaming "HERE!" before they had a chance to ruin my life. That pause, that silence, still happens when people have to use my government name. I love it. I let it linger, like the goddamn Cranberries,* and I do not help them. I let them sweat. It's a beautiful silence. The only other social silence I enjoy that much is the one that now exists in my life due to the lack of street harassment from men.

---

* "Linger" is both the title of the 1993 song by the musical group The Cranberries and a lyric repeated in the hook, sung by the late, great Dolores O'Riordan. "Do you have to, do you have to, do you have to let it linger."

Whew, y'all it's breathtaking! It feels like that scene with Jodie Foster in the movie *Contact* when she was describing a celestial event and says incredulously, "So beautiful. Should have sent a poet." The catcalling so graciously left my life three years ago. Oh, what a glorious time to be outside! I am finally completely invisible to men, and it couldn't be a more peaceful fucking experience. I know that Depeche Mode's song "Enjoy the Silence" is not about the glee of being a middle-aged, mostly femme-presenting person relishing in the tranquility of the external world without the cacophony of pestering men. I know it's not. But maybe we could petition for it to be the song for our new club. If you wanted to start a cool middle-aged club with me or whatever, NBD.

Maybe my new name will be a nod to me tossing away my desire to assimilate into African American culture. Or that it was the only choice I had, since I was not allowed to say who I was. But it has always been obvious that I am an outsider when I am in the rooms. I have felt it. Heard it. It has not been quiet. Sometimes I could pretend long enough to survive. Or study the things I could perform well enough to not be a culture vulture and not only exist in the spaces, but excel. Cooking. I can cook, and your grandmother will ask me back and let me in the kitchen and assign me at least two dishes, and one of them will be the mac and cheese. Boy, I really worked hard on that shit. So hard it makes me cry.

Assimilation has never gone well for me, and I'm finally all right with being loud about the me that I am. It did not go well in school. It did not go well in my career. It did not go well in dating. It has not gone well in friendships because I cannot relate. It did not go well when I was invited to any churches, because that is not my experience. It doesn't make me pretentious, it just makes me not an African American person with that very rich and deep culture. It is not mine to claim. I have experienced many parts of it; it is not a monolithic experience and it is still not mine to claim. It's not where I come from, and in order for a full understanding of me to be available, I really need to make this clear. So maybe my new name will hold some of that very heavy weight.

Perhaps my new name will speak to not only my new invisibility and silences, but also my old ones. I was invisible in my career the whole time. Never really being seen. Never really being heard. People do not listen to my lyrics and unpack them. People have never searched for the multilayered meanings and Easter eggs in my work. No one even noticed that, for the better part of a decade, I covered myself in faux blood onstage while elaborately cosplaying various characters from the movie *Kill Bill*. No one said a thing. Once, I asked a young Black woman in the audience of one of my two-hour solo shows if after the performance, she would sit at my merch booth and sign autographs for fans. I, of course, offered to pay her and soothed her fears that people would know she was not me. "They'll never know the difference," I told her. I will never forget the look of sadness she gave me after ten minutes of signing autographs and taking pictures. I wasn't far away, sipping a drink and watching. I have told some people this story and they thought it was funny. But it's not funny. It's fucked-up. And no, we didn't look remotely alike and no, we didn't do a clothes switcheroo. So maybe part of my new name will be a pause, or some large letter that is, for some reason, invisible to the naked eye? I don't know.

It might be that I'll choose to roll with a new moniker that makes it clear to not call me "Auntie." People really like calling women of a certain age Auntie. They just start doing it and no one asks for that shit. *whips around* *Where is the lady to be called this name? Is it me? You are mistaken on a grand scale.* I don't want to be called Auntie the same way I will, for certain, piledrive a youngster who will refer to me as "Grandma" in the future. Young people, if you are reading this— you're lettin' me down. I think you're so cool in so many ways and have done so much amazing self-work at such an early stage of life, especially in regards to how you correctly identify. And then in being strong and firm when it comes to demanding respect for how people must address you correctly. And yet . . . and yet I still see you out here in these no boundaries streets referring to every woman or femme-presenting older person as Grandma or Granny. Come on, y'all! This should be easier for you to grasp than anyone! You should know that not everyone wants, or has, kids. Is it that you should respect people's identities only until they reach a certain age? I don't know how to make it clear that if you do this to me, I will wrestle you to the ground. If it is a name change, then this could be the option for me.

I have thought about sticking with my old name. Not my old first name, but my old second name. I have thought about how it formed huge chunks of my personality in response to the world. The same way that a lot of my defensiveness and undying position of bullying the bullies in life comes from being ready to beat the brakes off anyone who spoke to my mother rudely. They spoke to her that way because they could hear her non-American accent and see that she was different. I'm sure I could think of some name that would reference that part of me too. Is it Beatthebreaks Offyou Barton?

The wonderful thing about identity and the way I understand it now, the way I claim things now, is truly the trope, the thing that you hear so much about aging. And I don't really use it in other ways surrounding my older years. It's the way you always hear people saying they "stopped giving a fuck." But, I do give *more* fucks about things in general now, so I don't use that term as often as one might expect me to.

I use it here. I don't give a fuck anymore. I don't give a fuck what people *think* I can't call myself. I don't give a fuck if they keep pretending to not see me. They're gonna have to see me, so they might as well admit it and make it hurt less. I no longer give a fuck about taking all the time to be all of myself. Because I am complex and long-winded and all the things. I don't even give a fuck if people can't pronounce whatever name it is I choose anymore. They can work on it. So when I get to my new name, maybe it will be so long and so complicated that it will take people years to understand. Fantastic.

For now: Hello. My name is Tsidi Azeeda Ibrahim. I am a gender-transcendent person of slightly indeterminable age most days of the month. I was conceived in, and almost born in, New York City, but my mom wanted me to be proud of where I was from and also say, "fuck you, Apartheid," so I was born in Cape Town instead. I'm many things, including my genetic and ethnic composition, which I will list for you now in order of percentage, not in order of when my ancestors copulated. I'm 45 percent African from many countries: Angola, the Congo, South East Africa, Ghana, Liberia, Sierra Leone, and Sudan. I'm 31.5 percent East, Central, and South Asian, from many countries: Southern India, Sri Lanka, Northern Indian. Pakistan, Bengal, the Philippines, Austronesia, Indonesia, Thailand, Cambodia, and Burma. And hold on to your butts! There's more! I'm 21.3 percent European, from many countries: England, Ireland, France, Germany, Spain, and Portugal. Then there's a chunk of me that no one can figure out yet.

What do I do for a living? Whew. Maybe I can buy you a drink or something. We're gonna need some time.

In my remaining years,
I'm gonna get that
DAMN
TWO THOUSAND DOLLARS

5.

Classic Jean

5A. The Gray Area

"Tell your partner what movie you would name your naughty bits afte—"

"*The Hurt Locker!*" I yell out as people turn around and someone close mutters, "What the fuck?"

"*Clash of the Titans!*" I yell out again and clap my hands together.

"You're only supposed to give one answer," says the woman on the couch to my right as she sucks her teeth.

"Ooh! *Watership Down!*" I am leaning in on my elbows like a football coach toward my date, who now has his head in his hands and is very sorry he brought me to this stupid event. He shakes his hidden face. "Jean, like a sexy movie. Not . . ."

"But *Clash of the Titans* is complimentary to both of us. And I would be the Kraken and the Kraken is *always wet*. Come on." I sigh as the woman next to me says, "*Who Framed Roger Rabbit!*" and smiles coyly to her date, who says, "Oh hell yeah" excitedly in response to her weird answer that doesn't make any sense.

"What? That doesn't even make any sense!" I turn to her.

"Ummm, yeah it does because like Jessica Rabbit, though!" she says and starts rolling her shoulders at her stupidly enthused date. "Oohh Jessica Rabbit is sexy as hell." He nods, reminiscing about a cartoon.

I am not done. "Yeah, but the name of the movie isn't *Jessica Rabbit*. It's *Who Framed*—is someone framing your vagina? That could be cool, but it doesn't make sense!" I almost want to stand up when trying to illustrate this point, but I don't.

"Yo, you said *The Hurt Locker*. How does *that* shit make sense?" Her date is now facing me. My date has gone to get another drink and clearly wants to be left out of this.

"Because it speaks to the power of my choche. It's funny." I shrug. And it *is* funny, I have used this joke before, and honestly, I've never seen *The Hurt Locker*, which makes it funnier.

"Motherfuckers out here trying to hurt dicks," her date mutters, and the two Jessica Rabbit fans move along with their sexy-date business.

"I mean, yeah. Kind of. Good for me," I reply quietly, shrugging and spotting my date talking to a woman at the bar, my eighteenth sign to leave. Which I did. But not before saying, "Who the fuck says *naughty bits* to an adult," in my former beau's ear on the way out. Whatever.

We had only been on two dates. Our first, the previous evening, had also held a lot of random vag conversation. I was a little upset that I had brought a (very handsome) dud to my favorite restaurant in the East Village, because I hate when people who can't appreciate good food get to have good food. It shouldn't be allowed. But it was too late, and he was eating his painstakingly prepared osso buco with an overhand-gripped fork and zero savoring. Ugh. Was I still gonna fuck him? Yes, yes I was. Because I was in my early thirties. Anyway, I had asked him about the few gray hairs in his well-manicured beard. He seemed too young to have gray facial hairs.

"You're thirty-three, right?" I tilted my head and sipped my very strong mojito.

"Yeah," he said, in between loud chomps. *Ugh*. "Jesus age." Seventy-two strikes. "Why?"

"Umm, just that you've got some grays already." I reached out and touched his chin, figuring I should get used to touching him. "Ohh, yeah, yeah. My dad's side of the family goes gray early. I've had these for a few years," he said, smiling with very good teeth. I smiled back, ready to flirt. "Ahh. I also have gone gray"—I leaned in—"early." He squinted his very nice eyes and waved to my hair with his fork. "What, you dye your hair black or something?"

I leaned back in my chair and took a heavy sip of my drink. "No. No, I don't." He squinted closer, and I thought he was going to poke my head with his fork, but he didn't. "I don't see any gray hairs though." He was confused and also still chewing with his mouth open. Damn that chiseled jaw and perfect skin.

"That's because I'm not gray . . . up there." I uncrossed my legs and looked down. "She . . . is distinguished." I raised my eyebrows. "A scholar. Very wise." I had finished my drink and set it on the table to prepare for my next move. "Who is *she*?" he asked a little too loudly for my taste. I held my right index finger up horizontally over my lip. It has a handlebar mustache tattooed on it. "*She* is *learned*." He frowned. I placed my left hand below my mouth. Between my thumb and index finger, I have a small triangle that looks like a villain's goatee. "*She* is a gentlewoman. Down there." I wiggled my eyebrows up and down.

"I don't know who you're talking about right now, for real. You mean someone downstairs?" This man was stumped. I dropped both of my hands and motioned quickly for the waiter. I was going to need at least six more mojitos to get through the night. I leaned across the table quickly and screech-whispered, "No, goddammit. I've gone gray downtown. Like not completely gray but a lot of gray hairs. She is wise. She is a scholar. She is well versed. Shit!"

"Ohhh," the pretty dullard nodded slowly. "That's wild!" He seemed impressed and also some other emotion I couldn't understand. "She's like an old lady!" He laughed. I banged my fist onto the table and loud-whispered again, "She is *not* an old lady! She is *distinguished*!"

When The Hurt Locker became "distinguished" I was absolutely sure that I would also get gray hairs early on, in the place I had expected them: on my head. And I was prepared to embrace them. "I'm a cool person," I thought. "I bet they'll know to grow in real fucking cool!" Please, give me grace. It's just what made sense to me at the time. "I have chosen a superhero name, so the hairs should act accordingly!" I waited. I waited some more. But by my forties, all my friends had gotten their up-top grays and I had gotten . . . nothing.

"No, no! Don't dye your gray hair, it looks so cool!" I have said to everyone I have ever seen with gray hair on their heads my whole life. Including my mother, my friends, and strangers on the internet. Because I do think that it looks so cool on other people, but zero percent of them said to me, "Yes. That sounds good. I will do that. Thank you." They did say, "You'll see when you get them and change your mind."

"Nah," I responded with the air of a person who knows things. Like Rob Base.° "I'm gonna let 'em grow in so that when I part my hair it looks sophisticated and like a wizar—" Again, I don't know why I thought I was going to get Doctor Strange's hair.† A couple of years ago, the wait was over. There they were. Guess what? They are not cool. They are randomly distributed around my head with no wizard, or chic, pattern to be seen. They are unruly, stiff, and I do not like them on most days. I wish I had just shut my mouth about other people's grays. To everyone I encountered: my bad. Do whatever you want to do with those fucking wiry demons. If they could at least move with the other hairs, that would be cool. But they don't.

I bought one of those root cover-up wands, because I wanted to see how much of a difference it made without having to go full dye. Y'all. Don't do that shit. It will make you feel a *way*. Apparently, it is a solid fifteen years shaved off without seeing the twenty gray hairs, which to be fair is kind of an act of wizardry, just not the one I was looking for. I am still early on in this portion of aging, so I can't say how I'm going to handle it in the years to come just yet. But I can tell you that there is a huge difference between the way I feel about Distinguished Downtown and this sparsely populated sprinkling of uncovered pipe cleaners on top of my head. Definitely not scholarly. Absolutely not learned. Just unkempt and a little on the side of "is she going to steal

---

° In the song "It Takes Two," Rapper Rob Base raps the lyrics: "Cause I'm Rob Base, the one who knows about THINGS."

† Doctor Strange is a comic book character from the Marvel Universe who has a fantastic gray hair pattern.

something from this store or not," the oversize clothes obviously not helping. And again. I apologize for anyone I gave my unwarranted advice to about their hairs. Maybe this will act as a public service announcement to not tell anyone what to do with their grays. It's along the same lines as saying "you don't need makeup" but much worse. Just, shut up. Me included. Sorry. I have learned.

5B. Not Vintage. Regular.

A few years ago, I was scrollin' through eBay in search of a very specific denim jacket from the 1960s. I typed in the words that I have always used to find vintage items, whether online or in person: VINTAGE DENIM JACKET.

"No!" I said strongly. "No, no, no." I shook my head at the results. Why in the world was my browser showing me denim jackets from the 1990s? Haha, silly mistake probably. Ahh. I should type in VINTAGE JEAN JACKET, which always makes me laugh and say, "Are they all mine?" to people in stores who have no idea what I'm talking about because they do not know my name.

VINTAGE JEAN JACKET

"NO!" I yelled so loud that my husband came in from the other room. "What's going on?" he asked. "When is vintage year what year is that when begin that?" I was so flustered I couldn't form a coherent sentence.

"Oh, you mean like, what is considered vintage now?"

I blinked and didn't answer, beginning to answer my own question. He started nodding slowly and drew his breath in sharply. He pursed his lips and kept nodding at me. I climbed up backward onto the couch and pointed at him. "I don't like what you're insinuating!" I was having a fucking moment. How. When. What had happened. "No! Not vintage! Regular age! Regular age!" I was still pointing, and he was still nodding.

"Yeah, it happens when I have to look for pictures for animations now." I wanted him to shut up. "I have to type in vintage for even early 2000s stuff."

I threw a pillow at him. "No! Regular time! Not vintage! Regular!"

Recently I commented on a TikTok post in which some child labeled a carousel of pictures of Marpessa Dawn and her husband (gorgeous couple) as VINTAGE ACTORS: I know that you have typed VINTAGE ACTORS in a search and found these pictures, but you cannot call these actual people VINTAGE as a descriptor.

The child who made the post argued back and forth with me that they were indeed VINTAGE PEOPLE, and then I asked myself what exactly I was doing arguing with a child on the internet that I couldn't actually fight in person. What was the point? There were other not-children in the comments also saying the same thing, so I figured I could bow out, but I still thought about it as I lay in bed the following few nights. "Vintage actors," I muttered to the ceiling. "Pfft."

A year or so ago, also on my TikTok, there was a post labeled ARCHIVAL UNEARTHED NYC 1980s FOOTAGE. "Unearthed? Unearthed? Like fossils?" The tears welled up in my eyes, not from sadness, but from wearing the wrong reading glasses, since my prescription ones had broken two weeks before and I hadn't gotten them fixed yet. Then the irony of the glasses actually did make me cry. Trying to argue that my life could not be of the olden times, when in fact I could no longer see, was a very futile position to take. "I hate this," I said to my phone screen and then typed I hate this into the comments on the ancient footage post of a deli I used to frequent. In less than an hour, someone replied to my comment with: this is the real NYC go touch grass transplant and it made me smile, because that was the right response to what I'd said. Good job, Old New Yorker maybe.

The only thing that has helped me get through being labeled as Vintage, Retro, Back in the Day, an Old Head, an OG, Old School, and Classic is that it has happened to every generation at some point. And I have definitely offended someone born before me by calling their shit "vintage." To which I'm sure they thought "fuck this child. Not Vintage. Regular." It happens to us all, and no one ever sees it coming. Because we all just stay regular age forever in our brains. That's how it works. There is no avoiding it, my fellow Gen Xers, it just happens to be our time and not in a cool way like "our time down here" in *The Goonies.*

"People used to get shot to this song. I have seen someone get shot to this very song," I whispered at the speaker in the supermarket that was blasting out "Brooklyn Zoo" by Ol' Dirty Bastard of the Wu-Tang Clan. "They're playing Wu-Tang in the supermarket," I said softly to a woman who passed by me and didn't care. "Uncensored." I sighed and started bopping to it, because what is there to fight at this point.

A younger person walked by me and said, "The classics." Out of pure defense, I whipped around and shot back, "It's not like oldies music, you know. It's *Wu-Tang.*" He frowned hard and pointed to my sneakers. "Your Reebok classics." I looked down, ashamed. "Oh. Yes. They are. You know, I've done shows with Ghostface, The GZA, and Method Man,* all separately. And once Ol' Dirty Bastard tried to talk to me in a Sam Ash Music store but my mom . . ." I looked up and he was gone. Classic Jean.

5C. The Pipe

A crowd of young friends sit at a hotel bar one evening. Over a table of drinks, they exchange stories and tales of vacations and dating. Of problems at their jobs and potential frenemies. They gossip and talk of new pop culture developments. New singles and videos. New movies and potential castings.

"I think Idris Elba would make a great James Bond, I dunno why they don't just give it to him."

"Yup, he would kill that. And you—"

"Idris Elba . . . owes me two thousand dollars." The voice comes from just a few feet away from them. The back of a chair that seems too elaborate to be in this setting slowly turns, as a large cloud of smoke billowing from a pipe held by a tattooed hand comes into view. I use my velvet slippered feet to slowly turn the chair I'm seated in until I'm fully facing the confused young faces.

---

* Members of the rap conglomerate: Wu-Tang Clan

"What?" says one of the young women. I throw the pipe to the side because I don't know how to smoke a pipe, but I continue my story. "Once many years ago, Idris Elba recorded a rap album. And I rapped on that album. After the recording session, Idris Elba, my manager, and I went to a small bar. Now, I did know that Idris Elba was on a very popular show at the time. A show called *The Wire*, but I had never seen *The Wire*. We sat in a small booth and drank alcohols, and many women stared at Idris Elba. I turned to him and said, 'You must be quite popular.' He nodded. Anywho, a couple of years later Idris Elba and I both followed each other on the social media application then known as Twitter. My friends were all very shocked that I knew Idris Elba and wanted me to ask him questions. But I wanted to ask him a very different question. Do you know what that question was, young people?"

The young people all shake their heads no. I sip my martini. "The question, young people, was: 'Idris Elba, where are the two thousand dollars you owe me for rapping?' And do you know what he said?

"Don't answer that. He simply unfollowed me. And that is why Idris Elba still owes me two thousand dollars and I intend to collect my money."

I don't mean to sound like I'm smoking a pipe and turning slowly around in a chair, like The Most Interesting Person in the World, but it's not my fault, and it happens a fucking lot. I can hear it happening when I offer an addition to any regular story being told in a group of people. I finally get old people. I get it. I get the stories. I get the "back in my day" interruptions, and I cannot pinpoint exactly when I became this person, but I can narrow it down to the past seven years or so. I understand when older people point at places from inside a car and say things like, "you know in the old days, we used to pee on that church and once I even saw a woman give birth on those very pee steps." Because I said that, that's my story. I fucking get it, and there's nothing I can do about it, because that's what happens when you've lived a lot of life very early on. I have stories for everything and everyone. It's too much, and sometimes I wish I could just say regular things, like a regular person, but those aren't the memories I have made at this age.

"Oh look, they're opening up a roller-skating rink by the pier and . . ." A billow of pipe smoke blows through the car. "Back in my day, the Chelsea Piers were not a place to go roller-skating. And the Meatpacking District, well, meat was packed. A lot of meat was packed, if you know what I'm saying." I have silenced the car. "When I was on tour with James Brown in Australia, he had a lady with him and I think she was his lady at that time, if you know what I mean. Anywho, she used to come out on the stage and roller-skate around him. She also pushed his wheelchair when he needed to get to and fro like, say, in the airport. But yes, tell me more about the roller-skating."

Someone stop me. It's too soon to sound like this. Too soon.

"You smoke?" Someone offers me a weed, however the weed is smoked nowadays. A cloud billows around me from no pipe, the smoke is coming from my body at this point. I wave the weed away. "Oh no, I smoked all of the award-winning weed in the world years ago and then quit. Because what do you do after that? Continue? I'm not Cypress Hill or Snoop Dogg. Once, I hosted the Cannabis Cup in Amsterdam. There's no way you can smoke all of the free weed that they give you. There were duffel bags full. But we did try. We really did try. We tried so hard, in fact, that we celebrated my birthday a whole two days before it was my actual birthday, and by the time the real day rolled around everyone was too tired to rejoice. Also, I had to bring George Clinton out on the stage and I couldn't concentrate on anything else other than trying to figure out if it was true that he has drugs of the rock variety stashed in his locs. I was really squinting and really too close. Anywho, you know how hard it is to perform when they're blasting cannonballs of weed smoke directly at you onstage? Very hard. So no weed for me, thanks."

Am I not supposed to say this shit?

"I guess no one really gets canceled. Because he's still out doing sets and—"

smoke "Jean, no." People are tired at this point.

"Once, this guy came to pick me up at my house and . . . *turns to camera*

Have you ever been on a date and not been able to figure out if it was a date? Is it a date if someone opens the car door for you?

*Anywho, we drove into the city because he was working out some new material at a comedy club I will not name and I could tell during the conversation on the ride there that he was having a real weird time. I was too. *turns back**

"On the walk from the car to the club the strangest thing happened. Now, I am famous to a few very niche bunch of different audiences. Sometimes I get recognized on the street and sometimes I don't. This man is famous in a more general, public sort of way, which is why what happened was so odd. A man ran up to me and said excitedly: 'Oh my God, are you Jean Grae?' He did not address the very famous person I was with. It threw both of us off, but we didn't speak of it. At the end of his set we walked back to the car, and I swear to you, a whole separate person ran up to me saying, 'Oh shit! Are you Jean Grae!' A fan, who also totally did not address the famed comedian I was standing next to. The whole night I had been tossing around the thought that I couldn't figure out whose 'show' we were on. Mine or his. At that moment, I knew it was mine. As we walked to the car, he turned to me. 'You're pretty popular.' And immediately I wanted to respond by saying, Do you know Idris Elba? But I didn't, I only said, 'Yeah. I guess.' And then he drove me home, did not show me his penis, and never contacted me again. But I did see him at the club a few years later and—"

"Jean!"

"Okay, okay. I'm done. But this part of the story has more comedians and a card game and a demon chant. Once, when . . . I'll tell you later."

So much of the beauty in aging is in experience and the great stories we get to gather along the way. The tales and weird twists. The unexpected characters who pop up in our lives and sometimes owe us two thousand dollars. By the way, I'm not sure if I actually *did* get paid that money or not, but at this point it's the principle of it, and I know he has two thousand dollars to spare. I do love the fact that being this age has made me less aggravated when people older than me start with a "back in my day we had to walk to school uphill in the snow both ways" story, because that sounds crazy! Tell me more. Not if it involves finally getting to said school and throwing bricks at Black children trying to integrate into schools (you never can tell with Boomers) but, you know, tell me the other stuff. Because I got a hot twenty minutes on how back in my day we couldn't walk to school because of the rampant kidnappers in aviators running the streets. Maybe next time you hear someone launch into a little tale about their lives while they smoke a pipe and cough like a war vet, don't write it off so quickly. You never know if Idris Elba might show up. He's pretty popular.

In my remaining years,
I will befriend the
DEMONS

6.

Free Mumm-Ra

I am the Alpha and Omega. The beginning and the end. I am the light, the darkness, and the all-enveloping spark and fire of the universe. I am an infinite entity that will forever be! Fear me!"

I proclaimed this out loud after drinking half a glass of water after an eight-minute workout. Breathing hard, with arms stretched to the sky in celebration of my remarkable achievements. A deity among mortals. A benevolent, hydrated God. The one. The only. All.

Hey, if you don't hype yourself up for your achievements, whatever size you or others may perceive these wins to be *shrugs shoulders* that's on you. It's not, as the kids say, "delulu." It's motivational, and you should give yourself credit. In addition, it is a very good time, and I am assuming that you are alive on this earth right now, thereby you could really use a good time to balance out the trash fire that can be *existing*. But I also know the personal hype-up can make some people very mad. I know this because I've received many "this has made me very mad" looks at the gym after yelling one. In fairness, I was probably pretty loud and possibly unaware of the volume of my voice due to my blaring headphones and adrenaline. But in all *not* fairness, people yell shit at the gym ALL THE TIME. I'm very sure that a fair chunk of the vitriol stems from the religious implications of the statement. Oh, no. Not the blasphemy. *Ahhrr naurrr.*

I can't do anything about the vitriolic feelings. I know that I'm powerful (I know this on most days) *and* "I am the Alpha and Omega" is a fabulous introduction line. I would, however, like to tell the people who "have been made very mad" that my speech is performed in a Mumm-Ra° sort of way, rather than in a religious sort of way. I *did* "get the chance" to explain this recently to a woman who served me disapproval face at my gym. Well, I attempted to explain it.

"You know, like Free Mumm-Ra!" I shouted at her across the short divide between the hip abduction machine, where I sat, to the elliptical, where she had fully stopped and turned her entire upper body toward me. I took one earbud out. Azealia Banks' "212" was still banging away on my Spotify, and my adrenaline was up from successfully completing reps with a newly upped (by five pounds) weight. I lowered my voice slightly to reaffirm my statement, but I was pretty hopped-up and still shouting.

"Free . . . Mumm-Ra?" Maybe she had forgotten who Mumm-Ra was. We looked like we were about the same age, but with Black people you never can tell. I raised my arms and outstretched them again. Perhaps a visual aid would be of assistance.

"Mumm-Ra, you know," still shouting. I growled, "The ever-living!" My best Mumm-Ra impression was being wasted. She stood stock still, staring at me. I continued. "The transformation happens when the spirits—" She rolled her eyes and turned back around, resuming her elliptical jaunt. I sighed and let my hands fall as a man passing by remarked, "Hey, Mumm-Ra from *ThunderCats*!" He raised his arms and shook them around, a little more like excited Kermit than Mumm-Ra, but close enough.

"Yes!" I had *not* wasted an impression. "Ahhh," I weakly growled, and he growled back. We did this a couple of times. He nodded and

---

° Mumm-Ra is a fictional supervillain and the main antagonist in the Thunder-Cats universe. *ThunderCats* is an animated television series that ran from 1985 to 1989. Not to be confused with Thundercat, a singer, musician, and guy who slap-a-the-bass really well and makes some great tunes.

crossed his arms, smiling at me. Oh no. "So, uh . . . what's your—" I blank-stared him, popped my earbud back in, and pried my jelly legs off the machine to limp away in confusion.

I am not used to getting hit on at the gym. I consider myself *fully* invisible to men. It's a gold star achievement in my ghost career of life. The highest level of apparition one can reach. The pinnacle of nonexistence. Middle-aged. Slightly muscular. Tattoos. Nonfeminine facial features. Baggy clothes. Unclear gender presentation. Assumed nonworking womb. I think about a date I went on years ago with an actor you don't need to know the name of, trust me. He leaned over his juice (just juice) and my cocktail and casually asked, "Do you have a working womb?" Casually. And then he took a sip of juice—*a store-bought, cold-pressed juice that he had taken out of his hiking backpack, which he wore on a date to a bar, at night, in the city*—and waited for me to answer. This memory makes me want to lift heavier weights.

At the gym and Keyser Söze-ing° over to the free weights, I thought about *why* this man may have been able to see me. I frowned like a confused ghost and determined that it was due to the Mumm-Ra impression. Ahh, yes. Men can definitely see a cartoon reference. Well, I certainly wasn't going to stop doing it, because if you have a good impression, you should do it often. If my impressions continued to reveal me to their world, I could always hiss to repel the men. I considered practicing my hisses.

The whole of my "Free Mumm-Ra" speech is how I identify and how I plan to continue identifying °*taps heart*° in here, as an ever-living being. A fabulous immortal God serving capes and lewks while flitting about my lair and the globe, excited to be grand and free. I'm doing all I can to also be this full-time on the outside, but I, like everyone else, lose the fucking plot sometimes. Thus, the hyping-up and pep talks. The affirmations. I'm working on minimizing the amount of

---

° In the movie *The Usual Suspects*, an actor, who we will not name, plays the character Verbal Kint. Only Verbal is also the villain of the movie: Keyser Söze. In order to appear "weak" and hide his true identity, Verbal feigns a limp, among other things. All are terrible. But not as terrible as the actual actor in real life. And if you're mad that I spoiled the movie for you, it came out in 1995. Stop it.

self-cheerleading that I need, but unfortunately I keep having to . . . do things. In the world. With people. And the things that happen. I keep having to exist in time and space, and frankly, it's quite bothersome.

You may have noticed that many people exist in time and space with their biological children, or children by other means, either way—children. Or in a marriage. Or with a gender. I have done two out of three and do not recommend . . . for me. I would also not recommend it for you, but as we're all different people with different desires and shit, that's your business.

The fact that I do not, and am not, having biological children means that I am the last of my bloodline. The buck stops here. Fin. Bloop. We done. That's all, folks. There will be no more genetics of this particular combination to spread about. This is it for the gene (Jean, heh) pool. End of the line. Peace out. You don't have to leave, but you can't stay here. Not sure if that last one applies, but it's a solid paragraph closer and a great callback, so I'm keeping it. Oh, I haven't forgotten that I have an older brother. He has no children, and I am willing to bet all of your (and your family's) money that the circumstance will remain that way, so bloodline go kaputzies.

Being the "end of your bloodline" is a conversation that's being had more frequently among the younger Gen Xers (like me), millennials, and the Z kids. You should take a little internet journey to seek out these discussions and opinions. It's an interesting rabbit hole to strut into and one that has truly helped reconfirm my feelings about the situation. It helps to have community so you don't think you're going completely fucking crazy.

That said, there's an overwhelming number of people online who rationalize being "pro-EOTL" (End of the Line) because of their own perceived insignificance. Saying things like "I'm not special! My genetics don't carry any amazing talents that need to be passed on, so who cares?" That's absolutely heartbreaking to me. You *are* special. It's a possibility that some talents weren't nurtured, explored, or supported, and I'm sorry for that. We all have talents and we're all painfully special. It's never too late to explore some uncharted dreams you may have.

Whether you're choosing to continue your bloodline or not, irrelevant. Do that shit for you.

The insignificance of self is a wild thing to state. There are people out there who have not chosen to become the EOTL, it's just their reality. For so many reasons, medical issues especially. But most of the people who hold the "I'm not special" torch are also pretty young and don't have the life experience to understand this concept yet. I wish we could all stop saying "I'm not special" about ourselves. Out loud or in our brains. If you're doing this, cut it out, or you'll stay there and have to reverse it all later on. Save yourself the work, the (expensive) therapy, and start saying you're a special, powerful motherfucker *now*.

Now, EOTLiners can be both couples and singles alike. Married people, unmarried people, planning-to-never-be-married people, or those with plans to be betrothed. #TeamNoKids is becoming a very popular team to be on. Some of the reasons people give for choosing to play on this team coincide with my EOTL reasons. On TikTok, there is a woman who's been making a list of reasons to remain child-free. Many people stitch videos of their own reasons why, and the list has grown to over two hundred items, probably four hundred things by now. At least 170 things on that list I had never even thought about, but they are right. I do not want to experience them. I didn't always feel this way though.

Flashback flashback flashbaaaaaack
wavy screen, smoke

The child tide shifted when I turned the age my mom was when she had me, forty-one. I was born in 1976, and it wasn't super common at that time—in the Western world—for women to have children at that age. Doctors told her about the high chance that her pregnancy would result in having a "mongoloid baby." So that's . . . does that give you an idea of what the era was like? It should. If my mother was still around to tell you, she'd say that finding out she was pregnant with me was "a surprise."

I'd say, "A surprise as much as common sense goes." I was born exactly nine months to the date after my parents' second wedding, and as far as I know, they were not in the business of getting down on a regular basis . . . so. My parents had also divorced in 1974 and remarried in March of 1976. I was born on November 26, 1976. There's some very easy math to do surrounding the convergence of all these events.

I've always wished for my birth time to be on my birth certificate so I could gauge how "on time" I tried to be, but as a Coloured baby born to Coloured parents in 1976's Cape Town, I'm lucky to have come out alive at all. As was my mom, who had been placed on a cot in a hallway, in labor for hours, ignored. We both almost didn't make it, and I wonder if my love of timeliness and hatred for being late stems from that remembered trauma. Apartheid made me late. How many of us are late for things every day due to some sort of global systemic racisms? Isn't it amazing how White supremacy touches all aspects of being alive? It is.

I started thinking about how to plan my motherhood around the age of thirty-five. That may sound a bit late for other people, but due to my history and experiences, it was right on schedule. At the time, I was in a partnership with someone who did not want children at all. In the early stages of our relationship, I had written off his decision as inexperience and assumed that our time together would change things. He was young, I thought. He just needed more life experience to understand that he did, in fact, want children. That he did, in fact, want to be a father. That he did, absolutely, want to be a father to *our children*. I held his feelings about parenting inside the same bubble I held his immaturity. If we both held each other tight enough, over time, the bubble would surely pop. Plus, at eight years younger, he was only in his twenties. He couldn't possibly know enough to make that sort of decision at that point in life. "Men mature slower than . . ." I thought. I could really go back in time and kick myself in the face for buying this stupid piece of patriarchy from the Patriarchy Souvenir Shop. I mean, I was wrong about everything I just said. I shouldn't have thought any of that craziness. We have really been sold all this socially accepted garbage for so long, especially that claptrap about men maturing more slowly than women. *So, you know, give them grace.* It's a fucking trick. A scam.

We struggled for a few years trying to come to some sort of compromise, but as I turned thirty-nine, I realized I wasn't prepared to accept the idea of not having children. He wasn't willing to budge, and we split up in early 2016. Later that year, on the night of the presidential election, things changed. He was living in another state. I had stayed in New York. That evening, as the unexpected political concern grew thicker by the second, we began texting each other. The texts shifted to a very long phone call. We yelled, we cried. We grew solemn, and before the official results were even announced, we had started discussing where on the globe we could move together. The world was about to go fucking nuts, and we decided we'd rather be a team in a potential apocalypse than alone because of a disagreement about hypothetical children. Seventeen days after the election I would turn forty, and potential children seemed like a really bad and unimportant choice to concentrate on for both the near and distant future.

We got back together, moved to a new apartment in Bed-Stuy that had much more room for both of us to create things in and live comfortably. We also started talking about getting married. Leaving America wasn't off the table as we dealt with our other plans, but realistically, it also couldn't be an overnight thing. It's not like we had *savings*. Our focus had to be on creating stable, long-term, creative projects so that moving anywhere wouldn't just be a terrible decision based on a lack of funds and the stress of said lack of funds. I had "New York City" things I wanted to scratch off my bucket list before I could even think about leaving.

At the top of that list: my one-person show with the Public Theater at Joe's Pub. I was also in the early stages of trying to convince the studio that had secured my adult educational puppet show, *That's Not How You Do That*, that I was indeed qualified to write the show by myself. My stress during those years came from a lot of having to continue proving that I had talent, through the burnout of fighting to be recognized for my skills, even when I already had the job. It felt neverending. But I suppose all of these work stressors, although different for all of us, are how all couples deal with life together. Seems like a shame to have so much of a connection based on trauma bonding.

Over the next few years, the internal pressure to have kids

returned. Our state of affairs shifted many times: Adjusting to getting married. Having a pet. Job transitions. Moving. Money. Deaths. Medical issues. Police shootings and being Black and Mixed people in the world, which, yes, is an absolute stressor. What a weird fucking time to hit middle age and have to make so many choices about so many things in the most ethical, responsible, and heightened—I mean *heightened*—stakes way.

Much like the 2016 heightened-stakes decision of getting back together, my resurfacing lean toward having children felt high stakes as fuck now. I also felt under the gun and at the mercy of my own body. "If not now, then never, right?" is what I kept saying to myself. I couldn't stand the idea that I wouldn't be in control of that decision if I waited any longer. Not after such a lack of control in so many other areas of my life so far . . . that couldn't happen.

In 2021, we were surviving in Baltimore when I found a new gynecologist. It was time to embrace the idea that this world we were in might be the new normal, which meant that we still had to go see doctors for shit, regardless of deadly germs. I was already forty-four and I made my appointment with the thought that this was gonna be "the" visit. I wanted to know the new odds. I was attempting to understand all of my new feelings about myself, my husband, and the world. Actually, a lot of the time, I was attempting to understand if I was even having feelings. I stared into nothingness a lot.

"What if we're dead? Have you thought that maybe we might be dead?" I was sitting in the living room, staring into nothingness, but I had seen my husband pass by the kitchen in my peripheral. He turned and answered so much faster than I thought he would have. "Yeah. I've thought that a lot."

"Where do you think we died?" I asked gently. He leaned on the doorframe, contemplating. "Ummm, maybe on the way out of Brooklyn. During the protests. On the bridge. Or maybe on the drive here from North Carolina. Just an accident."

"Huh," I said, making a very huh face. "Yeah," he replied casually. "It would explain a lot."

I nodded. "I guess that would mean Littles is dead too." I looked at the cat, cozied up to my hip on the couch, and brushed his head gently. "I'm sorry, honey," I cooed. He stretched his legs out in a *big stretch*, but I refrained from saying "big stretch!" I was stuck on the ghost part.

"I'm a ghost haunting my own house," I explained during a phone call to a friend who was still living in New York City at the time. "Essentially, we are haunting ourselves? Or there are people living here and we can't see them and that's how ghosts work? I honestly don't know what's real anymore."

I don't know what a good response is for that kind of statement, but no one else did either. Guess what? When you're unsure if you're truly alive or not, the world is still going on without you. And if you wait too long to tap yourself back into actually existing in time and space . . . you'll be pretty fucked-up. I was glad I had made the appointment with a new gynecologist in a moment where I'd thought I was, indeed, a living being. And besides, if I *was* a ghost, it would be a fabulous weigh-in before the checkup.

"Yeah. Back at my *I'm just a concept* weight!" I'd . . . not yell, 'cause I don't think ghosts can yell.

See. That's a positive thought.

"Mumm-Ra didn't have kids," I said quietly to my gynecologist.

Her head popped up from between my legs and responded in a soft tone, "Pardon?"

"Mumm-Ra. The ever-living. He didn't have any children." I repeated it matter-of-factly, in case she had forgotten who Mumm-Ra was. I know that we were the same age, but if you had tried to guess how old we both were, you would have failed, because: Black people.

"I don't know who that is, but all right." Rightfully so, she returned to poking around inside of me.

Afterward, sitting in her office, we would discuss age, IVF, and non-Mumm-Ra-related things. I wasn't sad. I'm trying to find a good word for the feeling I had. It wasn't sadness and it wasn't regret. Not disappointment or joy either. Ahh, proud. I was proud of myself. I briefly thought about that juice-date man who had asked me about my womb. I wished I could travel back in time real quick and say, "No. My womb *doesn't* work great. So there." And then smack his stupid juice onto the ground.

I knew that I was not willing to put my body through rounds of IVF for the next few years. I thought about all my dreams and hopes, even in an uncertain world. I could not believe how fast I knew, without any question, that *I* was more important than hypothetical children. I was more important than my marriage, than outside opinions, or even hypothetical outside things. I was proud of the voice in my head that was right there, so fast, that said, "No, I won't be doing that." And I think it's pretty rare to be proud of the voice in your head. It's not always the best.

When I got home, after an unsurprising lack of any nuanced conversation with my husband, I googled: DID MUMM-RA HAVE KIDS?

As far as Mumm-Ra answers go, first off, I had forgotten about him having a dog. He was totally a dog dad. All right, he spent most of his time in his tomb, replenishing his energy. Felt. His power comes from four huge statues that surround his tomb. In these statues reside the Ancient Spirits of Evil, his MASTERS. He submits to them and does their bidding without question . . . Wait, what the fuck. I leaned back on the couch. Wait. What? All at once it came flooding back to me—

"*Ancient Spirits of Evil, transform this decayed form . . . to Mumm-Ra, the Ever-Living!*"

He did, y'all. He certainly did submit to those evil spirits. I had only remembered the James Brown-esque throwing-off-the-cape move he did to reveal the super-ripped physique and the growly speech, but I had not been paying attention to who Mumm-Ra was or remembered the intention of the words correctly at all! I was so disappointed in myself for wrongly perceiving Mumm-Ra for so long. Was I just like the men who found me imperceptible? I thought about the woman in the gym and her look of disapproval. Maybe it wasn't about blasphemy but, instead, shock at my apparent want to align with a weak, controlled puppet? Well! All right, it was most likely the blasphemy, but I'm just saying.

Lemme put it out there that I'm totally cool with Mumm-Ra being evil. It's the "controlled by outside evil" that loses me. Why had little me felt such a connection to Mumm-Ra? I came up with these things:

• He was just kicking it, being evil, ruling Third Earth. Now, here come these assholes, the ThunderCats. They say they've come to "liberate the planet." Sounds like missionaries to me. Sounds like, "hey colonizer." Mumm-Ra is now forced to spend all his time coming up with plans to defeat them. Super fucking annoying.

• There's a great speech he gives: "I have lived here for a thousand years. I am not the intruder, it is you who have disturbed my rest! But I . . . have . . . time." Mumm-Ra has time today, henty! He has time every day, what with the being immortal and all, but sincerely, great speech.

• Perhaps little me internalized my mother's exhaustion. Her exhaustion from being a mother and from having to constantly explain herself to the world, as an artist and a woman of mixed heritage. As a businessperson and an all-around motherfucker who had been forced into believing that marriage had to be part of her journey. Knowing we, as kids, had contributed to her annoyance isn't the best. I know we're all not here to fix our parents' choices and bullshit, but that doesn't mean that I can't recognize the issues. If I can't recognize them, I'm a part of the problem. I think of me and my brother as the very annoying WilyKit and WilyKat ThunderCat children. Ugh, hated them.

• Even in his "weakest form" he wears a very good red cape.

• Great symmetrical fang teeth that are not too small for his head. (My teeth are very small.)

• As noted above, he is highly irritated by the ThunderCat children.

• He loves spending time in his tomb taking naps.

• He's lonely, because literally everyone else on the planet is inefficient, including his henchmen. This makes him generally upset.

• His weakness is his own reflection. Mine isn't (all the time) now, but I very much understand how little me could have felt this last one hard.

I sat and thought about Mumm-Ra for a while. I think about him often. Not the Mumm-Ra that fell into the hands of evil, but the Mumm-Ra that could have been, if he were free. A servant, bound to his submission in exchange for his immortality and power, he became dependent on the system. When he saw his own reflection, it made him weak. Being able to see himself drained his power. It's a pretty easy parallel to capitalism. To colonialism. To White supremacy and the idea of legacy creating. In my mind, I have freed him.

In my mind, I visit Mumm-Ra's tomb. I bring snacks and make martinis. We sit for hours and gossip about the bitchass ThunderCats. I tell him that he is not invisible, not a ghost, not an apparition, even though a group of motherfuckers landed on his planet like he didn't exist and declared themselves the leaders. *I* can see him, but he needs to see *himself*. We build up his tolerance to mirrors. Every day, we stare into them a little longer and repeat positive affirmations until his reflection actually makes him stronger. We spend hours discussing what immortality actually means to both of us. I tell him about existing at all points in time. I know it'll take a while to break his indoctrination, but we'll get there. I explain that it's not always about needing to fight people, or to prove his skills. They have sold him a bum idea of immortality, chained him to servitude, but he was already the *ever-living* and *all-powerful*.

"In here, Mumm-Ra." I tap his only-bones chest and dust flies everywhere, some bones crumble. "Well, I guess not technically, in . . . but you know. In there."

He nods and lowers his head.

"Are you crying?" I ask.

"Yeah," he says somberly. "I don't have . . ."

"Tear ducts. Right, right." I finish his sentence, and his fragile shoulders heave. I hug him. "You cry like a reality show housewife. No tears," I offer, and we both explode into laughter.

In our talks, Mumm-Ra says he hates how he's always compared to the ThunderCats by the outside world, by people who will never meet him. People who will never take the time to know him. Compared to the ThunderCats bright colors, communal living, and kids running around. Compared to their "traditional family values." But those things don't appeal to him. He loves neutrals *and* pops of red. His place is dimly lit, and he loves a fire—

"Same!" I scream, interrupting him.

"Just because I'm a *mummy* doesn't mean I need to have children. The word has two meanings! Just because I like to serve looks, doesn't mean I have to serve. Just because some people choose to not see me, doesn't make me invisible. I am the end of the line, but also the beginning. I am Free Mumm-Ra. I am an infinite entity that will forever be! Fear me!" He says it into the mirror and I stand behind him, tears in my eyes, completely blown away. He turns to me, "How was that?"

Turns to camera

Can you tell how
many remaining years
I have left?

7.

Eye Cream

jrrrr. jrrrrrrrrrrrr. jrr. jrr. . . . . jrrr jrrr. . . . . . . jrrrrrrrrr
rrr. . . . . jrr.

My silk-gloved finger hovers above a button, pressing it intermit-
tently. I don't want to rest my finger completely on the button, as my
finger pads should not be overworked.

jrr. jrr . . .

I press the button that lowers the window so that only my oversize
glasses are visible to the outside world. Did you know that when people stare at you too long, it can cause wrinkles? Well, it can. However,
I am smoking cigarettes in the back of my Tuesday sitting car and I
don't want the smell to linger on my robes, so I must open the window.

jrrrr.

Jeffries—my eye cream butler—stands at a respectable distance
from the car and sighs gently, without looking at me. I allow him two
sighs per year because self-expression is important. No matter how

much money I have, I will always remember that. He is not allowed to make eye contact with me.

"Mm," I grunt shortly to let him know I'm ready and also in such a way that doesn't overstimulate my vocal chords, causing interior wrinkles.

In his thirty-seven-piece suit, Jeffries carefully rushes to the car. He lowers a diamond-encrusted silver tray perched on his white gloved hand to the window. On it, a single, small, black jar. The jar opens itself as I remove my sunglasses and close my eyes in order to think the cream onto my face. You do pay extra for the Think version of the cream, but what's twenty-five thousand dollars? You're not supposed to touch your face, you know. Spending the money is a no-brainer. "Mmmm." I smoothly moan as the eye cream penetrates my thin face skin. I open one eye briefly, to make sure Jeffries is not looking at me. If he was, it could cause the cream to malfunction. When men look at you, it causes wrinkles, and the octopus collagen in this cream is extremely sensitive to the destructive properties of the male gaze, as it should be. I then laugh very slightly, again, the wrinkle risk, as I recall that I had Jeffries's eyes removed last winter solstice.

"Ahaha. Oh, Jeffries. I had forgotten that your eyes are in the trash now!" I sigh and close my eyes, which are still in my head. "Oh, Ole Trash Eyes." One never can be too careful. Best to remove all threats.

This is who I envisioned myself to be, when I would become a woman who used eye cream. Women who used eye creams were grown and rich. They had opera gloves and cars reserved for sitting in their estate driveways whilst they reminisced about removing their butler's eyes. Or they were women like my mom and Nancy Kwan. They were *real* adults.

Nancy Kwan is an incredibly beautiful, multitalented, mixed Chinese-American-British woman, who became the spokesperson for a facial moisturizer called Pearl Cream. If you're around my age or older and grew up in America, you're probably familiar with Pearl Cream infomercials. The way that Nancy pronounced "pearl cream" might be your first go-to memory, and that makes you a racist, you racist. My *non*racist memory is that Nancy was a mixed woman who was also not from America *and* was willing to share her beauty secrets with me. She was a fancy, beautiful, rich, successful woman who was selling cream to White America based on the proposed fact that "people are always wondering why it's so hard to tell how old Oriental women are." When Nancy says that phrase in the infomercial, it's the greatest marketing shade imaginable. It almost makes me not hate hearing the word *Oriental*—HOLD ON NOW—in this very specific instance. The exoticization coupled with the read and watching Nancy deliver it with a smile—gold. Or . . . pearl. Now, while Pearl Cream wasn't exclusively an eye cream, it was a *fancy* face cream. You can argue that there are fancier ingredients in face creams, but selling the experience of *rubbing real pearls* on your face in the 1980s at 10:00 p.m. to White America was pretty damn fancy. I wanted to be that kind of fancy too.

"I wanna put real pearls on *my* face someday," I muttered quietly to Nancy Kwan's image. Her nonwrinkled face, bathing my nonwrinkled preteen face with flickering TV light as I sat cross-legged on the edge of my mom's bed. I was sitting a reasonable distance from the TV, as I was ordered to do, but close enough to still feel the electricity of both the TV and Nancy's hustle.

My mom sat up in bed behind me. She was in her early fifties and also had a nonwrinkled face. Her reading glasses were perched low on her nose, and she wasn't paying attention to the television. But she was involved in analog beauty marketing. Her well-moisturized hands with their perfectly shaped almond nails (without a manicure) flipping through a thick *Vogue* issue. She would rip perfume inserts and pass them to me, and I would frown and say they were "too floral" or "not sophisticated." She'd give them a second smell and place the scents she approved of in her bedside drawer, sometimes taking my advice. The inserts lived in the drawer next to a smattering of cosmetics and skin care ads ripped from fashion magazines, torn pages displaying elixirs and creams from Shiseido, La Prairie, and Clarins. They served as her analog likes. Her version of an abandoned shopping cart on some skin care website, whose page has been lingering in your laptop's dock for months.

In those preinternet days my mom bought her creams in person from the Holy Grail of department stores—Macy's. Macy's, a short eleven-block walk from our apartment. It was the Macy's from *Miracle on 34th Street*. Macy's from the Thanksgiving Day Parade. *The* magical Macy's. Macy's and its otherworldly fifth floor for kids, with its small magical malt-shop-like eatery. My mother took us to lunch there often. My brother and I, sometimes with our friends, ordering our staple meal of a hot dog, potato chips, and bread and butter pickles. To drink, we'd have the most perfect root beer floats. Or, sometimes, vanilla Cokes made the old-school way. The round marble tables felt cool against my forearms, and I dreamed of performing a tap routine on the (also) marble floors that would end in me splashing into the large patinated fountain that sat in the middle of the restaurant. It's one of those childhood memories that seems false, since I can't find a picture or mention of that restaurant anywhere. But I can still smell, feel, and taste every ounce of that place. It taught me a lot about how spaces can become the enchanted sensory corners of our minds, and gave me a lifelong appreciation for well-crafted and intentional experiences. The cosmetics floor was equally iconic.

Located on the ground floor of Macy's, the cosmetics section held the real hustle and bustle. The zones of fragrances formed territories, as if they were ethereal gangs. The strong smell of loose powders and lipstick wax with 1980s formulas of ingredients, crafted to drown out cigarette smoke. The evolving, dancing scents of the women who breezed past me and the very distinct smells of each cosmetic house's counters. La Prairie was creamy and smelled exactly like two thousand dollars. Dermablend was thick with the scent of "performance," since it was my mom's makeup of choice for the stage. It's a full-coverage makeup she used to conceal her many freckles and the port wine stain on her cheek. The light music in the air and chatter among the counters, where saleswomen pitched products in melodic, alluring high and midtoned siren songs. The *juj-juhmp . . . juh juhmp* of the wooden escalator on bass and drums. Light taps of polished fingernails and deeper *clanks* of big rings hitting glass counters. My mother's own silver bangles jangling their own tune as she reached for jars and passed them to me to smell. They smelled complicated, involved, and important. The whole experience smelled rich. Sounded rich. Felt rich and fancy to all my senses. You know, *fancy*. *Fancy*, for real adults. I would be a real adult someday. I would have my own smells and creams and jewelry songs.

Though I did have smells, creams, and jewelry songs before my forties, the quality of those things improved as my knowledge improved. Knowledge of ingredients, what worked with my body, and what I would like as my life plundered on. Oh! Also as everyone poor (I mean you too) gained access to better quality products. In the 1990s and early 2000s, many of us endured "The Years of Fire." Our skin burned and shrieked from the likes of Sea Breeze, Stridex, Noxzema, Queen Helene clay masks, and, of course, the face-shredding violence of St. Ive's Apricot Scrub.

If I had a time machine, I'd risk disrupting the time-space continuum to slap things out of my hands and steer myself in the right skin care direction. Sometimes I think about the skin I would have if I'd thwarted my St. Ive's and everything-camphor-and-alcohol-based youth. I'd have let teen-me keep the Amber Romance and Pear Glacé flammable-as-fuck Victoria's Secret sprays though, which truly really enhanced the smell of the many Newports we were all chain-smoking. What a sweet, fruity, smoky, and on-fire time to be alive.

In my thirties, after I had Ghost Rider-ed* my face off, there were pricey facials and some midrange face/neck products that were . . . fine. I dabbled in eye serums but never had great results. I tried a gaggle of horrible DIY exfoliants and treatments that only exacerbated my already damaged skin barrier. In my defense, I had been touring for two decades and you know what they say: "There's no better way to have access to fabulous skin care than being an underground rapper who tours internationally with large groups of men." Obviously, no one has ever said this, because it's a horrible environment for skin care and . . . life.

In my thirties most of my energy and spending were aimed at

---

* Marvel comic's character Ghost Rider (there are a few Ghost Riders) has a flaming skull for a head. He is going through menopause and the flames signify hot flashes—I'm kidding. But that would be a fun character. I'm looking at you, Marvel.

having a "young, good, rock star time." I spent my funds on flying myself and friends out to drunken beach and spa vacations. Or on buying a pool table to put in my living room so that I could host billiard tournaments, much to the chagrin of my upstairs neighbors. Or on solo trips to Las Vegas, where I'd rent out a hotel penthouse for a week, just so I could experience popping bottles and spraying them on myself in a private rooftop pool. All of those times and the money spent were absolutely worth it. But being married, in my midforties, with a gaggle of irresponsible tales already behind me brought my fancy, *real* adult fantasies to the fore.

"If not now, then when?" forty-three-year-old me thought as I stared at my supposedly real adult reflection. "Pearl Cream," I whispered softly at myself. Funny, I hadn't anticipated that I would really *want* better products for myself. Only that I was *supposed to be* using them at a certain point in life. I was supposed to be, expected to be, taught to be, a certain type of woman who did these things at a certain age. Many a friend, upon reaching their midforties, have said to me, "I guess I need an eye cream now. Something that costs real money. What should I get?" So I know it's not just me thinking that we were all supposed to be *someone* by now.

I wish it had all been described to us differently. And I don't mean the way that poor Gen Z is having it described to them. Those kids have caught the fallout from the skin care and social media bomb. There's so much pressure to use all of these products and treatments at such a young age. To have so many procedures and surgeries, and shit, so many people commenting on how they look all the time. All the time. To be told that they look "so old" at twenty-fucking-six. Good lord! I wish we could just let them be young in peace.

I hope that Gen Alpha punches the whole system in the trachea. Their experience will be so different and likely based on never seeing *anyone's* real face, which is its own separate nightmare. What can skin products even do in the face of a computer-generated image? It was quite possible for me to attain skin results like Nancy Kwan's, or my mom's. Fuck, it's even possible to get close to social media–perfect skin results right now, if you have enough money. But it is an unattainable goal for the younger generations to become AI flawless.

What fancy cream could possibly do that? None. It is impossible, and I worry about them.

Gen X, we think we're tough, and we are in many ways. Sure, we'll beat people to death with a brick. Sure. But the majority of us had some time off in our youth from the scrutiny of our images and the bullies. At the very least, we didn't have to show ourselves to the *entire world*, every single day, as flawless beings. Okay, we were around for the beginning of social media—Friendster, Facebook, MySpace, BlackPlanet, MiGente, Asian Avenue (I belonged to all)—but let's be for real: our cameras were shitty. We didn't have to be in fucking HD videos detailing the minutiae of our lives while wondering if our existence was good enough to share. If we were pretty enough. If we looked young enough. If our skin was good enough. If we would be ripped to shreds by millions of people in the comments for having acne, a hair out of place, or a single wrinkle. We had the freedom and we had a romanticized version of skin care that had a clock. On second thought, I suppose I would have to send another time travel Jean to stop the first time travel Jean from slapping the face-burning products out of teen-me's hands. Leave her alone. Besides, what was she going to do? Ask mom to buy her a bunch of La Prairie face care? No! Can I bring her skin care products from the future to use? I'm not doing the math on those quantum physics, but I'm pretty sure the answer is no! Besides, that many Jeans would definitely create a selfish black hole. Use the Sea Breeze, little me. Be free. We have time.

| | |

I have spent a lot of time since reaching my midforties figuring out exactly who I am and who I want to be. There was a portion where I looked back at all the things from my youth I had held in such high esteem regarding presentation and femininity and threw them in the garbage. The angsty puberty of middle-aged righteousness, still tossing antiquated ideas of society and our parents' desires that live in us into the trash. But like a box with a recipe on the back that we chuck into the bin too soon and then have to shamefully retrieve (more than once), I found myself dumpster diving my experiences after being too fucking hasty. And too fucking socialized. Because I absolutely love so many of those things. Some of them in their original form and some of them modernized and tailored to grown-up me. And that feels like being a "real adult" if nothing else ever will. Knowing yourself and understanding where all your likes, dislikes, and behaviors come from. Being able to say, "I want to keep that," and "This makes me feel good," if it's not things that are hurting people. I'm not saying to go retrieve your mom's collection of Nazi memorabilia, do not do that.

I don't identify as "a rich grown-up lady," but I don't think anyone truly does, not even rich, grown-up ladies. We're just all out here doing our best to keep it the fuck together and find things that make us feel like the most beautiful people in the time we have. I know that my mom liked all those products and fashion and lipstick, but she was also just trying to find time for herself. And I think we all realize at some point that the thing we are trying to buy most is . . . just time for ourselves.

I practiced for many years, waiting to be ready for my eye cream moment. When my bracelets would jangle and sing their own song. When my rings would clank against glass as I made purchases at cosmetic counters. It took decades for me to find my signature perfume. Years of finding all the right creams, lotions, and potions for my face. And I only got it right when I truly stopped thinking about who I was supposed to be. Stopped focusing on the actual items. Stopped copying. Paid attention to the way things really made me feel when they were on me. Around me. When I made them a part of me.

My bracelets don't jangle at all; turns out that I hated that song on myself. I have black wrap Hermès leather bracelets that I wear every single day. They make no sound at all. In fact, I'm not big on jewelry, so there are no rings to clank. I tried wearing them, but I feel better when I don't. I no longer put pressure on myself to keep buying large Iris Apfel statement necklaces like that's the shit I am supposed to start wearing. That is someone and I love it for them, but it's not me. I found my signature perfume, La Vie Est Belle, in my late thirties, and *nothing* else I have ever worn has the same effect as that damn perfume with my body chemistry, my mood, and the world. But I layer it now. I wear other perfumes, and I keep searching for new ones that create a lasting, enchanting moment of me. It took years of trial, error, color theory, and understanding of undertones and my own presentation to find my Perfect Red lipsticks. And you know what? I don't even wear them on my lips half the time. I smear them across my eyelids, bold and fierce. In doing that, I'm decolonizing my mostly Westernized outfits and reclaiming something for my ancestors. It makes me feel so powerful and so gorgeous. Would my mother, or Nancy Kwan, have ever attended a gala with half of their faces encased in red lipstick? Well, I don't know about Nancy Kwan, but I'm gonna tell you my mom would rather you call her a slur than do that. But she would have loved it on me. Loved it.

And as for the eye cream, well, you don't *need* a specific eye cream. WHO KNEW? I tried many, and I keep one in the stash that Tracee Ellis Ross recommended, because we still have our Nancy Kwan kind of women who we trust. But I do have many a fancy cream and lotion in double-walled heavy glass jars that do the job. The kind that clank well on a vanity, or a silver tray, and have deliciously weighted tops that swivel with just the right feel and sound. I'm a sucker for clean packaging and beautiful fonts. For rich oils and emollients and dripping amber liquids from small glass bottles. For expensive combs and brushing my waves out before oiling my scalp and braiding my hair up at night. The act of opening a medicine cabinet to see all my beautiful things. Putting on all my body lotions and layered potions while I'm in boxer shorts and a tank top, and then topping it with a silk robe. I do love a skin routine and spending money and time performing my "fancy lady" rituals. Who cares if I'm an actual fucking "lady" or not. I still love a lot of that shit. I forever will.

I'm still working on gifting myself some La Mer, for the fuck of it . . . maybe next year. But the reason I would buy La Mer now isn't because it's expensive. It's the intention behind the process of making their product. It has lore, it's involved, and I am into that kind of shit. Things are fancy to me because of their intentions, and I don't care if that sounds pretentious *fart sound* suck it.

So don't feel bad if you think that you aren't the "woman you were supposed to be at this age." Or that you're not grown-up enough. None of us are and no one ever fucking has been. Besides, the journey doesn't end here. There will always be shifts into new things that make us feel good. And it's always okay to dream about what those fantastical things might be. I'll keep imagining myself in my sitting car with my eyeless butler and my transatlantic accent, because I love that part of me, and goddammit, it's a good time! And definitely don't feel bad if in your bedroom, or bathroom, you are just like me. Calling for your White servants and wearing opera gloves in your mind as you layer on creams and serums. Taking your well-deserved time. Then turning slowly away from your mirror to say, "People are always wondering why it's so hard to tell how old I am" as you hold out one of your heavy jars with both hands, to absolutely no one. Fancy. Like a real adult.

In my remaining years,
something will be better
than birds.

8.

Church of the Infinite Me

I roasted half of a single, very large beet. I cut it into cubes, with a little olive oil, salt, and pepper. And at around five o'clock in the early evening, as hazy light poured through my large, rear-facing loft apartment windows, I ate the half beet while standing at my kitchen island. It was good. I didn't bother to sit down at my big dining table, which took up so much space in the large room. I didn't bother to plate it: I just pierced the little magenta squares with my fork and ate them all relatively fast, in between large gulps of a really smoky cabernet that I didn't let come to room temperature. I'd bought that wine the day before and wished I'd had someone to split it with me, so I wouldn't have to gulp two-day-old wine. I didn't really want wine with my beet today, but if the wine stuck around until tomorrow, I'd have to figure out how to use it in a meal because it would be undrinkable, or at least, not as yummy anymore. I would have to make a beef stew with it, probably. But then, I'd have to eat beef stew for two days, and I didn't want to do that either. It was summer and only psychopaths want to eat hot beef stew *in* the hot beef stew that is NYC summertime weather. I did love making a big pot of beef stew, having it simmer for hours, but it just wasn't the right time to do that. Not only because of the weather. It wasn't the right time for me to cook *any* of the big things I loved. They required more love than I had to give. More good feelings in the air. They required more of *everything*, including ingredients, and I was doing my best to buy only those quantities of everything that reflected being a newly single person. A single beet was the right quantity of beet for a single person.

After I'd stacked my single fork in my single-person-capacity dishwasher, I cleaned and seasoned my tiny cast-iron pan. It was a cute pan, just the right size for a single person, making single-person meals, except for the time I had used it to make mac and cheese. I had wished that I owned an even smaller pan, because this pan held the amount of mac and cheese that made it seem like I was depressed. I mean, I *was* super depressed, but I didn't need a food-portion size to reinforce that feeling.

"Ramekin," I thought. "I should get a ramekin." But I wanted a single ramekin, not a set of ramekins, as stores tend to sell ramekins. A set of ramekins would serve only as a persistent reminder that no one was ever coming over for dinner. It's serving loneliness, henty.

"Goddammit. Where does a person buy a single fucking ramekin in this town that is a good ramekin and not a Dollar General ramekin," I muttered. I ordered a single Le Creuset ramekin online, instead of adding to my single-item collection of Dollar General goods. I just wanted something nice. One nice, single thing.

Two days post half beet, I stood hovering over my open fridge, avoiding eye contact with the now probably not delicious bottle of wine. I stared at the box of arugula I'd bought three days ago. It had been wilting when I bought it but had also been the freshest of all the arugula boxes in the store. All the leaves and veggies go bad so quickly nowadays, as if avocados had a talk with the rest of the produce section and they collectively decided that humans have a two-hour window after purchase in which to consume them at peak freshness. I was annoyed that I somehow had to finish a box of arugula in a day, or suffer the sliminess of leaves. The time restriction always feels like a threat. If I could have bought just half of that box of greens, a smaller portion of cilantro, or *not* eight hundred baby carrots! I could see the full bag of unopened carrots I had bought a week ago, sitting at the front of the Forget About Me drawer at the bottom of the fridge. I kept buying a bag of eight hundred baby carrots, thinking that some version of me was finally going to "snack on a handful of baby carrots." I don't know who that baby carrot snack person is, but I have never been one. Bag 'O Carrots had been easier before, when I lived with my partner. We would agree to, and subsequently fail at, snacking on a handful of carrots together. But those days were over. I'd thought about pilfering a reasonable, single-person number of carrots out of their package at the supermarket, but I couldn't think of another vegetable, or herb, bag to hide them in to pull off a successful heist. I did, however, finally start stealing dill from the supermarket. Because even if you have a family of eight, absolutely *no one* is getting through that bushel of dill you have to buy. It's absurd. I pluck a palmful of dill off its massive bunch and hide it in my cilantro, or parsley, baggies. It's not stealing. It's correcting the system.

It would be really great to be able to buy only half a bottle of wine too. I know that they sell little wines in the cans, but that's not good wine. I'll have a wine in the can if that's the choice at, I dunno, a nightmare event where I can't ask anyone for good wine. Maybe it's an event run by children. I don't know why I would possibly be there, but I would drink that canned wine . . . very reluctantly. I'd also searched both my neighborhood and delivery services for a single slice of good chocolate cake. I just wanted a slice.

Or even one of those tiny Ne-Mo's chocolate cake squares, which you used to be able to get at every bodega. I would have accepted that happily. But my neighborhood was somehow both too gentrified and not gentrified enough to know that they needed to keep nostalgia items in stock. I couldn't make the price of a delivery order for a single slice of chocolate cake make sense either. I tried to solve this cake puzzle for a full month before I gave up and made a whole chocolate cake at home. I thought I wouldn't feel as terrible, throwing out a five-dollar cake after eating only one slice. But nope, I had lied to myself about being able to do that and instead ate the whole cake by myself over three days. Then, I felt terrible about the amount of cake I had consumed and had to go buy more large portions of salads and vegetables that I didn't finish before their rotten threat kicked in and *then* felt even more terrible about myself. ARGH!

Why can't there just be a store for single people, with single portions and single items? A Half Foods?

I would buy a bag of only thirty baby carrots, I could definitely eat fifty—okay twenty. Twenty baby carrots, I could eat that. And there would be no family packs of anything in stock! Fuck that. You want to shop for your family, you can go to the traditional supermarket. Ooh! Maybe we could have the single-people liquor store next door? Half bottles of great wine especially. Low pressure, low stakes, high-quality things.

I would walk down the aisles of my local supermarkets and, at every turn, find myself questioning my decision to separate and ultimately divorce. And these thoughts weren't being prompted from inner me. Inner me knew that I had made the right decision and inner me knew that I was in a time of transitioning lifestyles. Those periods of adjustment are always difficult, but this breakup felt especially rough and different in an *outside* way. We had been together for almost ten years, and *yes*, readjusting to single life after such a long relationship, a marriage, is absolutely not the same as breaking up with someone you've been dating for a few months, or even a couple of years. It's *a lot*. Taking all of that into account, it still felt . . . choosing to be single felt like a judgy punishment. And not just from outside *people*. Did my choices also need to be judged by giant broccoli crowns and ridiculously sized bunches of fennel? What are single people supposed to do with all that fennel? I don't need fennel judgment! What, I can't make a nice fennel and apple salad for lunch one day without having the 98 percent of the fennel that's left threaten me for the next week? Isn't the judgment from society when deviating from traditional Western values, isn't that enough? Is "just a little bit of something" too much to ask for? I don't wanna bother the rest of y'all, with your babies and spouses and shit. I just wanna live with my small amounts of nice things in peace. I just want to take my little *New Yorker* tote bag to Half Foods and be able to fit all my single-person-portioned things for the week in it. Must I be cursed with rot? *Sheesh.* May all my wines oxidize and all my greens wilt. A rotten pox upon my independent household, I guess.

Before I had even moved back to New York, I'd spent so much

time daydreaming about what my new, independent single life would be like. Inside the house, I imagined myself doing a lot of somatic therapy, in front of large wall-mounted mirrors. Ooh. I would order a ballet barre! Livin' my NYC dream of *LOFT.* I imagined myself meditating with sound bowls. Doing free flow on a mat, underneath a giant birds-of-paradise tree. I imagined Littles coming to visit, stretching while I was stretching, or lounging on the windowsill, watching me as I cooked dinner. I imagined cooking for myself, alone, and I imagined cooking for a large group of my friends, often. Many times I had thought of a fire crackling, jazz playing, candles flickering, and the snow falling softly outside the big windows as ten of my friends sat around a huge dining table. Their laughter and conversation filling the air and my heart as I smiled from the stove and plated so many gorgeous things.

I imagined hanging out in the living room area with just one friend, sharing a bottle of wine. Talking so much that the time escaped us until we'd laugh about it being three in the morning. I imagined being in my happy place, not just physically, but mentally. Fucking spiritually. I love being alone, I truly do. But I also love being with community and breaking bread. I love hosting a dinner party. I love being able to curl up on a rainy day, eat trash panda food, and fall asleep to rom-coms, by myself. I love meeting friends for a late-night dinner somewhere in the city. I love to talk and share, but I also love to shut the fuck up and be at home doing a lot of nothing. I thought I had done what I needed to do, to give myself the opportunity of being at my best. Getting there was hard, actually literally. The apartment hunt, the move, the emotional trip of leaving a life behind. It was hard, but I did it. Had I done it all so wrong?

New York has always been able to deliver a beautiful balance of being alone, but never *really* feeling alone, even if you weren't surrounded by people you knew. People relocate to New York from all over the world to experience that feeling. *I* had come home for that feeling. I had expected to combat all my current feelings that came with all my changes, by embracing them both alone and with community. And I had known before I arrived that I would be trying new things. Things that New Yorker lifers take for granted. I had promised myself that I would do stuff that a tourist, or a fascinated transplant, might do. Maybe I would even go see the Statue of Liberty for the first time, wild! Just kidding, fuck outa here, I'm never gonna do that. I mean other things that a tourist would do, like go to a museum. Or sit on a park bench and people-watch. I would do things that people do. In a city. But not really New Yorker things. Probably.

I sat on a park bench and tried to enjoy sitting on a park bench. That's what people do sometimes, right? Go to a park, sit on a bench, and people-watch. Or feed a fucking bird, or something. I sat there and waited to feel like how sitting on a park bench looks in a movie or when I see people doing it in person. I saw a few other people sitting on park benches alone and wondered if they were waiting to feel like how sitting on a park bench looks. I wondered if we were all looking at each other and wondering the same thing, all of us playing out some sort of "being outside" scene and not actually wanting to be there. There were a lot of dogs, too many dogs. Ugh, too many large dogs without leashes. I stopped being able to concentrate on my "park bench act" and wondered what would happen if one of the three unleashed pit bulls ripped my face off. Dammit. I had just started a new skin care routine, and that would be a real fucking shame, to have no face. I watched a rat climb out of the garbage can ten feet away and start a fight with a plastic bag. One of those invasive spotted lantern flies aggressively jumped on my lap and I hopped up, flailing wildly to get it off me. All the dogs turned to look at me and I carefully and slowly backed out of the park. I sighed loudly all the way back to my stupid loft. I guess I wasn't a park-sitting kind of bitch, but I had known that in my heart.

I stood on the newly opened roof deck of the Metropolitan Museum of Art and nodded to myself at the sights. "Yep, that's art," I thought, looking at the art. I looked out to the streets of New York City and Central Park. "Yep, there's the park." I nodded and sighed. Well. I kept nodding. Umm, was that it? Again, I felt like I was supposed to be feeling some other sort of feeling that people have when going to museums by themselves. My feeling was simply, "I guess I'm here now."

I took a couple of pictures, because then I could show people on social media that I had gone to do a thing, at a place. I was taking my second uninspired photo when I realized that I didn't want to engage with strangers online at all. I didn't have it in me to pretend, in any format. I sighed deeply and pulled my coat around my shoulders, at least MUSEUM had given me the opportunity to wear my new coat and my new Chloé boots, which had never been out of the house before. That felt nice. Maybe I could focus on the small joy I had and try to expand it into a larg—medium joy. I could go home, clean myself up, put on something I hadn't worn before, and do a good face. The ritual of getting ready to go out always brings good feelings. Like kitchen prep. A mise-en-place, but on your body!

I could wear something black with a plunging neckline. A long braid. Heavy sprays on my perfume. A great sitting shoe° that did its best work with a crossed leg. A red lip. I could go do a "mysterious sitting" at a bar, or a restaurant. I loved a mysterious sitting, right? That wasn't like "park bench" or MUSEUM. It was a tried-and-true activity that always made me feel like . . . me, anywhere in the world. I remembered watching a horror movie a couple of years ago, and as a hooded, tall, skeletal demon floated out of a dark corner in a cave, I sat up and pointed at the scene excitedly. "That's me!" I shouted. "That's me in any bar or restaurant!" I got really excited about doing *something* that was an alone activity, but not a lonely one. I got really excited about the prospect of not hating myself for a few hours.

Halfway through the train ride home, I had abandoned my mysterious sitting plans.

"I'll go to Bemelmans at The Carlyle," I had thought as I left the museum. That would be a real New York old-school mysterious sitting. I would sit in a dark corner and drink a bunch of filthy martinis. But after I had calculated the price of Ubers between the Upper East Side of Manhattan and where I lived in Bushwick, Brooklyn, *and* added to it the cost of "a bunch of" Bemelmans martinis, I'd compared the outing total to the price of my sanity and happiness. The outing still

---

° A shoe that is difficult to walk in, for whatever reason. Heel is too high, too thin—it could be anything. However, the shoe is still fabulous and must be worn. This is solved by either wearing a more comfortable pair of shoes to an event and then changing into your sitting shoes, or very strategically planning your outing to only do minimal walking and standing in said shoes.

won. Then, I compared the outing total to the total amount of money in my bank account. Half an hour later, I lay curled up in my bed, scrolling through TikTok. I watched the newest batch of New York City transplants flit around the city and call it "En Why See" like no one had ever called it. No one.

I watched a girl and her boyfriend enjoy a bunch of martinis at Bemelmans while saying that the bar was located "in Upper East Side." I furiously typed, it's *THE*. IT IS THE UPPER EAST SIDE into the comments and threw the phone to the other side of the bed.

"GET OUT OF MY CITY, YOU FASCINATED TRANSPLANTS! THOSE ARE MY FEELINGS! AND MY MARTINIS!" I yelled at my invisible, mortal enemies and went to sleep. Crying, but at least crying into my good-quality pillows, which wouldn't get moldy.

| | |

"Twice-divorced birds. Look it up, it's a thing," I'd told everyone I ever spoke to, after I knew that divorce was imminent. And it is a thing. And it is actual birds. Birds who look, you know, twice divorced. They're very fancy and have an air of experience. They look as if they're wearing expensive scarves and coats. Fancy hats and jewelry. "That's me," I would say as I watched people gasp at the birds on their phones. "That's me."

Only, there I was. In a sparsely furnished loft, eating half beets and feeding my shared-custody cat. I did not have "shared-custody fur child" on my middle-aged fucking bingo card. There I was, randomly singing original songs of depression out loud to myself daily. Songs like:

What the fuck have I done? I'm a piece of shit!

Walking around and I wanna kill myself!

*Being so lonely but what am I lonely am I lonely
cause I made a really dumb fucking choice and I
make stupid choices because I am stupid I'm a stupid*

*fucking bitch I'm a stupid fucking loser I'm a stupid
McGupid A STUPID MCGUPID A STUPID STUPID
FUCKING STUPID BEYAAATCH*

And then maybe it would end with a yell, or a scream. Or a mouth drum solo. I sang a lot of songs and talked to myself a lot. I hadn't anticipated how much I would talk out loud to myself at all. None of the conversations even started at the beginning of a thought, just straight in the middle of an idea. Sometimes it was just a maniacal laugh. This was not . . . this couldn't be right, right? Was this it? Was this what it was gonna be like? Is this what my fabulous, twice divorced bird, loft-living in New York fantasy had been reduced to? A maniacal, single father who couldn't cook and was silently pitied by their shared-custody cat child? I felt lied to. I felt indeed, like a Stupid McGupid, loser stupid beyaaatch.

"I should just stop this and try to make the marriage work," I thought again, now not only when I was in the supermarket. I looked at people around me who were getting in new relationships and sighed heavier. Everything in the world seemed to be telling me that I had made the biggest mistake. But everything in the world wasn't being honest. What a surprise.

I bet you didn't know that 46.4 percent of adults in the United States are single. That is 117.6 *million* unmarried people, including divorced people, widows, and those who have never been married. Yeah. Now, you would *think*, you would fucking think, by the way we are made to feel, that the number of single people would be *three*. There are only *three* single people in the world and you're one of them, you fucking loser. Get it together. Well. Seems like my Half Foods wouldn't be such a damn bad idea after all. I mean, I know that profit-and-supply chains and other shit factor in, but I'm saying . . . it doesn't sound so fucking wild with this new information. I hope that if you're somewhere feeling like a stupid McGupid loser beyaaatch about being single, that the real stats make you feel less loser-esque.

In any case, I wish I would have looked that stat up while I was in

New York City, feeling like a piece of shit. Ultimately, it wouldn't have led to me staying in my apartment, but it could have provided some temporary solace.

I don't have all the answers, I'm learning them as I go. And I'm learning them as I go, because the representation of single women and femme people in their forties and beyond is trash. It always has been. For fuck's sake, I was looking at BIRDS. I was looking to *BIRDS* for some sort of relatable experience. I dunno, seemed reasonable at the time? We don't have to look far to know that women and femme people who choose to be single and childless are under literal attack from the media. Literal attack and threats and insults. "You'll die alone, you childless wench." "Childless cat ladies" came out of the mouth of a thing unconvincingly posing as a human being and running for the office of vice president of America! "What a fucking loser, you have to be with your stupid cat and no man" are sentences very commonly said to people like me. So it's no wonder that I was hitting myself with my own hands, trying to figure out how to make it stop. It's hard out here, but in order to make it not hard, we do need to utilize kind words, honest sharing, more representation, and more community. I am so desperate for community and I know that so many people are deeply feeling this as well. I know this because I accidentally started a cult in 2016.

My accidental cult, the Church of the Infinite You, began as an ode to a scene in the movie *Fight Club*. In it, the character Tyler Durden takes a cashier from a convenience store into a dark alley at gunpoint. He then takes his wallet and tells him that he is going to die. Tyler spies an expired community college identification in the cashier's wallet and asks him what he studied. Turns out, he wanted to be a veterinarian, but it was too much schooling and he didn't finish his studies. Tyler takes the cashier's license and tells him that he's going to check in on him, and if he's not on his way to becoming a veterinarian in six weeks, he will kill him.

"Well," I thought. "I would also like to threaten people to live their dreams. Probably without the gun . . . but yeah, that's a great idea!"

For the next few years, I would talk to anyone anywhere and ask them what they "really did." Not the job they were currently doing, but what they really wanted to do. Comedian. Baker. Painter. Artist. I met a lot of people with a lot of dreams who had all either abandoned them because of capitalism, or never even tried. Yes, I checked in with them, without the threat of death. And it was the greatest thing in the world when someone said they had started painting again. Or finally done a comedy set at an open mic they had been afraid to do for years. People started pursuing their dreams, and I didn't even have to pistol-whip them. But, doing this one at a time wasn't enough. I needed . . . I needed a basement where I could threaten a bunch of people at once to be brave. I do understand that this sounds a lot like *Fight Club*, and that is because it was purely and 1,000 percent . . . intentional. In the winter of 2016, I held my first service as minister of Church of the Infinite You in Brooklyn's Union Hall basement, usually reserved for comedic performances. (I had done many of my own comedy things there for a few years.)

The room was packed. It was one in the afternoon, and day drinking was happening. I'd asked many of my talented friends who sang to be my choir. They would later name themselves The Intersectionals. I started my one-hour sermon by saying, "If this is your first time at church . . . you have to fight." And I did mean that, but not in a physical way.

Church came at a real fucking weird time in America. Trump had just been elected. I had not expected to deal with so much trauma, in such a big way. I had only thought, "I would like creatives to see the power in themselves and for all of us to not have to look for a savior. A superhero. Not even me." I was just there to organize a meeting and give reminders. If we were all the superheroes together, as a community, we could change the world and not feel so alone. And people did change. They quit their jobs. They got divorced. They went and traveled the world. I took the Church on board my friend Jonathan Coulton's nerd cruise that he does every year. Built more community. I took Church to the Broad Museum in LA, but I don't think they understood what the fuck I was doing, that one was weird. I did Church online again in the early days of quarantine and lockdowns. It was hard, but it felt fucked-up to not connect and help people not feel so alone at that time.

I did my best to not be the leader of a cult, but after someone came to me and asked to be a true disciple, I thought, "Oh, this may have gone too far." COTIY had no religious element. I'm an agnostic atheist, but that wasn't important to mention either. It was truly about people just recognizing their own power and then translating that to being a powerful community. I don't have it in me to be an evil leader of a cult though. I have a great ponytail for it, but I don't have the fucking ego. I also didn't like feeling like a *magical negro*, and that definitely started to happen.

I don't miss being a minister, but I had a really good time with my choir rehearsals. I arranged all the songs we sang, from Radiohead to Queen to Bell Biv DeVoe. I miss picking the soloists based on what I knew they needed to get out onstage. I miss hanging out with my friends and serving them really great charcuterie boards and drinks. I miss. My. Friends. I missed them then, and I miss them now.

I thought that I'd be in New York with three homies at brunch, cackling over separations and divorces and our middle-aged woes because that's what I had grown up to expect. Where were my Sex and the Fucking City brunches, drinks, and sex-pun-filled happenings? Why would the world lie to me about that being a thing? Why did no one want to talk about this? It would have even made more sense if we weren't in the right city for these activities, but shit. That was the biggest letdown. Not the separation. The postseparation experience. I just didn't want to do *that part* alone. I know, now, how much the pandemic made people lean into isolation. And I understand that too, but what's missing is the part where we gather and talk about how fucked-up we are about being alone. I wish we could do that. I wish everyone wasn't so burned-out from work, because it stops our ability to spend time together. This place is killing us.

America doesn't promote community building, and I know why. I know that sometimes when you're in long-term relationships, you forget that you are still part of a community. And a successful community doesn't just have to be a marriage and kids and a fucking HOA. It can be the rest of us too. We don't have to be alone, simply because we are single. And maybe just letting people know—especially women— that you don't have to be in, or stay in, relationships for fear of being alone . . . that there is a promise of having your people . . . that could change everything. Even if we're not sitting together at a long dinner table in someone's home—though I do want that—it doesn't even have to be all the time.

Maybe we could all meet up at Bemelmans. We could all make our own reservations, one person to each table. We could all get dressed up in our finest Twice-Divorced Birds outfits and slink quietly into our chairs. We could all order a bunch of drinks and not even have to talk to each other! Just slightly nod and smile and wink, looking mysterious and fabulous. We could all enjoy our roller-coaster lives, by ourselves, but together. I didn't think that this is what I would be searching for when I arrived at this age.

This is probably the most unexpected twist of all.

But I do know that I will do whatever I need to find it. And them, whoever they are. And I'm fine with that sounding like a threat. It absolutely is.

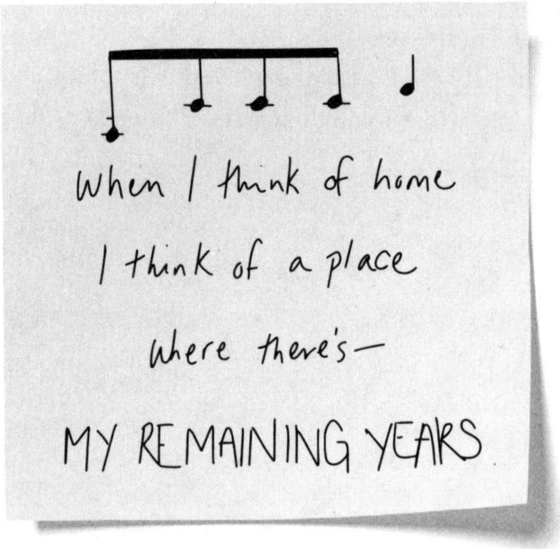
When I think of home
I think of a place
where there's—
MY REMAINING YEARS

9.

Home

I am on one of the Nour El Nil's luxury sailboats that cruises down the Nile River.

More specifically, I'm on the Nour El Nil's *Adelaïde* sailboat—in my opinion, the most fabulously designed and decorated sailboat out of the company's small sailboat fleet—cruising down the Nile River.

I'm booked in one of the two panoramic rooms on board but have moved to the deck to watch the sunset paint the sky in red and gold tones. The hazy light bathes the surface of the water as it also performs duty highlighting the sun-faded carmine stripes of the soaring sails catching the wind, carrying us along this ancient waterway. It's odd how the sunset steps in to seemingly soothe and calm the fabric of the sails after its harsh, glaring treatment has been stripping its brightness away all day. The sun, in its other form—hot, bright, relentless—seems very toxic. For a moment, I am saddened that I find so much beauty in sun-faded things. That I understand them deeply. The moment passes as I remember that I'm not looking at either the sails or myself with pity, or in a way that they are beautiful despite the abuse. Nor because of it. Only that I am able to acknowledge the experiences and how things look in the aftermath. I wonder what will step in to soothe and calm *me* and immediately laugh softly, as I am currently experiencing such a meta-answer.

My straw hat is barely able to contain the wispy tendrils of curls that hug my ears. A single jet-black braid rests on the back of my favorite white Ralph Lauren Yarmouth shirt, damp with sweat. The buttons open to my sternum, the oxford fabric relaxed and thinned against my skin. It's a well-worn-in shirt, now. Soft, creased, loved, sun faded. Sparsely spotted with specks of paint from my last gallery show. The cuffs of the shirt, rolled up, sit just inside my folded elbows. One arm rests on my double-cuffed, vintage Ralph Lauren Andrew trousers, the other slung over the back of my chair. I normally shuttle between the Andrew and Hammond as my favorite cuts of vintage Ralph Lauren pants, but on this trip I have packed only my stash of most-worn Andrews. Both cuts of pant have pleated fronts, but the Andrew is a bit lighter, a bit higher in the waist.

If one were to not have this information and simply look at my pants from a distance, they could say (and have), "I don't see the difference. Those are the same pairs of pants." And one might be satisfied living their life with that level of knowledge. But when I shop for vintage pants, I am a hunter who has to be adept at discerning brands from a distance. It would take too long to sift through racks that contain hundreds of (to the untrained eye) the same chino trousers. I can pick out the vintage Nauticas, the Eddie Bauers, the Brooks Brothers, Banana Republics, and Ralph Laurens from a distance. I can weed out the Ralph Laurens from those options at a closer distance. I first learned to discern the Hammonds and Andrews from the RL Ethans or Prestons by touch. Now I can also do that by eye. It's a skill I value and utilize in all of my professions. The eye for detail, fabrics, clues, and stories told by items. It's also a skill to be utilized when reading people, from a distance or by touch. But I digress, this is Egypt and it is hot. Even a slight change in the thickness of a fabric could ruin everything.

I slowly swish the lemon peel garnish around the surface of my coupe glass. In it: my still ice-cold Vesper Martini. One ankle rested on the other thigh, my legs create a wide figure four. A sitting position that I understand could be called "unbecoming" for someone who looks like me. My black Hermès loafers with their understated black logo have become soft from walking the grounds of many lands. They echo my hair in contrast, and as I slip my well-moisturized heel out of my perched shoe, the other passengers on board enter the deck for the scheduled evening cocktail. They're surprised to see me here early.

I am not surprised to see them. I speak without looking up. Softly, but projecting a confident, indistinguishable accent well enough to carry over the soft sound of the river cruise.

"There's been a murdah."

There are only fourteen other passengers on this boat, but the way they gasp and clamor so loudly in response to my statement, you would think there were seventeen. I break their noise.

"Yes. That's right." I chuck the entire lemon peel into my mouth and chew. "Ahrr murderr." I grab my martini and sip it. I begin to choke on the peel and bang my fist into my chest repeatedly until the threat of dying is gone. I then raise my head slightly to look at the shocked guests and continue my news. "And I, Dr. Umentray, I intend to solve this mystray."

One too-tanned White man steps forward. "This is ridiculous! Preposterous! You're no doctor! What is the meaning of . . . and why do you have your drink before any of us do! I demand to—"

"Hush up, George Hamilton!"* I yell, before returning to my calm, down-to-business demeanor.

"A murder that I intend to solve. A. Murder. Mystray." I say it gently but firmly, before whipping around to reveal a typewriter on the table beside me. A typewriter on which I begin to type furiously, with only my index fingers and a glaring absence of paper. It's what I do. And no one, absolutely no one else, has the skill set needed to solve this murder mystery . . . besides me.

---

* American actor George Hamilton, known equally for his acting as he is known for his entirely overly tanned appearance. I first became aware of Mr. Hamilton in the 1979 comedy/horror *Love at First Bite*. A very tan vampire? That's a fun gag. Love that movie. You go head, Ole Leatherface.

"It's Doc, by the way," I say quietly, still jamming away at the keys. "Doc Umentry."

I need a lot of conditions in order to be calmed and soothed. To then bloom like a flower, or just . . . to not cry heavily and daily on any city's given form of public transportation. The conditions don't *all* have to happen at once, like the situation I've just detailed, which combines many of my loved things: global travel, luxury travel, sensory satisfaction, being fucking silly . . . murders . . . but they do have to happen. It takes experience and living some life to figure out all the things that keep you calmed, soothed, blooming, flowering, and growing. And then it takes some more experience and living of life to figure out how to make those things a regular part of your . . . living of life, because you *have* to.

I had always considered "global travel" a regular part of my life. It wasn't so much a necessary requirement for happiness as a necessary requirement for work and survival. But when it stopped being available, I realized how truly integral it was to maintaining, thriving, living.

Did you know that you can still ride the Orient Express? Well, you can ride the modern version of the train: Belmond's Venice Simplon-Orient-Express. You can adventure through Europe for one night, four nights, or five nights of fanciful travel. You can also take the Eastern & Oriental Express through Malaysia! Kuala Lumpur! Bangkok! Am I thinking about being draped in silks and linens, sitting in the open-air observation car, sipping a cocktail as our train crawls through the jungle, the sunset's golden glow reflecting off the brass railings? You fucking bet I am.

There's Belmond's Hiram Bingham train that goes through Machu Picchu—please, I need this. There's the Rovos Rail from Cape Town (my hometown) to Dar es Salaam—sign me up, but I might have to bring someone to monitor my rage at the White people on that train. There are so many luxury railway and sailway (that's not a word, but why isn't it) travel options around the world, and I want to go on them all. Sooner than later as a kickoff, but as long as global luxury train/boat travel is a thing, get me on those motherfucking Monday-to-Friday° modes of transportation most expeditiously! Get me there quickly, please. So I may be alive.

BOOK NOW TO AVOID DISAPPOINTMENT

This message is on the Belmond Venice Simplon-Orient-Express landing page of their website. "Yes," I nod to myself and twist my mouth in contemplation. *"Entendres."*

I get that Belmond has placed this statement on the page to ensure that people understand the importance of booking their journeys far in advance to avoid being left out. Space on their trains and boats is limited. Dates for all prospective jaunts are also limited. At the same time, I think about the message being so all-encompassing on the "disappointment" tip. I think about having to finish my literal *book* now to *avoid disappointment.* I know their disclaimer is not on their website specifically for me, but I take a snapshot of it and type "JEAN" after their words.

I save this Frankensteined photo and smile to myself. In a couple of weeks, I'll swap this creation in place of my current phone's wall-paper, an unidentifiable person filling out a crossword puzzle as they lie on the deck of a small boat off Italy's Amalfi Coast. I change my phone's wallpaper regularly to reflect the motivation needed at differ-ent times. I'm currently bouncing between that Amalfi Coast joint, André Leon Talley in his living room (in his iconic red Norma Kamali sleeping bag coat) looking at me sternly, and a shot of Grace Jones at the 1983 Grammys wearing Issey Miyake. All these snapshots serve as nudges, in case I forget what the life plan is as I plod through the survival of it all. Maybe I can photoshop ALT's glaring figure onto

---

° This family-friendly phrase was famously used to replace Samuel Jackson's use of "motherfucking" in the iconic 2006 movie *Snakes on a Plane*. Second in great-ness only to "mickey fickey" as an overdubbed replacement for "motherfucker" in 1989's classic film *Do the Right Thing*. "D, Mickey Fickey! D!" I'm not doing another footnote for that, go watch it.

the Belmond snapshot, because I fucking hate when he looks at me with such disappointment.

"You know you must, must travel, Jean," I imagine him saying to me. "Go and see the world again! Paris! You must go back to Paris with matching luggage. What kind of international traveler doesn't have matching luggage!"

| | |

"I was just six months old when I came, by myself, to New York City, from Cape Town. My parents and brother came later." I have told this joke to strangers many times.

"You came . . . by yourself?" they respond, with puzzlement.

"Yes, I swam all the way here," I say, straight-faced. "Took a long time, what with the baby arms and all." I paddle my hands only, my elbows tucked into my sides. "A long time."

Even before my six-month-old self arrived in the States (with my parents and my brother), I was travelin' in the womb. I have always had a passport from somewhere. Never a driver's license, always a passport. Growing up with international musicians and activists as parents meant that I traveled all over the world throughout my childhood.

I was used to gigs, tours, and residencies, both domestic and foreign. I was used to sound checks, rehearsals, and recording studios. Planes, trains, and tour buses were things that constituted a "normal life." Add to that royalty checks and contracts, press clippings and interviews, photo shoots and backstage green rooms in venues around the world. All very normal and constant things.

In addition to performance-and-work-related trips, my family also traveled to Germany, Dakar, Switzerland, London, Mozambique, Australia. And, of course, as the four of us were the only members of our extended family living in the North American continent, we traveled to Cape Town to see family. Infrequently, but we did go. I grew up in airports, on planes, and in hotels—in addition to the one we already lived in. I can still smell the difference between a suitcase that belongs to a passenger who has just traveled internationally versus domestically. *Airplane scent* is still one of my favorite scents, second only to the chemical smell that used to pump out of dry cleaners and apparently causes cancer. Airplane scent always makes me feel right at home, wherever I am in the world. When I began traveling internationally by myself, as an artist beginning my own career, I would always get so excited to get back home to New York and open my suitcases, the lingering smell of adventure permeating my apartment and my clothes for weeks. A living memory of my accomplishments. An addictive, captured fragrant flashback that, after it dissipated, could be collected only by creating more adventures. "More." I can feel myself fiending for it like a junkie, longing to take in a large whiff of the fix. "*I need more!*"

I was nineteen when I first went to London by myself, in 1996. I was recording some vocals for the UK group The Herbaliser for their upcoming album *Blow Your Headphones*. I had been to London many times before with my mother—and I assume with both parents sometimes—but was ecstatic to finally be going alone. Did you know that you could still smoke cigarettes on airplanes in 1996? Hell *yeah*, you could and hell *no*, it didn't make any sense to have a "smoking section" on an airplane. If there's a smoking section, the entire plane is the smoking section. But did *I* smoke on those planes? I sure did. My favorite-ever international smoking flight was flying from NYC to Japan in 1997.

My rap cronies and I had a whiskey-, sake-, and cigarette-filled blast during that flight. As a person who still smokes cigarettes, even today in the age of vape popularity, I cannot imagine myself as I am, being stuck in a tube for fourteen hours with cigarette smokers. I hate the smell of cigarette smoke and don't wish it to linger like airplane scent, or perfume, on the second wear of a black turtleneck.

After 1996, I continued to globe-trot on my own work accord. I was now an established artist in my own right, out in the world. I was part of a new genre of music but, technically, continuing the family business. I had many dips of adventures in between my strictly occupational trips, but until 2020, I had never stopped traveling internationally for work. Twenty-four years. Twenty-four years is a long time. That's a whole-ass adult! I always find it so confusing when people say that I had a "short career in music." Math isn't mathing for y'all.

Regardless of whether people can solve basic addition problems, I have been around the world many, many times so far.

On my ways around, on music tours specifically, I always knew that I was experiencing places and spaces very differently from how those traveling with me did. More likely than not, I wasn't encountering things for the first time. Not the hotels we were staying at, or the venues we were playing. The restaurants, bars, the sidewalks. I was flying, walking, standing, performing, even sleeping in the echoes of my parents.

"Have I been here before?" I'm whipping around in the doorway of *[insert any performance venue]* especially in Europe. "No, I really feel like I've been here before." I've said this many times.

This feeling happened so often and usually during sleep-deprived, long stints on the road, so it was easy to question my own mind, even if briefly. When the movie *Fight Club* came out, I related so much to The Narrator's insomnia. His travel and waking up in a different city, constantly switching time zones. The question he asked himself about potentially waking up as a different person, while maintaining this kind of unsustainable schedule. Questioning everything, even your own existence and the validity of your own memories. I felt it *hard*. Many, many times I was correct. I *had* been there before, but as a child. I stared at posters of my parents performances in the backstage hallways of venues I was going to perform at that night. Trying to think what my mother's rider° might have been, while I enjoyed items from my own. Wondering if we used the same microphone or if I would trace their footsteps on the stage.

Some of our rap tour promoters had also booked my parents. Sometimes, the feeling of me being there before wasn't right, but my *father* had been there. My *mother* had been there. I just felt it in my bones. Other than the times I toured with The Roots, Okayplayer

---

° A rider is a list of wants/needs provided by a performer, band, or artist team to a venue. Stuff for backstage, stuff onstage . . . food, drink, etc. If you're ridiculous like I was, you can put an Optional section on your rider full of silly things like: 12 *Planet of the Apes* towels, or a cattle prod. Please ask me about my rider adventures in further detail. I beg of you.

crew, and Questlove, no one else experienced these feelings. Questlove's father was also a musician, and he too had been out on the road
with his parents when he was a child. I wish we'd talked about that
more at the time. But young people don't know that they should be
connecting and sharing those things until they are older people. We
were young.

On the road, everything was so bright, shiny, and new for most
of the group. Nothing felt new to me, and although it didn't feel like
Fight Club's "a copy of a copy" phrase in a bad way, it was an accurate
description most times. Add to that, it was just me and a bunch of
men. I was not trying to do what they were trying to do on tour. Rap
travel was always "an othering, on an othering." The sense of isolation
was terrible for a little over a decade until I realized all I had to do was
get to the shows, or whatever else was truly mandatory on the itiner-
ary, which, eh. An interview maybe? All I really needed to know was:
Does the mic at the venue work? Is the music loud in the house, and
do the onstage monitors work? That's about it. My new travel mode
epiphany sounded so reasonable. Thus began my "C U iN The next
place" tour era.

"No one needs to do anything or help at all. I know how to travel
and book flights. Just leave me alone and I'll see you at the next show,
in the next city, or country. Go play with groupies in Berlin. I'm gonna
go hang out in Dublin," I'd say, replacing *Dublin* with each new city
on my journey.

I never just left without saying anything either. I wasn't rude. I
was just *doing*. The phrase "on some Jean Grae shit" became a thing
that people said around me. It referred to changing one's travel plans
or showing up in a new city on your own time. The whole thing was
very reminiscent of how I dealt with high school, once I understood
that it was offering me less than a positive experience: excel and don't
overextend yourself in a situation that does not value your gifts. Find
your exit as fast as you can.

"No. This is not recommended for *you* to do," I would always say
to the male artists wanting to rebook their own itineraries. "Since everyone has made it clear that *we are not the same*, let's stick to that." I
would add, "And you definitely cannot travel internationally without

any identification like I am doing."° They were actually very aware they couldn't do that.

| | |

In November of some year in the early 2010s, I was with a touring rap party in Melbourne, Australia. It was my birthday. I'd traveled to Australia and New Zealand over the years and was so excited that my birthday finally fell on a day off. The promoters took us to a fabulous Italian restaurant with a private dining room and a gorgeous rooftop. I got dressed up. I was feeling wonderful. It was so nice to not get "rap ready" but instead get "actual dinner ready." As we sat at the long communal table, the waiters brought gorgeous dish after dish out. The owner began serenading me. I tried to enjoy his performance, but my eyes darted around at my tour party with anxiety and suspicion. I hoped that they wouldn't do anything fucking stupid at this dinner. Not even twenty minutes later, they were screaming at each other over the food. I was fervently apologizing to the staff, to the owner. I was livid. This birthday debacle was *absolutely not* the worst thing that ever happened to me on tour, but it stays with me as much as the other things do. I wanted to stand up and scream, "I just want to have a fucking good time and be fabulous! What the fuck is wrong with all of you!" And then, I wanted to Dr. Manhattan† *poof* everyone out of existence and transport myself to Mars to sit quietly and build beautiful things. Or, reverse Dr. Manhattan and only *poof* the rappers away. Either *poof* would have been acceptable.

| | |

° You should ask me about this.

† Dr. Manhattan is a fictional DC Comics character who resides in the Watchmen universe. He's a doctor who had a lab accident and has the ability to observe and manipulate matter at a subatomic level. He has famously °*poofed*° himself to Mars before, because people are annoying. Felt.

"I just want to have a good time and be fabulous," I exhale my new favorite phrase out with smoke and flick my stub of a cigarette out into the cold, dark, rainy street outside of City Winery in NYC.

I turn back to my agent and pull my vintage Burberry coat a little tighter around my waist. "You know?" I finish. I thought about *not* saying this to her, as she has just asked me what I would like to be working on next. But I had assessed myself quickly and decided on transparency. Two seconds after I uttered that cool-ass shit, I ruined myself and fell into "productivity guilt" as I rattled off a list of shit I'd been working on in the three years since we had last seen each other in person, in early 2020. If she asked me that question today, I wouldn't rattle a motherfucking thing off.

I would end with "you know" and tap-dance out from under the awning where we stood, into the rainy night until I was out of sight. All the while knowing that I was sacrificing my beloved oversize, black cashmere, limited edition Made for Barney's New York coat for a *moment*.

Moments in clothes are held in high value to me. Not necessarily the label, designer, or house the fancy items come from, but the moments and adventures that I have in them. The knowing of which items go with which moments for maximum joy. When I look at clothes and accessories, I think, "Is this for a sailboat going down the Nile? Does it want to go on an adventure with me? Does it communicate who I am immediately? Is this a suitable fabric to wear for solving a murdah mystery?" If the answer is, "No and it also doesn't work for going to the supermarket. It just has no moments," then it's not mine to be had.

That Burberry coat of mine, if it had not been cashmere . . . I would have tap-danced then. But that wasn't the right adventure, or a rightful sacrificial-coat moment for who I was in that moment either. I was in the middle of a trauma about the loss of so many things, including my own physical items, so all of my belongings were deeply precious to me. Maybe the tap act could have served as an additional tale to weird stories that executives relay about me in their meetings. Maybe, but I also didn't feel as if I had enough leverage to pull that off.

Why would my tap dance in the rain happen today without a

second thought? Not because I'm over the trauma and fears of losing everything I own—I still have a lot of work to do there—but because the moment, the adventure, the sacrifice, the destruction of one beautiful physical thing to create a beautiful moment doesn't hurt anyone. Similarly, my good times, my worldwide adventures, they never hurt anyone. They might ruin some clothes, or break a pair of glasses. They might confuse the people I'm talking to. Sure. But for me, there is a home to be found in these moments of pure absurdity and freedom. I suppose I was trying to compensate for my lack of travelin' adventures by fantasizing about this unfettered "tap away." Maybe.

I haven't left America in *years*, and I can feel a light inside of me growing more dim by the second. I miss making unexpected friends. I miss thrilling conversations and connections and the smell of my suitcases. I miss clutching my passport in hand, and still printing out a paper ticket to tuck safely inside of its pages. I miss luggage tags and the group excitement and anticipation when the food cart arrives in the airplane aisle. Shit, I miss that first whiff of gross airplane food that we lie about and say doesn't make us excited. Mingled with that airplane air. That weird smell of the plane bathroom and even the wait we might do as a small group in the middle of the night on a long flight. We do tiny stretches and weirdly huddle by the drinks station, just hoping to hear the click of the door, to see the sign change to a green VACANT on the restroom. Maybe someone from the flight crew offers you a little biscuit that you would never eat outside of this airplane, but you are very happy to grab this tiny treat and eat it like a rabbit, once you are back in your seat.

I miss the air and smell of a new country that hits you smack in the face when you exit airport doors in a far-off land. Each place smells very different. I miss unpacking my robes and clothes and dresses to put on adventure display in my room, or house, or villa. I miss staying at hotels and single-serving amenities and judging the rooms and standard of snacks in minibars. Judging the tiles and insufficient bathroom countertop space and if they supply a black makeup towel, gross. If they have a lighted makeup mirror that swivels out from the wall, I know I will have a better experience. I miss being upset at a too-thick hotel hallway carpet as I drag my suitcase to the room. Why would they do that? Please offer me a smooth tile experience for suitcase wheels' sake by the elevator bank, but then in the hallway you should lay a *thin* carpet that dampens sound but still allows for easy suitcase wheeling to rooms down the long corridors. I miss shifting my flights and making jokes with flight attendants. I miss new crisp sheets and kicking my legs free from the trap of a fresh, tightly made hotel bed. I miss waking up and being confused about where I am, for just a few seconds.

I miss sitting at foreign cafés, drinking coffee or wine, and people-watching. I miss strolling the streets of a place I have never been, without consulting my phone for directions and instead trusting the universe will take me where I need to go, with no fear. I miss being everywhere and nowhere, everyone and no one, on my own time in a very Dr. Manhattan sort of way, I suppose.

My brain works better when I have travel. My ideas are better when I'm actively living that way.

My body feels better. And I'm never lonely when I travel, how could I be? There's a whole world of people to meet and talk to, and they talk to me a lot. There was a time where I tried to figure out how to stop this from happening, but it's never going to, so I embrace it.

Is this not the whole point of living? The moments. Textures, smells, time.

The need to be "of the world" *does* begin with my parents self-exile and their artist history. It *does* have roots in my touring years and solo adventuring. Some of it is a reclamation of time and sullied places, yes. Of course it is a reaction to having a home taken from me repeatedly. A reaction to my inability to return to my childhood home. A reflection of watching "traveled and worldly" older women be so understandable and aspirational. Mmhmm. It is also a deep ancestral pull that wants me everywhere, experiencing everything freely with joy, for always. And I suppose also a way to answer my "where do I belong?" question that has always plagued me. "Where is home?" has been a difficult question to answer because I do love nesting and building a stable home in one place, as equally as I do galivanting around the earth and solving fake murdah mystrays like a complete lunatic. I can acknowledge all of these things now.

So, everywhere. Home can mean "everywhere" too.

I am soft, flowing, and draped. I am tailored and heavily fragranced with intentional, multiple sillages for all moments. I am sometimes new, but mostly secondhand, quiet luxury. Robes, tassels, and trailing trains that might be destroyed on these adventures. I don't shout, or scream with anger. I echo. I imprint. I am tapestries, open-air sunsets with gentle breezes, and intimate dinners. Martinis and soft jazz. Trails of cigarette smoke that snake through the air on a hot summer night, in a dimly lit bar with chipped marble tables. I am sun-faded, broken-in oxford shirts rolled up at the sleeve and unbuttoned down the chest. A line of sweat visible on the back, haggling at an outdoor market in a small foreign town, over the price of silks and various textiles to be shipped to my home base. I am deep base notes of amber and leather. Saffron and incense. Animalic labdanum. Tonka and ylang ylang in a black dress that fits like a glove. I am all of the places my ancestors are from, called exotica and reclaimed in my hands stained red to the tips and wrapped around a cigar. I am the reminder of every place they tried to destroy, even the place inside of me. I am all. I am home.

"Madame, I was only asking the name of the reservation." The host at the restaurant is confused.

"Oh, yes. Sorry, that's *Denise Denephew.*" I pull in my arms, which have been outstretched wide in a Jesus pose for the duration of my lil' speech. I'm using one of my favorite fake adventure travel names and pronouncing it painfully French-ly, since I'm in Paris to begin my Paris-Budapest roundtrip on the Orient Express. I only make use of "Dr. Umentary" when it's time to solve a nonexistent murdah mystery, and "Denise" holds no stress in an introduction, compared to offering up my nonexistent PhD.

As the host leads me to my table, a red velvet booth in the darkest corner of the room, I get that old familiar excitement. Someone in here besides me has been traveling internationally. Even through the fragrances of many foods surrounding me, I can pick out that unmistakable suitcase scent. I breathe it in deeply as I toss my Burberry cashmere coat off my shoulders and onto the floor behind me. I keep walking. And even though I am thousands of miles away, I truly, once again, feel right at home.

Eggs
Tube

~~Romen~~ In my ~~Broken~~

REMAINING
years

I will - ugh... (WHAT)

rmember : meraki
      pswd : Fuckyou029483

10.

Peri-Peri

Did you know about perimenopause? Have you heard of this? Do you know about this?"

I am screaming.

"We have just fucking found out!" has been the unified, resounding cry from all the people I know who have the corresponding parts on the inside that might be affected by said "perimenopause." How. How are we all just finding out? Don't tell me. I know the answer. Anything regarding women's health, especially women's reproductive health, is dealt with in a very "We Don't Talk About Bruno"° sort of way.

I have always known this, I just thought we'd have a different answer by this era of Earth, what with all the advances and . . . robots and shit. Robots have been very busy of late. The humanoid robot ARMAR-6 has been able to wipe counters down for a few years now—please send that robot to my house. There are self-driving cars. Chat GPT can pretty much run your entire life for you—don't do that—but it could. We should have been talking about perimenopause before

---

° Song from the animated movie *Encanto*. I don't have kids, so I didn't have to listen to *Encanto* a bazillion times. Maybe you did. I dunno. This reference is less about the song's innards and more about the title.

this very late period in time, all puns intended. We should have been alerted en masse by, oh I dunno, *from our doctors*? They should have said something to us. Even if that something was "Perimenopause! Watch out, nah" as they shot finger guns at our cervixes. That would have been unprofessional and wildly inappropriate, but *informative*.

We shouldn't have found out about a major life change that is relevant to more than half the population of Earth, via . . . TikTok. On second thought, let me correct myself. Women's reproductive health is regular information that is always relevant to *everyone* and should be taught to *everyone*, like menopause, but with far fewer jokes and erring on the side of facts. For the most part, we have all been aware of and anticipating *menopause*, right? But no word of a potentially lengthy opening act that hits the stage before menopause shows up? A performance that may last months or ten years? Which is a very large difference in times. What if a stranger showed up in your house and said they might stay there for four months, or . . . I dunno . . . TEN YEARS?

"Hard to know," they'd say, shrugging casually after you'd inquired about the length of their stay. "Oh, also. Could I stay *inside* of you?" They wouldn't wait for your answer. "Great," they'd reply to themselves. They'd unhinge your jaw and climb into your mouth, whispering along the way, like White people do when they're trying to move past you. "Lemme just . . . just gonna climb on in here. Lemme just scooch on in." Once inside, they'd turn on a fog machine, making it impossible for your brain to function.

"What's going on in there?" you'd scream.

"What?" they'd respond after a minute of being eerily quiet. "Oh! I'm doing a magic trick that makes you forget everything and feel terrible in every way! You're gonna love it!"

"Who's that?" you'd wonder. The brain fog now too thick to see the memories of what had just occurred. "What was I saying?" you'd repeat quietly to yourself as you wandered around your apartment, picking up random objects and hoping for clues to solve this mystery.

Maybe some of you want to tell me that perimenopause is just PRE-menopause and we did know about that. I would like to tell *you* that no one consulted or notified us about the changing of the name and absolutely no one was up front about any of the peri info at any point in time. There have been no pamphlets. No cops came to our schools to tell us about the Perils of Peri, the way they came to let us know that there were cool stickers adults might give you that could get you high if you touched them. High from LSD, which by the way, never fucking happened. And we tried really hard to find those stickers. Some kids even pretended that regular stickers they got out of twenty-five-cent vending machines and put on their hands were acid stickers and that they were tripping balls all through Mr. Cassidy's social studies class. Some. Kids. That I may or may not have been.

In any case, I've been waiting since my preteen years for *only menopause's* terrible magic acts. In school, I belonged to "Old Parent Gang," a special gang for children. OPG refused membership to kids with parents who were perhaps five or six years older than the "Regular-Age Parent Gang" (RAPG) kids.

"My parents are older too!" they'd exclaim, trying to build a connection with us. I would step forward as OPG chairperson. "Really? My mummy is *fifty*. How old is *your mother*?"

"Thirty ei—" Denying them the grace to finish their statements, my OPG would turn away sharply. Cackling. "Can you imagine?" Mimicking the transatlantic speech learned from our forced watching of Turner classic movies.° We'd saunter into the distance of the school halls, smoking our candy cigarettes and pulling invisible long fur coats across our shoulders. Triple points in OPG for having old, *immigrant* parents. Because that is a whole other ball of old, hard-to-relate-to-other-kids wax. Or yarn. Or whatever ball you might have, I don't know! *tosses candy cigarette, climbs on moving train*

My mother was born in 1936, in Cape Town, South Africa. I was absolutely not having the same parenting experience as other 1980s and 1990s New York City kids whose parents were born in America in

---

° Notoriously "good at racism" American mogul Ted Turner bought the MGM film studio in 1986 and eight years later launched Turner Broadcasting System, on which he played his new library of movies. Ironically, Turner colorized many of these Black-and-White films and I'm leaving those words capitalized to highlight the joke.

the 1950s or 1960s, or even my nonimmigrant OPG compadres. While my mom was cool about a lot of things, she was still very strict about "regular things" I wanted to do. Like sleepovers.

Or *going places* with my "little friends." Somehow, she did manage to acquire the lingo of *all* parents across the globe with that one phrase. Her use of the phrase actually made me feel like part of the RAPG, but I was quickly reminded of my nonmembership whenever she utilized words like *ruffians* and *hooligans*. It's hilarious that as a child in 1980s NYC I said sentences like, "My cronies are not hooligans, Mummy!" I sounded like a time-traveling street urchin.

Being a part of OPG meant that I would be present for my mom's menopausal years. Kids in RAPG (in America) are usually not living in their childhood homes for this experience. But in our household, my mother and I were both having "coming of age" moments. Thankfully, my mother's progressiveness in many areas led her to being very open about menopausal discussion. She talked about what was to come for her and what it felt like. Also thankfully, albeit sparsely, there were a couple of television portrayals of women experiencing menopause who didn't gloss over it, or make women the complete butt of the joke. By "didn't gloss over it" I mean that they addressed it with a single episode. There were no shows called "Menopause Manor," well . . . kinda.

In the 1986 episode of the television sitcom *The Golden Girls*,[*] "End of the Curse," Blanche Devereaux played by Rue McClanahan shockingly reveals to her housemates that she is pregnant. After a doctor visit, she discovers that she is not with child but, instead, with menopause. Hilarious! The audience thinks, "Haha, silly Old Lady!" Blanche's sex-positive character descends into a dramatic southern sadness, greatly dismayed at the imminent loss of her femininity. After her doctor recommends that she "find some other value in herself,"

---

[*] *The Golden Girls* was a television sitcom (1985–1992) about a bunch of middle-aged White women (three widows and one divorcée) who share a house in Miami, Florida. "Golden" like in their Golden years. Word? We all thought they were so old. Blanche was forty-fucking-seven when the show started. Bitch, me? I am Golden Girl? Fuck off.

Blanche and The Girls have one of their kitchen roundtables. They discuss periods, menopause, and everyone's varying experiences. Blanche is still confederately verklempt. To cure her Dixie melancholy, she goes on a date with a young veterinarian.

When she appears again in better spirits, she tells the rest of the *in their goddamn early fifties* Golden Girls that it was not the date that perked her up, but the talk they'd all had together. This was pretty good content for the 1980s. The fact that a bunch of women had decided to build community and support each other was outstanding. As a member of OPG, I didn't think it was weird that Blanche could've been pregnant, so the joke was odd to me. That episode aside, *The Golden Girls* were a bunch of White women living in Florida, and, well, they weren't very relatable. Plus, there's an episode of *The Golden Palace*, the spin-off of *TGG*, where Blanche hangs a Confederate flag to welcome the Daughters of the Traditional South, and Don Cheadle's character has to stop his day to tell Blanche why she's a piece of shit. So, sad to say it, but fuck Blanche. Love Bea Arthur, but you never can tell which White women are problematic so . . . eh.

Next, in 1990, television's *The Cosby Show*° episode "Clair's Liberation" aired. Clair Huxtable (wife to Cliff Huxtable, played by Bill Cosby) was played by Phylicia Rashad. The Huxtable's were Black professionals who owned a beautiful brownstone in Brooklyn, NYC, and had too many children. They were caring, attentive, and involved in their kids' lives. Cliff and Clair were aspirational as a couple, always finding the time to slow dance to jazz in their living room at the end of an episode. Always finding romance and intimacy in between the five kids and their respective careers. "They have it all," we viewers

---

° Listen, I don't wanna talk about wretched-ass Bill Cosby, and I apologize if my mention of him is triggering to anyone; it's also triggering to me. But it is important to acknowledge the effect this episode of the show had on my expectations in life and not in a "separate the art from the artist" way. Even forcing myself to rewatch this episode was rough. Sincerely, fuck that man and fuck anything he has ever done, or will do. And, fuck Phylicia Rashad for her private and public support of him. And fuck anyone else who still supports him and remained complacent and silent about his actions for so long. My absolute heart goes out to all victims and their families. Absolute.

thought as we watched the TV couple sway to John Coltrane's "Dear Lord" next to their couch, under dim lighting.

Especially to nonrich New Yorkers, the show was satisfyingly voyeuristic. We could finally see inside all those rich people's brownstones. Trying to look into rich people's brownstones is a New York City pastime. We walk by slowly, craning our necks from the bottom of their stoops with the rest of the poors, to catch a mere glimpse inside their palaces. The soaring ceilings and wide staircases; shoot, most of us don't have *other floors* in our apartments. What a life! Although I couldn't relate to a lot of Black American culture in the show, like having extended family nearby, fraternity, and HBCU culture, it *had* to be close enough to qualify as representation, or I'd have nothing. Just like when that lady on *Romper Room*° would look into her Magic Mirror and never say my name, I'd accept her saying "Sadie" as a win. It was close enough. The TV Cosbys were . . . close enough.

The Huxtables had *everything*. And Clair, well, Clair Huxtable was "goals." She was a brilliant, beautiful lawyer. She was kind but would read a motherfucker for filth. Clair reading Elvin, the beau of her oldest daughter, Sondra, for filth, was a regular occurrence. Elvin was deeply misinformed and misogynistic, always questioning how Clair managed to "have it all" and still do things like "serve" men drinks. As balance to the era of the "how can a woman have it all" struggle movie trope, Clair never struggled to maintain her marriage, five kids, career, *and* being fabulous. So when the show tackled Clair's experience with menopause, we knew she would read it . . . for filth.

In "Clair's Liberation," Clair mentions casually that she is going through menopause. The teenage kids are stunned as Clair flippantly says, "Don't be silly, it's just a part of life." The menopause news sends the kids into a panic, and they begin to dissect all of Clair's behavior

---

° A long running (1953–1994) children's television show. There was a segment at the end of every show where the host would look through her Magic Mirror, which enabled her to "see the friends at home," aka the viewers. She'd call out names and say she could see kids having a special day. But she never said my name, which meant she never saw me. °*emotional piano music*° I was always there, but she never saw me.

and share urban menopause tales. Stories about women who have "cried so hard they had to have surgery on their tear ducts" are shared between them. The children begin to treat Clair as if she is insane. But Clair peeps game and ropes Cliff in on pulling a prank on the unsuspecting kids. During dinner, Clair acts out menopausal tropes, resulting in television high jinks. She forgets names. She sticks her head in the freezer to relieve her "hot flash" and cries when offered some corn, saying, "I was hoping we would have carrots! I wanted something orange!" She finally delivers a gotcha moment with her perfectly white-toothed laugh as the kids look on, horrified. This felt like a more relatable menopause experience to me. I too would enjoy pulling a prank on children. Not specifically my children, just *any* children. And when my mother's time for menopause rolled around, I knew not to be stupid like the kids on the show.

My mom wasn't Clair Huxtable in all ways, but she did balance business and family, and she *was* fabulous. And there was a lot of jazz played in our house, even though we didn't live in a brownstone. Close enough. "I'm just so fucking hot!" my mom exclaimed, sitting on the edge of her bed, her shirt off.

Wearing only a bra and flowing skirt, she would slump forward, looking defeated. My mom treated her hot flashes by dabbing cool washcloths on her neck and chest. She'd then throw massive amounts of Jean Naté After Bath Splash on her décolletage with fervor. She fanned herself a lot, and I'm unsure if this move was nabbed from Clair, but I definitely found her standing in front of the wide-open freezer of our refrigerator more than once. I remembered her always telling us kids to "stop standing there with the fridge door wide open!" But I wasn't stupid like the Cosby kids, so I didn't say anything about the unfairness. I talked to her with kindness, support, and her favorite delivery of chat: dark humor. For someone so kind and soft, my mom's love for sarcasm, straight talkers, and dark jokes always amused me.

"You know, some people just burst right into flames from hot flashes," I'd say. "They get so heated from the inside out that they *poof* explode." I nodded with certainty. "Hope you don't explode. Who'd clean all of that up?" She'd laugh until she cried and sometimes I'd draw tiny diagrams of the self-explosions.

Hot flashes aside, we did talk a lot about her fear of losing her femininity. I thought about Blanche. We talked about her fear of her voice changing and how that could affect her singing. We talked about her fear of weight gain, her fear of "becoming an old witch," and we talked about how happy she was to not be getting her period anymore. And, and . . . before the menopause happened, we talked about her being premenopausal. PREMENOPAUSAL for SIX MONTHS. At no point did we discuss that premenopause might appear *ten years* prior to menopause, and at no point did we call it "perimenopause."

None.

Maybe after the gynecologist did the finger guns to our cervixes, they could have said, "Oh, PRE. I mean, PRE menopause." And it still would have been unprofessional and wildly inappropriate, but still . . . *informative.* Also, why PERI? *Peri* makes me instantly think of South Africa's famous peri-peri° condiment, and I'd really rather not think about a bird's eye chili pepper sauce in relation to my ovaries.

Maybe you too have found yourself scrolling through the algorithms of perimenopause edutainment late at night only to realize that, yes, in fact, perimenopause has come for you. Perhaps you too have screamed at the heavens, "Is there no fucking break?!" I yelled at the heavens, aka the ceiling, "Can I just have a fucking second to be a person? Goddamn!"

This is a very fucking valid cry. I don't know about you, but I've had a twenty-one-day menstrual cycle since I was sixteen years old. This means I have one week (if that) out of a month where I'm slightly peachy. All other days of the month include bloating, cravings, sadness, anger, and then . . . bleeding. Bleeding like a stuck pig for four days, sometimes five. Bleeding through my clothes, my nice sheets. Bleeding through super-plus tampons and overnight pads. Bleeding like the

---

° Nando's is a famous chain of flame-grilled chicken restaurants that specializes in peri-peri chicken. It's delicious and you should try it immediately if you haven't. I like the lemon and herb better than the peri-peri flavors though. Not because of the ovaries, just 'cause it's yummy.

elevator doors in *The Shining*.° Hey, fun fact: a twenty-one-day cycle can sometimes hit twice a month, 'cause that's how numbers work. Fun fact, fun fact, fun fact!

At my current age, the whole period situation is less of a discomfort and pain issue and more of an annoyance. I'm annoyed at the whole process and everything it entails. Annoyed as I snatch a box of tampons off a store shelf, muttering, "Can't believe I'm still doing this fucking shit," as I suck my teeth and leave the store after checking out, naked box of tampons in my hand. Put it in a bag for *what.* I'm annoyed that we're still even *paying* for these things. I've tried period panties, but those quickly became annoying and not practical without a washing machine. I tried jamming a menstrual cup into myself, my anxiety couldn't fuck with that, annoyed. Is it me, cursing up a storm as I change my tampons and use wipes and ruin pants? Yes. Cursing at the toilet seat I have to clean whenever Redman† is in town, yes. Extra washing hands and washcloths and towels—RAAAAAR!!! Annoyed at the process, the extra work, the thinking, the planning—RARRRRR!!!

"Just a second," I sob into my good pillow. "A fucking second to be a person? Goddamn."

Oh, to be a person unplagued by hormonal shifts, pain, and unwanted emotions. Couch, sad, bad brain, tapeworm like binge eating. And real me inside my head who wants to get up and do things. When your annoyance from the outside world joins forces with your PMS annoyance, it fulfills The Great Yelling Random Things Prophecy. Sometimes it's just sounds. Sometimes, unintelligible words. Sometimes, a singular obscenity. It's so hard to tell what the culprit is, because there are so many possible assailants. There's no way to pick out the criminal from the lineup. "It's all of them," I imagine myself saying, waving my finger around at the one-way mirror in the police station of life. I turn and nod at the cop. "They all robbed me."

° Sigh, really? *The Shining* is a very famous movie and this scene is very famous and a lot of blood pours out of elevator doors and yes that sounds insane with or without any further context.

† Redman is a rapper, but I use this reference far more than Aunt Flo. You're welcome. Someone should tell him. Maybe I'll tell him.

- Brain fog
- Anxiety
- Depression
- Weight gain
- Insomnia and interrupted sleep
- Mood swings and "irrational" annoyances
- Questioning self-worth
- Hair loss
- Difficulty concentrating
- Social withdrawal
- Intrusive thoughts
- Loss of interest in pleasure
- Reduced sex drive
- Headaches
- Exhaustion

"Fuck," I mutter to myself as I reread all the symptoms out loud. "Well, yeah. I have those things."

The list above is a super cool compilation of things I am experiencing, taken from a much longer "possible perimenopause symptoms" list. Actually, it's from a few lists that I hobbled together. ACTUALLY, it's from a few lists that I hobbled together and only one of them was a list of perimenopause symptoms. That's right.

Severe work burnout. CPTSD (complex post-traumatic stress disorder). Habitual burnout. Straight-up depression. Late-stage capitalism. Assimilation trauma. Patriarchy stress disorder. Structural racism burnout. Midlife crisis. Long-term effects of gaslighting. And lastly, perimenopause.

Well.

I texted one of my friends I'd been sharing "what the fuck, fuck this shit" perimenopause videos and thoughts with: What if all of the things we're being sold as "perimenopause symptoms" aren't solely that. I'm not saying hormonal changes don't exist, but we're all suffering from multiple systemic burnouts and have been for years. At a certain point, you can lose your mind and become incredibly fatigued. It just seems too easy to dismiss this time of life as women/perimenopause. The same way men have always weaponized "you must be on your period."

She answered that she hadn't thought of it in that way yet, but yeah. Sounded fucking reasonable.

We are so tired from our collection of experiences. We need. To shut. Down. Even for a little while. And we cannot. I typed that and just lay still for a long time, until I had to get up and do an unreasonable capitalism.

I'm gonna be super honest: I would love to simply say that my issue is perimenopause. I love having an easy answer. It might be? My period now has a twenty-four to twenty-six-week cycle range, which I'm actually not complaining about. I am the right age for the perimenopausal experience. But again, my symptoms are impossible to separate from all the other potential causes. I don't have hot flashes. I don't have itchy ears, or frozen shoulder, both of which I've heard are peri-peri jams. I should probably go have some blood tests done to figure it out, but until I can work out my relationship with the other villainous possibilities of why I feel this way, what would it matter if I did also have perimenopause? Is hormone replacement therapy going to stop racism? Capitalism? Livin' in America constant feelings? If it will, please give me the juice. I will even withstand the annoyance of the fight that people of color have to do in order to explain their way into getting medical care. But I feel as if many of us simply can't identify our issues as being one thing.

If you've also received the super fun bundle of Earth gifts I just mentioned, maybe you could let me know what your proposed solution is for handling them. I'd love to bounce some ideas off of each other. The solution I came up with is to do my best to first eradicate as many of the other potential criminals from affecting me as much as possible. And I'm getting there, but unfortunately it is hard work to stop doing so much hard work, isn't it? And then, it is also hard work to reposition yourself to . . . what was I explaining? Do you remember what it was? ARGH. I can't tell if the brain fog is perimenopause, or my thoughts need to power down for a while. Ahh, thank you. I got it. To reposition your . . . nope, it's gone again.

Let's just move on. I'm working on lessening the work so I can see what needs to get worked on. Does that sound right to you? It all feels like such a losing battle, because if I am one of those people who isn't getting peri symptoms, I still have the main act of menopause coming up at some point. And I have considered going through the wretched act of begging a doctor to perform an elective hysterectomy just in case I might feel slightly better, but then I would just launch right into menopause, so—reader, can you just move a little over to the left so I don't hit you with this *throws table* I don't know!

Regarding menopause, I'm not afraid of losing my femininity in a lack-of-estrogen kinda way. Or my voice deepening. I'm not afraid of being unfuckable. It is a very interesting journey to be having as a person who no longer subscribes to the gender binary, and I wish there were more spaces where I could find people like me to discuss that.

I know that there are so many of us who don't fit in with groups of women who are having these kinds of conversations. And that's a modern issue that could use some more public addressing. I'd like to encourage those of us who are comfortable saying these things out loud to say them a little louder. I also hope that shining a light on our collective traumas can help us all better identify what the fuck is happening to us. Whether it might be a shitty magician climbing into your body and living there for a decade, or the fact that we haven't openly and effectively dealt with the rest of our Earth CPTSD. The multiple ongoing genocides. The fact that no one can afford to pay rent and that aluminum foil costs eight dollars now. Eight dollars! And then just regular at-home shit, like your cat keeps throwing up from eating random plastic around the house, and some days, it's just the last fucking straw.

It would almost be the most welcomed thing if *only* perimenopause was fucking my life up every day. "Turn the fog machine up," I might even say to my unwanted body house guest. So that maybe, for a few moments, I could drown out the world and have a fucking second to be a person. Goddamn.

In my remaining years,
I will not order any
more piña coladas!

11.

HJGHGB

My friend and I are texting about "taking vacations." It's in quotes because everything is uncertain and never-ending. Any sort of vacation seems like a fantasy. It's sometime in late 2021 and things are "2021 bad," personally and globally. That term has the bite of a bottomless bowl of exhaustion, peppered with two full cups of cayenne, fresh arugula, and radishes. I am experiencing waves of sadness, and these are not the "waves" I requested. I remind myself that when you ask the universe for things, you have to be very, very specific. I did not want waves of mental unwellness. I meant ocean waves at the beach. I really needed to go to the beach.

I probably said, "I need to go to the beach really fucking bad. I'm gonna rip my skin off!" because my friend sends me a picture of the *How Stella Got Her Groove Back* movie poster, followed by the text: All of the remedies are in Jamaica.

I immediately yell, "NO!" out loud. Not at the general "being in Jamaica" part. That sounds wonderful. The flora and fauna. Mountains and beaches, a combination reminiscent of Cape Town. Bombay mangoes and plantains, food, all the food in general. Waterfalls, music, and fuckin' Grace Jones! Jamaica gifted the universe with Grace Jones! Jamaica, yes! But it seems as if my friend may be referring to a Jamaica that is more of an all-inclusive resort, "these drinks are made entirely out of sugar," Jamaica. It seems as if she is suggesting a vacation where Taye Diggs might be involved, and Taye Diggs might be a portion of the remedies. But I do not want to imagine spending any amount of time with Taye Diggs. I'm not a betting person, but I'm willing to bet an exorbitant amount of money that he also does not want to spend any amount of time with me. Which is great.

"Yeah, Taye Diggs blocked me."

Which he did. Years ago. Right after I tweeted something to him about his "constant fedora." Being blocked by celebrities on Twitter was not a thing I aspired to or would ever brag about. I've had people do that to me and I'm not doing it now. The blocking is just a fact. As is the constant fedora.

I'm expecting my friend to respond to my statement with shock. Taye Diggs *blocked* me? But, Taye Diggs notoriously follows EVERY-ONE! Taye Diggs probably follows Taye Diggs! He did, in fact, follow me, but his follow was quickly followed by the *blocking* of me.

I'd seen his follow and just couldn't hold my water about the fedora. Because if you're going to wear a fedora like, a lot of the time, would you not expect anyone to ask you about said fedora(s)? I dunno. I start typing "What's with that fucking hat, amirite" to my friend but delete it, as her next message is not about his always-chapeaux.

"Okay, replace Taye then! It's not about him. Just Jeannie Basset with a rum punch and a twenty-one-year-old!"

I am immediately dehydrated and exhausted by these replacement ideas and consider accepting the TD original scenario instead. Or, just dying.

In general, I don't like sweet, fruity drinks. I like refreshing, smoky, bitter drinks. Crisp or spicy. Citrus squeezes and herbaceous elements. I like to taste the ingredients, including the alcohol. I don't understand drinks that are attempts to mask the alcohol in the alcohol beverage. Don't give me a simple syrup, or a liqueur. I will sometimes accept a Manhattan, or a Negroni, and that sweet red vermouth is where I draw the line. I'll admit to enjoying a Luxardo cherry, or a candied gin-ger piece, if it appears on a corresponding beverage. I like my white wines like I like my White people, dry and crisp. Reds, I want funk, dirt, earth, oak, smoke, chocolate, fullness. Maybe a nice Gamay. I wasn't always like this. In my early twenties I was attached at the hip to Southern Comfort, 100 proof. I used to drink it straight from the bottle, like a lunatic. I cannot imagine doing that now—pouring a vat of sugar down my throat. I definitely wouldn't have a rum punch. It is not a refreshing beverage, which is what the beach calls for.

Refreshment.

This is not a knock to any islands and their rum punch. It's a personal preference. That drink is cloyingly sweet, and sticky—but not in a sexy way. Plus, I am imagining the rum punches in reference at this all-inclusive Taye Diggs resort. *So much juice,* with a *tourist* amount of rum involved. In the past, I have gotten caught up in the "I'm on vacation" thrill of it all and ordered things like this. Arriving at the bar, I smell like coconuts and heat, my cover-up swinging open. I rest my elbows on the sticky rim of the beachside bar, I prop a single flip-flopped foot on a brass footrail.

I watch people order piña coladas and rum punches as I stare at the chalk menu, unsure. I bite my lip and feel full with social pressure indecision. These people all *look* like they are on vacation, walkin' around with their piña coladas and rum punches. They look like they are having so much fun, with their souvenir glasses the size of vases. Jugs full of tepid juice, accompanied by trinkets. A wacky straw. An inedible, old, warm slice of pineapple. A plastic monkey draped over the edge of the glass. An elusive maraschino cherry and a paper umbrella they attempt to stick behind their ears because that's what you do when you're "on vacation."

I have known that I really wanted to get a vodka soda, or even a Vacation Jean compromise of Wray & Ting with lime, because Ting is a delicious grapefruit soda that isn't overly sweet and the acid from the lime provides balance! I have wanted this, known myself, and failed to order it. Blurting out, "uhhh, uhhhh, a piña colada" at the last second and instantly regretting my decision but refusing to rescind my statement. Best to not let any of these strangers I'm probably never going to see again think that I can't make up my own mind!

"But can you pour more rum on the top? Like a lot? I'll pay extra!" I have added, thinking that will fix my stupid choice. Sure. I will pay you more money because I don't want you to think that I am indecisive and that I don't know how to enjoy myself on vacation like everyone else here. Makes perfect sense!

I have received my now thirty-dollar drink and slowly pulled out the loopy straw, drawing it through the viscous mixture like pulling a sword from a wound. I've pulled myself up on a stool to dance this plastic, whimsical tool across the surface of the cocktail, where the hardly two shots of pooled rum sits, and sucked it all up, before exiting the awning of the bar and walking out on the sand, into the gorgeous sun. One short minute later, after taking two long sips of the actual drink, I have softly exclaimed, "Ughhh."

I am hot, which is great. But now the drink is lukewarm and thick. "Milky" is not the adjective I would use to describe a good drink for a hot day. "Thick candy drank" is not what I desire in my mouth when the sun is beating down on my shoulders. Even worse are the tiny plastic cup versions of these drinks, that cost *not tiny plastic cup drink* money. Now I'm all the way out on the beach, I've finished my drink on the way to my chair, and my mouth feels like I've been chewing towels.

No.

I have done all of this and wondered how everyone else is enjoying the same things I am hating. Are they for real having a good time, or is it all purely performative vacation stage plays? Because that umbrella will always betray you and fall to the ground. Or stab you in the neck. And now you have to carry your stupid souvenir glass vase. If you put it in your bag, it would magically spawn more hot red juice that would stain your passport and/or all of your fabulous belongings, including the bag. You wanna walk to the water and crouch in the ocean, rinsing out the glass? That sounds like thinking, work, and tasks. That is the opposite of vacation. The opposite.

I've only seen the movie *HSGHGB* one time, many years ago, so I don't remember exactly how the whirlwind romance began. I imagine that Angela Bassett was lying on a beach chair looking like Angela Fucking Bassett and then Whoopi Goldberg sat up from her beach chair, looked into the near distance, and pulled her glasses down to perch midnose. She nudged Angela Bassett with the exact force that your friend would use to let you know you need to look at a hot person right away. It's a very specific touch. Cut to slo-mo Taye Diggs walking and dripping out of the ocean, all the way to Angela's chair. A popular R&B midtempo jam plays as Angela feigns disinterest. TD reaches the chair and a single drip of water falls onto her incredibly supple at-any-age leg. He bites his lip.

"Sorry," he says, in a terrible Jamaican accent. "I didn't mean to get you . . . wet." This elicits a tiny cackle from Whoopi, and TD smiles, the brightness from his teeth drying the drip instantly.

"Every ting irie now," he says as an unseen disapproving woman sucks her teeth in the background, because he is *so* young and Angela Bassett is *so* old. I think about this happening to me. TD reaches my chair and a single drip of . . . "Hey, get the fuck out of my sun, fam!" I reach down and throw a handful of sand at him. It gets him right in the eyes. I suck my teeth in disapproval as he grabs his sand-filled eyes and flails down the beach, screaming. I turn to Whoopi Goldberg. "What is it with men and personal fucking space? Like . . . get the fuck out of here!" I use my biggest New York accent. "I know that's right," says Whoopi. We both laugh and smoke cigarettes.

I don't know if you can tell, but I am not a good candidate to be the recipient of this All-Inclusive Beach Cougar Fantasy. Even though my friend very sweetly offered it to me, and I appreciate that! If I had to be located anywhere in this fantasy world, I would not be Angela Bassett. I would be Whoopi Goldberg. The supportive friend who . . . wait, does she die in the end? Okay, even better. The supportive friend who provides quips, snark, and then dies. Love zippy one-liners and support for someone else's need to have a rum punch and a twenty-one-year-old boy, then a funeral. We all need different fantasies, because our life experiences are not the same. I will bring my friend a rum punch. She will have a fabulous time, and I'll have one too. As well as a vodka soda. And then I will go home and perish in three months to ten years, because again . . . I do not remember the movie that well.

Two years later, a different friend would send me a clip of dumbass Piers Morgan interviewing Whoopi, with the text, I had my eyes closed and thought this was you. I had actually just watched this clip the previous day. I had watched it no less than twenty times and cried because I am an easy crier and a lot of things that Whoopi said resonated with me. It felt good to hear her be "ahead of her time" in thinking about men, love, relationships, and being happy to be by yourself. Of course, stupid Piers Morgan was so taken aback at her views, because he is stupid. But she looked so beautiful, *stunning*— remember they got us to think how not beautiful she was—and so, so comfortable and confident. Except . . . it still wasn't *exactly* relatable.

Because while Whoopi did talk about enjoying being by herself, being in love, and past marriages all so casually (samesies), it seemed as if men and relationships were still a part of her life. And y'all. I . . . that's not the fuck where I'm at. Or where I plan to be in the future.

| | |

"You need three different men."

I am ten years old and my mother is talking in low tones to me and my friend Nadxi. We stand on the threshold of the tiny kitchen in my childhood apartment. We are both rapt, wide-eyed, and fully confused at this random-ass information we are being told. All we wanted was a snack. My mother continued, "One man to talk to. One to have a beautiful romance with. And one . . . to take to a hotel."

What. Was. Happening.

My mother turned her back to us and stirred the chicken curry she was making for dinner in the big pot. The big scratched-up and well-seasoned pot, where so many of our trillion-spiced meals were made. The scent was as thick and complex as the also well-seasoned words she served up. "Because one man isn't going to do all of that." She faced us again and leaned in. "If you want a man at all. You don't *need* one, but if you do . . . you need three men." She returned to her stirring, and I'm not sure if we got the snacks or not. I like to think that we turned on our heels quietly and went back to my room to lie down in silence.

For years, I was so confused by what my mom had said. Her statements were so far outside of my idea of how I thought she viewed marriage and partnership. There were no other men in her life; there were no affairs. My parents had divorced and *remarried*. And my mother didn't just say this to us *once*; her "three different men" speech happened many times, with no previous context and as a little low-toned aside, or later on in her Wine Era, loudly with laughter. It would be a long time—after Wine Era and after my mother's passing—until I understood how my mother could feel "three men" as a truth and also stay in her marriage. It would take a lot of experience and living for me to truly get how complex love, abuse, and longing can be. It would take a long time to understand that "three men" was a cautionary tale of how men are incapable of fulfilling women's needs, wants, and desires. It would take a long time to know that the statement didn't have to apply to me.

I've been married twice. I've been engaged a trillion times. I've collected engagement rings (none of them good) like Pokémon. I've had a lot of relationships. I've had all the sex. I've been dating since I was a teenager. There's a scene in the olden times *Sex and the City* HBO series when everyone's favorite traditional and ever-optimistic character, Charlotte York, exclaims with utter exasperation, "I've been dating since I was fifteen! I'm exhausted! Where is he?" Well, I deliver you an updated version—"*I've* been dating since I was fifteen. I'm exhausted." Full stop.

I've slept with more people than I've dated, but those affairs were mostly in my late teens and early twenties. Everything after that was unwise serial monogamy, or terrible attempts at dating either very minimally, outside of the entertainment industry or, very horrendously, inside of it. None of these options have yielded good results, so it would seem that not wanting to date anyone would be the logical choice to make now. Why in the world would I keep trying something that has never worked for *checks birthdate* over thirty years? Actually, "never worked" is far too tame a description. "Been an absolute nightmare" is far more accurate.

In my late twenties, I once was *kinda* dating this dude who drove a PT Cruiser. Now, when you say, "Jean, the PT Cruiser ownership should have been your first red flag," I say, I hear you, but no. My first red flag should have been that he was too handsome. But handsome in a way that translates to me as "corny." Some of you know exactly what

I mean. He was also just corny in general, minus the face. He was an insipid human being, and we had nothing in common. Our conversations were nonexistent and the sex was definitely not good enough to ignore these other things. In general, good-looking people tend to not fuck well. Not all, but most. Anywho, I was continuing to spend time with this person because I was in my twenties. That's the only reason. About two weeks or so into this experiment, PT Cruiser decided to accuse me of an action I was physically incapable of doing.

"And then my brother said he saw you driving *[insert famous rap producer's name here]* car, in the Bronx! Jean, if you're going to lie to me, I just can't fuckin' do this!"

I was silent for about a minute. I kept trying to open my mouth to respond, but I couldn't figure out how. I had to say something, so I just began very slowly, as I was thoroughly confused.

"I . . . I have never met that person. For one." I was making eye contact with PT, but it was the first time I'd noticed that he had crazy eyes. "Ohh, I see," I said, quietly, acknowledging the eyes before continuing. "But more importantly, sir. *I* . . . do not know how to drive a vehicle of *any* sort. And you know this. So, you think that I have fibbed about not knowing how to drive. So I could go to . . . lemme get this straight . . . the Bronx?"*

PT was smiling, but also frowning, which was very unnerving, but I had to get the last point in there.

"Because even more important than the nondriving . . . which seems like it should be the most important factor here, is the fact . . . that you think . . . that I would . . . GO TO THE FUCKING BRONX."

I have also dated a lot of people who I never even dated. By this, I mean that there was never a clearly defined relationship. I *think* that I dated one specific man for a couple of years, but we never had sex. We did sleep—actual literal sleep—in the same bed often. At my apartment and his. We spent most of the hours in the day together, every

---

* For all my Bronx readers, let's just be honest. No one from outside of the Bronx without a car is trying to date you in the Bronx. I'm not talking shit about the Bronx, but let's all be reasonable and agree that it is like living in another state to everything below it, in NYC.

single day, whenever we were both in New York. When we were both traveling internationally, my phone bill was so fucking high because we were always talking. He once came to my apartment in Brooklyn to carry my suitcase down my stairs to a car. At a ridiculous time of the morning. And then left. Also, he is a recognizable figure in the entertainment world, so the young people in the building next door freaked out when this happened.

"Did *[insert name here]* just carry your bag to a car and then leave? You know him?"

"I guess," I responded, shrugging and getting into my car to the airport. Because they were right, it *was* weird. That was the strangest dating and absolutely not-dating experience I have ever had in my life. The more I look back on it, I wonder if the issue was simply, "I wasn't the right look for his status."

I don't think I need to talk about the fact that dating physically abusive men is not a thing I want to do anymore. I made so many excuses. Like showing up late with a black eye for my *L'uomo Vogue* shoot. "I was in a bar fight," I said. "Ooh, I love this sheer scarf as an accessory I can place on my face for this photo! No reason!"

I've had neighbors who heard everything. I know, because they tried to stop it all the time. And they knew exactly who I was. I had four of those relationships back-to-back. It would take an entire book of juicy details to go through my tales of dating all these worthless men. Most of them never even liked me. They just wanted to know what it was like to fuck me. Or say that they had. Sometimes, people just lied to the world, and said they had slept with me. Good times!

I will most certainly write a whole book about these things in the future, because that book is a goddamn bestseller and it would be very freeing. But, you'll publicly find out that many of these currently unnamed by me people are supervillains far before I tell you. There appear to be reckonings a going. Love that for them. And some of them will simply die, because we are of that age now. Most important, this moment is about *me.* So . . . no, I do not want three men. That's three too many men. The thought of three men just made me lean my head back into the couch and let out a guttural sigh for all my ancestors who were forced to be with men. I don't even want *one* man.

But all my experience and sound reasoning, apparently, still don't create a real and acceptable answer to give the world, after you have separated from a relationship, long-term or not. I should either be "finding myself" or "getting my groove back." Getting over someone by getting under someone, even if it's just a little fucky fling. But I'm not in a place where I'm trying to "get over" the relationship. I did that and I did it alone. And if I were, I wouldn't try to get over it by masking it with another activity similar to the original activity. That seems, like, unwell behavior.

And to be quite honest, my sex drive is just not there. There's the couple "Days O'Horny" right before my period, but besides that . . . nah, that shit left my body when I turned forty and has never returned.

"You'll see, it'll hit you again at forty-five!" said a woman who needed me to join in the older-women-wanting-to-fuck gang, for some reason. "No, I don't think so. I'm cool with that." I shrugged truthfully.

"No, you'll see! You're gonna want it all the time!"

But I *don't* want it.

Can I just have money instead? That would be great. And I know, I know I could have *one* man, with money. But that's a whole performance to pull off, and it's not my money, or really my man if it's *that kind* of a money man—ahhh. °*throws table*° Trust me, I have thought about how much easier I could make parts of my life with MONEY MAN, but . . . nah. Not worth it. Like a rum punch, all of this sounds so dehydrating and draining. Thinking about a man makes me feel so dehydrated. And I watch all of the people walking around with their men and wonder, How is everyone else enjoying the same thing I am hating? Are they for real having a good time, or is it all purely performative MAN stage plays? Like the Piña Colada People. Because I have had MAN and I *know* it isn't refreshing. People with MAN have suggested that maybe I just take a break. But I don't want to take a break and Eat, Pray, Love and then MAN. I don't want a MAN Recess. I want NOT MAN in perpetuity.

"I want to spend my time searching the world for textiles and buying amazing clothes. I'm in my Iris Apfel Era, but just without the man and the Trump-supporting. I did not know she was a Trump supporter

until after she died though, but I'm running out of role models, sorry,"
I tell people, blithely.

"Ahh, yes. Retail therapy to soothe your aching heart." They nod
slowly.

"No." I am puzzled. "I just love fashion. And travel. And fabrics."

Not everything is *therapy*. Can't I just enjoy things without them
having to be categorized as activities that are fixing something within
me that a man broke? I mean, they have broken many things, but I
liked the stuff in the china shop before the bull wrecked them, ya
know? Can we decenter men from all of the things, including basic
enjoyment of personal interests? I'm not choosing an alternative lifestyle. I just want to live well, have a good time, and be fabulous. And
I understand how much people can yearn for deep connection, for
partnership, and for love. I do too, but I just don't think it can only be
satisfyingly found in MAN. I am not giving up on love, I am just giving
up on pursuing an intimate relationship with a man. I love love. I love
myself. And there are people that I love, other than MAN.

Under the Tuscan Sun is a very popular rom-com that came out in
2003, starring the gorgeous Diane Lane. I have watched this movie
many times. I just rewatched it again last week. It is also another
movie I am coming to terms with, now that I am older than the main
character. The way I've understood *UTTS* over the years has evolved
so much. The expectations and aspirations that young me felt about
it are all gone.

In the movie, Diane plays Frances, a literary critic who discovers
her husband's infidelity and is having a really shitty time dealing with
the divorce. Through a bunch of rom-com hijinks, she ends up finding
and purchasing a shitty villa in Tuscany. She hires a ragtag bunch of
misfits as contractors, and they become a little community. But Frances's vagina starts to ache, and she fucks a handsome dude and then
wrongly thinks there is a future in their fling. More stuff happens and
then the house is finally in decent condition, because they all worked
together as a community. It's the end of the movie and there's only

about two minutes left. Will it end with Frances realizing that she actually does "have it all"? She even says quietly to herself, "I got my wish. I got everything that I asked for." As she sits back in her beautiful garden, hosting the wedding of one of the contractors on her villa grounds, she seems so content. Effortless and beautiful, filled with the joy of community, she sips a martini. There is forty-five fucking seconds left in the movie. Have we finally excluded MAN from joy—oh no. There's a dude, there he fucking goes. Look at this fucking loser introducing himself to her. Goddammit.

Young Jean and even Slightly Younger Than Now Jean didn't mutter "you silly, silly bitch" at Diane Lane, right before the credits hit. I thought it perfectly fine and so lovely. I am disappointed in it now. The same way that I am disappointed in Stella, because girl, leave that man-child alone. These are all older movies, but I am shocked that as a generation, we are still looking for "the MAN at the end."

Maybe I'll date again? LOL. I truly can't see it. Relationships are work, and I would be a terrible partner. I am aware that I barely, barely want to work at anythi—okay, I *don't*. I don't want to work. Not a job, not a relationship. I don't want the mental load, the decision fatigue, or the physical presence of a man. I don't want to ask him anything about his life, or his interests. I don't wanna meet his old-ass parents, if they're alive. I don't want the care of being responsible with another human being's everyday feelings in that way. Not even with something as small as asking, "How is your day?" because I would really have to care and have to listen. Rather than pretend I am up for that task, I feel like being alone is a far more responsible and mature thing to do. I do want that kind of check-in with my friends, but not with a person in an intimate relationship.

Even my fantasies have changed! I used to dream of having a platonic fling with a rich, older Italian man who owns a yacht. Now I just want the yacht to be mine. *I'm* the rich, older Italian man—you know what I mean. I might see a good-looking dude while I'm ordering my vodka soda on the beach and say, "That's nice," and that is the end of that. Because I do not want the rum punch of his existence. I do not want to order what everyone else is ordering, simply because that's what I'm "supposed to do now," and even if their choices look so fun from a distance, I have experienced the drink many times and I know better. I do not want to put that giant souvenir glass in my lovely bag, only for it to spill all over my fabulous things that I just spent so much time searching the world for. And for it to leave all of my silks sticky and . . . unfabulous.

I just want to fucking feel . . . *refreshed.*

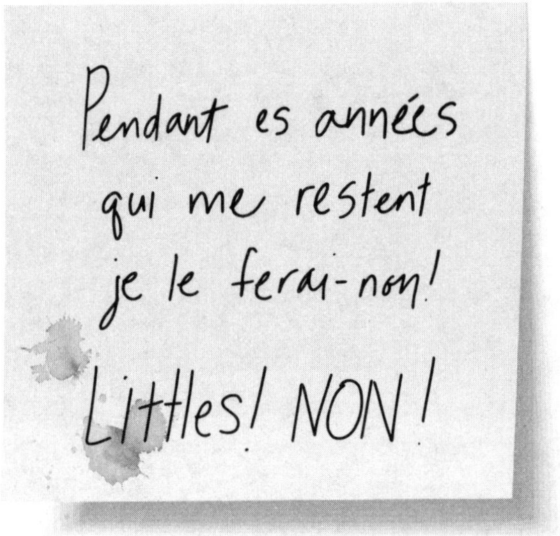
Pendant es années
qui me restent
je le ferai-non!
Littles! NON!

12.

La Vie Est Belle

Le *temps est bon"* plays from somewhere in the near distance. The weather is perfect. Not perfect for all occasions, cities, or times. Not for every age group or hair type. Perfect for me. Me, right here and right now. Choosing to enjoy all the moments in life, particularly the "right here and right now" portions, has been a huge part of the past few years in my personal journey. It's just past two in the afternoon, around seventy-six degrees and breezy. I know it's breezy and haven't even been out yet to run my one errand. I wanted to create a space for myself that gave me exactly this experience. I have done it. I am standing in it.

This is my favorite room in this house. The kitchen, with its large French doors that open up onto the garden. The breeze in this space carries the scent of lavender and rosemary. I planted those specific things in this area, for wafting purposes. Wafting keeps me sane. Sets a better mood when I don't have the capacity of manufacturing one inside myself. If you have French doors and private acreage, why not waftage? Honestly, if *anywhere,* why not waftage . . . but we're not *anywhere* right now. We're here.

I lean against the rustic marble and wood counter that I built (and sourced) myself. It's more refined than my Italian kitchen, but it's not stuffy. Nothing in here ever feels like a museum, where it can't be stained. It can't be touched. I like things to be both refined and undone. That type of living makes me feel my best. I love expensive things, but I want to use them. I enjoy a patina. A beat-up, buttery soft leather. A worn edge. Hands that look like they've built something. Mary-Kate's iconic black Kelly bag. My face with a little bit of nose peeling after my irresponsible time spent sunning on the yacht. Visible evidence of life well live—

"Littles! No! Not the fucking Restoration!"

I clap my hands and glare at my cat, who is digging his claws into the kitchen couch. He turns slowly to look at me, removing one paw slowly and furrowing his brow in confusion.

"Just kidding." I tilt my head and smile, waving off my faux anger.

Littles smiles, nods, and turns his paw over in an "of course, you were kidding" gesture.

We both laugh softly at our inside joke. He removes his other paw from the couch and turns to me, sighing. Meowing once and shaking his tiny head, he wanders outside to plop in a sunbeam just outside the door.

I watch him and smile. We share this joke *at least* once a day. I pretend to be angry at his attempted destruction. He pretends to be offended. It reminds us both of a life we lived just a few years ago. He, just trying to do regular cat things. Me, always mad that we "couldn't have nice things" because he would scratch them to bits. Now, mind you, there's definitely shit in the house that I don't want claw marks in, or hair all over. He doesn't have access to those things, so it's no longer an issue. Worn in, timeless pieces of furniture fill the portions of our house that he can reach. The kitchen couch is especially one of my favorite items. Last winter I rescued it from my friend François, a well-to-do French artist who has a penchant for disposing of expensive furniture violently.

We'd been sitting on the couch in François's second solarium. Smoking cigarettes, drinking wine, and listening to obscure experimental jazz on a transistor radio. All of a sudden, he stood up and looked at the couch with French disdain.

"I must burn this couch?"

I couldn't tell if it was a question or a statement. Sometimes foreign inflections can get confusing. He took a long drag of his cigarette and extinguished it on the arm of the couch, next to a multitude of other burn holes. It seemed unnecessary, as there was an ashtray right there, but François is eccentric. He turned and threw his entire glass of red wine into the massive fireplace. The smashing of the glass hitting at the same time as the building hi-hats in the music. We both nodded in approval at the timing.

I, who was not going to throw my wineglass, ran my hand over the cigarette burns on the couch arm and shook my head.

"Not this couch, François. This one is beautiful. Why not one of the others?"

I motioned to the rest of the room, because François had forty-five couches. The room was massive, and there was always a new place to sit, but the whole idea was a little bit unhinged. The first time I visited his historical château, I questioned his seating collection. François immediately responded by bringing up the fact that I owned six hundred robes and had brought twenty of them on the yacht that day.

"Well, that's different." I crossed my arms defensively. "They're all for different activities-and-and-rooms—and sea levels and moods!"

"It is the same for these couches, *ma cherie*." He held both arms wide.

A cigarette between each pair of fingers. The gesture had the air of a magic trick. I waved the smoke cloud out of the way and nodded. It was absolutely not the same thing, but I guess everyone collects what they enjoy.

That night, I had easily convinced François to give me the couch instead of setting it on fire, by saying, "Why don't you give me this couch instead of setting it on fire."

"Okay," He shrugged and lit three more cigarettes. Later, I helped him drag a vetiver-hued Songololo ten-seater couch out onto the lawn by the moat. We set the furniture on fire and drank more wine. The heat from the expensive inferno warming our bodies. The fire lighting our cigarettes.

"*Oui.* This was, indeed, a better couch to burn," Francois whispered into the embers. "Restoration couches . . . they burn without passion."

"Mmhmm," I agreed. "It's the patina." I wasn't sure about that at all, but I was drunk and excited about getting a highly coveted piece of furniture into my home.

I had always wanted a good, patinaed Restoration couch. For friends who understood that they could hang out in the kitchen, at a distance. For plopping down on, while things were simmering and wafting. For Littles to keep me company and have naps while I prepared evening meals. And most importantly, for Littles and me both to feel soft, comfortable, and not uptight in our surroundings. That kitchen couch saved our relationship and became a turning point for how we appreciated both of our needs.

In the afternoon light, I walk over to the couch, dig my finger into one of the burn holes, and smile. "Meow? Mmm. Mmm?" I look down to see Littles, who has wandered back into the kitchen, standing at my feet. He's rightfully asking about our plans for today.

His fluffy white tail dances against the black Baba Chic tiles that I laid (by myself) last summer. Most of the château's renovations I did myself. I attempted hiring a team of ragtag French misfits to do the work, thinking the experience would be something like *Under the Tuscan Sun*, and we would become family. Unfortunately, the ragtag misfits were slightly racist and fully misogynistic. It wasn't a French thing; I enjoy the French attitude very much. It's a huge part of why I moved here. It was just that some people are slightly racist and fully misogynistic, and also that you should not expect to have the same experience overseas as a fictional character in a romantic comedy, especially one played by the fabulous Diane Lane.

"Brrrp," Littles chirps to interrupt my reminiscing.

"Oh!" I say. "Yes."

I look at my Cartier Ceinture and tap the face. It's now two thirty. "You're right. I'm ready. I'll meet you out front."

"Mep." Littles turns and exits through the doors, disappearing around the corner by a tall lavender bush. I snatch my glass of Gaía Monograph Assyrtiko and chug the last bit. I hadn't been able to find this particular wine anywhere near me, so I had it imported by the case. A great knock-around table wine that makes everything feel crisp. Pretty. Unpretentious. It's still slightly cold and matches the feeling of my bare feet on the tiles. I wiggle my toes and glance at the fireplace, but decide against smashing the glass. I don't do that at my house.

Grabbing my giant sun hat off a hook by the doors, I slide my feet into my favorite Balenciaga mules. After spending a year and a half falling into the fields, I now opt for only flats during errands. I love all my summer platform sandals, but they're just not practical for CHORE.° I tie the silk scarf attached to my four-foot-diameter sun hat under my chin and put on my vintage Dior oversize butterfly sunglasses with category four custom lenses. Now, you're thinking that category four glasses are illegal to wear for driving, because they're the darkest sunglasses and absorb so much visible light. That's fine. I don't drive.

Tripping over the threshold, I emerge into the garden and feel my way past the twenty-seater dining table. Littles immediately begins meowing (as we've practiced) so that I may follow the sound of his voice to reach our means of travel. It takes a few minutes to traverse the path, but soon enough, my hand grips a leather streamer, then moves upward to a handlebar and an approving "meow."

I remove my glasses and place them in a titanium case on the back of the tricycle. They've served their purpose, as this repeated sight/ trust bond activity between myself and Littles is imperative to our life together. In case of any French or other apocalypse, we train in these kinds of activities every day. Maybe it sounds silly to you, but what sort of plans do you have in place for you and your fur companion in case of a blackout? Probably none.

Littles hops up into the large front basket on the tricycle as I unstrap my sun hat and deftly flick it clear across the garden and back onto the hook by the door. That hat would be completely unpractical for this ride, but it does protect me from the birds that nest in my hazelnut

---

° There's only one chore a day.

trees. They poop relentlessly, and I'm not riding into town with my Johanna Ortiz chore dresses covered in poop. Anymore.

"So then don't have hazelnut trees!" you scream at me.

Well, how would I make the hazelnut butter that I bring to town and trade for cartons of cigarettes every other month? Please. I know what I'm doing. Please.

Littles turns in circles, searching for his best positioning, as I yell "CHORE PLAYLIST FOR SEVENTY-SIX DEGREES ON A TUESDAY" into the air. One of my favorite functions on this custom tricycle is the voice-activated (*don't even think about trying it, it's only calibrated to my voice. If anyone else attempts to utilize it, the tires shoot poisonous darts into their shins. François still has scars, but now he knows to leave my vehicle alone*) music function. The tricycle has a huge memory bank, with playlists for every temperature and day of the week. I know that I'll probably never get to listen to *all* of them, as I doubt it will ever be 167 degrees here. But again, in an apocalypse, could it not be? If you stay ready, you ain't got to get ready. I also know that some of you are wondering why it's not Celsius. Please. Maybe when *you* get *your* custom tricycle playlist, *you* can do that.

"La belle vie" by Sacha Distel begins to play at the perfect volume, seemingly from every part of the tricycle. There are four hundred minuscule hidden speakers built into the frame, all equipped with a distance limiter of two feet. No noise pollution, no rudeness. When I designed this tricycle, I thought about everything. *Everything.*

"Ready?" I check in with Littles, who is curled up with his chin resting in his (perfectly sized for his chin) chin rest. His eyes are closed as he rocks back and forth. I'm happy with this body language answer and don't need a vocal response, so I begin to pedal off down the road.

When I began the online consultations for the bike build, the tricycle company had wrongly assumed that I would want some sort of motorized function for motion. "Why would I want that? Do you think I'm lazy? You think that I'm lazy and don't want to pedal my own tricycle? Because I'm Black?" By the last sentence, I was leaned in so far to my computer that I was blocking the camera with my whole mouth.

They apologized nervously and profusely before I told them I was only joshing. We had a hearty laugh, and I was then able to feel confident that I had chosen the right custom tricycle company.

The ride to town is always gorgeous but is especially beautiful today. I'm not pedaling fast, but combined with the breeze, the speed is just enough to lift the hair from the back of my neck and make me feel especially light. There's never anyone else on the road to town, since I bought up all of the properties along the way. Sometimes I stay at my other houses, but mostly I just enjoy the fact that I take up space and no one will bother me. I enjoy community, but I want it at a distance. Ten minutes of distance is just perfect. Ten minutes of riding through the lavender fields and inhaling all the wafting that money could buy. It brings me immense peace and joy, and truly, at this point in my life, that is priceless.

I pull up to the boulangerie with my hair in just the right state of "undone." Littles's long fur is also slightly in disarray, but we both enjoy this state of freedom. He does a big stretch and hops out of the basket as I dismount the tricycle. I reach for a velvet case in my dress pocket for my "buying bread"* sunglasses and put them on as Littles runs ahead to the shop. They always have a new piece of French plastic for him to play with, so he loves coming here. I catch up to him, where he waits excitedly just outside of the front door.

Wind chimes play the sound of Edith Piaf coughing as we enter the boulangerie. "Sous le ciel de Paris" (the Juliette Gréco version) plays. I've never been able to figure out where the speakers are located in the shop. The music always seems to be coming from the croissants, but I don't understand how that would work. I'd long since stopped trying to figure it out and just enjoyed the atmosphere . . . and the incredibly fresh baked goods.

"Bonjour!" Littles and I both call out.

He immediately runs his tiny legs to the back, where Michel will have a French-manufactured plastic strip and treat ready. I stand in

---

* Sunglasses only to be worn when doing buying-bread chore. Unsuitable for all other activities.

the front, twirl once, and pose. This dress is good for both twirling and posing in French bakeries. Always live the moment.

"Bonjour," Loulou replies from behind the counter without looking up from her book.

Loulou owns this shop and the bookstore down the road. You have to make an appointment to go to the bookstore, since she's always at the boulangerie. When I first learned about this scheduling issue, I asked her why she didn't just let Michel run the bakery. Wasn't he the baker, anyway?

She had stared at me for a solid five minutes in silence, before uttering with quiet disgust, "*Un homme?*"

There was no need to discuss the matter further, as this was an excellent point. She had then asked me if I had a husband, or boyfriend.

I replied with my best French quiet disgust, "*Absolument pas. Dégoûtant. Je m'aime.*"

Loulou peered over her glasses at me, a slight smirk. I didn't pay for my baguettes that day, and I've never paid for anything else there since. I longed to be her friend, but the one time I got up the nerve to ask her over for dinner, she laughed at me, responding in English with a heavy accent, "The bread is free, but I do not like people."

Again, there was no need to discuss the matter further, as this was an excellent point. It made me like her even more, but I understood not to push it. The gift of free, delicious baked goods by the tricycle basketfuls was enough. I felt seen and valued.

Today I was in the shop to pick up a dozen croissants and two armpits of baguettes. As usual, my order sat on the counter, ready to go. I stuffed all the croissants into my pockets and began tucking the baguettes strategically under my arms. I can carry about ten on each side—if I keep my arms stiff enough—before unloading them all into the Baguette Basket on the back of the tricycle. If you're wondering why I wouldn't bring a bag of some sort, well you just don't understand how inauthentically French that would be. Also, I tried that. Loulou jumped over the counter as if it were a car hood in some buddy cop film and slapped all of the baguettes to the ground, screaming at me to get out and not come back until I could "respect the process."

I didn't understand a lot of French at that time, but the sentiment was felt.

Tucked and ready, I call out for Littles, who rushes to hold the door open for me. Upon our exit, the wind chimes plays the sound of a wheel of Camembert casually rolling down a street in Belleville, admiring street art.

"Au revoir, Loulou!" I yell over my shoulder.

"Eh," she softly grunts back.

The ride back home is even better than the ride into town. As always, I place one baguette in the front basket for Littles to rest on. That's his personal baguette, and it also serves for fresh bread-wafting purposes. The many speakers play "Chhh" (Mathieu Boogaerts) on repeat, for the duration of the trip, and Littles falls asleep almost immediately.

With my bread-buying glasses off, tossed onto the side of the road for some French animal to wear and enjoy, the sun is in my eyes, and I mutter "J. J. Abrams lens flare" with quiet excitement. At some point during the third playing of the song, I take my hands off the handlebars and close my eyes, pedaling while stretching into the sun. I breathe in deeply and think about all the terrible things that had to happen for me to get to this perfect moment. I quickly realize what I'm doing wrong, breathe even deeper, keep pedaling, and don't open my eyes for the next two repeats of the song. I just. Ride.

In the evening, after Littles and I have tended to our wounds from the accident—I slightly veered off the path when my eyes were closed and we ended up in a large lavender bush—we meet in our favorite place again, the kitchen. "*Que reste-t-il de nos amours*" softly plays from an undetermined location in the room. Littles loafs on the couch as I prepare dinner. A spatchcocked chicken with herbs, potatoes, and carrots (all from the garden, of course). The waft quality from all directions could not be better. The lighting over the large island is brighter than the rest of the space, lit with small antique lamps and the flames of a few candles, just out of Littles's reach. The whole area dances with warmth. Every source of light bounces off the tiles. Off the marble insert on the counter. The Mauviel cookware. My wineglass, full with my favorite Gamay, glints as I pick it up and take a big sip. A ring underneath the glass has formed on the wood. I dab my finger in the corner of it and scrape the same finger across a heavily buttered piece of bread with apricot jam, before shoving it into my mouth.

Littles and I exchange slow blinks and *"Samba Saravah"* (Pierre Barouh) begins to drift in the air. I tilt my head and hold my hand out to my friend. He untucks a paw from his loafing position and extends it in my direction. I rotate my wrist into a hand flourish and curtsy before making my way over to the couch, arms wide. Littles does a small jump into my arms and I carry him to the garden doors, still open for evening wafts. He leans his body against mine and sighs with contentment. I feel deep gratitude for his love and friendship, as a wave of happiness washes over me. His deep exhale makes me do the same. I pet him gently as we sway in the doorway, both doing our best to live in the moment. Knowing, but not dwelling, on how many terrible things had to happen for us to get here. Right here. Right now. I wanted to create a space that gave us exactly this experience. I have done it. I am dancing in it. We are dancing in it.

We dance in it forever.

FADE TO BLACK
MUSIC CUE: *"Si tu vois ma mère"*
CREDITS OVER BLACK

In my remaining years,

the most important thing
to know about fashion is

13.

The Problem with Being Fabulous

People always like to think about how much cumulative time we spend in our lives doing everyday activities. How much of our lives will we spend waiting in lines, or taking a poop? How many hours will we have spent sleeping, eating, cleaning, or watching television? How will all these numbers add up when it's our time to kick the bucket? Personally, I'd like to know how much cumulative time in my life I will have spent thinking about ways I could possibly die, when it's all said and done.

I feel as if my answer to this query might be up there with the provided "time spent sleeping" numbers, which, if you're curious, is allegedly one-third of our lives. I say "allegedly" because I don't know from what privileged demographic they got that number, since most people are out in these global streets very much not getting the recommended amount of rest required for optimal living. But maybe the lack of sleep is what cuts their life span short, and the number becomes relative to the situation. Sure. In any case, judging by studies, my How'mi Gonna Death Thoughts number is both currently and will be much higher than the average human being in Western society. Apparently (and again, allegedly) here, only 11 percent of people consider death in their daily lives. They're only gettin' morbid with it around three or four times a year. Really? Hmmm.

While I am more than sure that I'm deathin' it up at rates far greater than most, three to four times a year seems . . . Well, it seems like someone's lying. To me, the numbers in the study represent the stigma that society places on discussing our own expiration dates. The act of this discussion is deemed "not right" or "too dark." Merely thinking about your own death, in what is considered excessive amounts, is seen as a sign of mental illness. But, mortality salience—simply, the awareness that death is inevitable—seems like such an incredibly healthy and normal brain function to have. Are we . . . *not* all going to die? If not dying is a new option, lemme know, as I didn't get the guaranteed immortality pamphlet, but would love to check it out!

I'd truly love to know what the upside is to not embracing the promise of death. Things don't just go away when you ignore them. You think that when death comes for you, you're just gonna stick your fingers in your ears, close your eyes tight, and "nah nanny boo boo, I can't see you" the reaper away? What, are you gonna hold up one finger in a "just a second" extended-for-years moment to Hades?

I don't think it works that way. In fact, I *know* it doesn't work that way, but it does align with the Western world's ideal ways to cope with all of its societal issues and woes. Don't think about it, don't talk about it. Too uncomfortable. Do not confront. Definitely don't tell people who are conducting a survey that you are constantly filled with existential dread. Definitely don't do that, weirdo.

Burnt umber and ochre autumn foliage cover the ground, under and around the railroad tracks. The trees surrounding the rail path are tall and slender, not yet bare, and some, holding on to the waning presence of summer, still glow emerald green. The branches reach high into the sky and bend just enough to gently kiss. To form a delicate canopy far overhead, one that isn't averse to allowing breaths of spaces where the blue sky breaks through. You can feel the crispness of the Catskill Mountain air through the phone screen. That first chill of the season that can turn you around to return home for a sweater you haven't worn

*since last year. You glide down the railroad's pathway, pedaling
a scarlet vehicle. The tandem seating of the rail bike invites you
and a partner to share in the magic of adventure, with no need
for either of you to steer, or to utilize your hands for anything
other than possibly taking snapshots of the glorious scenery to
commemorate your experience. As Nat King Cole's version of
"Autumn Leaves" plays softly in the distance, you explore the
calmness of your surroundings and feel nothing but peace.*

Oh no.

I wish I could go enjoy this and not imagine a bear running out from the
woods, tackling and *Revenant*-ing me.

So far, 1,061 people have liked this comment, which I left on the
TikTok video of Rail Explorers Catskill Mountains Ride. Ride? Experience? Either way, the rail bike thing is exactly as described above. In
replies to my comment, people have tagged their friends, suggesting
they would also voice a similar concern. Typing something like: you af.
Another person responded: Wait I am crying bc I didn't know someone
else's thought process was like this 💀.

I nod and smile at all the comments, saying, "See? SEE?" I knew
those death-thought survey numbers weren't correct. I feel proud
that I've made some people feel comfortable about embracing their
own death thoughts publicly. Plus, I think it's very reasonable to refuse Woods Trips, due to bears. I have refused invitations to hiking
and camping excursions. People laugh and tell me I shouldn't worry
about bears. They start explaining the difference between black bears
and brown bears, but I have already researched what kind of bears
do what kinds of bear things. They tell me that bear sightings are
rare, but—

"*Rare* means that there *are* bears," I interrupt quickly. They roll
their eyes and say something stupid like, "There are some bears, but
those bears will stay away from people and—"

"Do you know the odds of being mauled by a bear in New York
City or Paris?" I have interrupted again. I quickly follow up with, "It's

zero possibility because zero bears. See? *Some* bears versus *zero* bears. Do you see?"

They do not see and ask me how could I be afraid of hypothetical bears and not afraid of big-city, human murderers. Well, because I can possibly win a fight against a human murderer, I am from New York City. A bear is . . . BEAR. I have zero-win chances. Let's be real about this.

I don't feel as if I'm missing out on the woods as a life experience, the same way I don't feel as if I'm missing out on the Catskill's rail bike. Or a roller coaster. Or skydiving. I like adventures, mine just don't involve potential wild animal attacks. Or heights, drops, speed, even ski lifts. Jet Skis—no. None for me, thanks. I *know* someone who went skydiving and had their parachute malfunction. Yes, they lived and yes they broke . . . how many bones do we have? They broke most of the bones out of the total of body bones. Besides, I don't even have to participate in activities that would provide "reasonable" anxiety surrounding injuries or death. I just do that every day, with everyday things! With age, I have become my own parent: "No. Put that down!" I swat my hand away from booking a trip to an amusement park. "We have *death* at home!"

| | |

In February 2023, I attended The Collection of André Leon Talley viewing at Christie's auction house in NYC. When I'd learned of the upcoming auction, months prior, I'd wept. Wept for the loss of Mr. Talley's general presence. Wept for the lack of proper treatment he received in the world and in his career. Wept to express my gratitude for the expansive knowledge I'd gained (and continue to) from studying his work and contributions. I wept with extreme gratitude at being able to see someone like him, to have that kind of representation, if you will, in the form of someone so passionate and meticulous about their work. Someone who wasn't "expected" or welcomed in their field by so many people, because he was so brilliant and so Black. I started planning my outfit for the collection viewing months in advance. I had to pay my respects correctly. I had to bring the fashion.

I walked through the collection space with an abundance of reverie and emotion. I'd invited my friend Joyelle to attend the viewing, and we did a full walk-through twice. Once, just to see and feel things. The second time to take pictures. I was floored and entranced, weeping openly behind my blackout shades.

Joyelle and I held anger for people who touched Mr. Talley's clothes with their grubby paws. We snitched on them to security. I can only explain seeing Mr. Talley's belongings as "looking at the items of a deity." The unbelievable grandeur and intentionality of his things. The sheer size of hats, gloves, and especially caftans. Some of the capes and caftans were suspended in the air and felt ten feet tall. As I marveled at every piece, I couldn't help but silently wonder: How many times had Mr. Talley tripped, fallen, gotten a sleeve caught in a door handle, or had any sort of extended "whoops, whoopsie daisies" stumbling from wearing such billowing, fabulous clothes. I could not stop thinking about Mr. Talley entertaining his good friend Diane von Furstenberg in his wonderful home.

"Would you like some biscuits, Deyaan?" he might ask her, with his signature lilt.

"No, André. You know I don't eat biscuits. Look at me," Deyaan would reply, waving a delicate hand across her lithe body.

Mr. Talley would slip his feet gently into a pair of custom Manolo Blahnik house slippers and brace his arms draped in billowing sleevery on the arms of his custom-ebonized Oscar de la Renta chair.

"Well. I shall have the most *wonderful* biscuits by myself, then. They're resting in the butler's kitchen. I will retrieve them now, Deyaan." As he stands, his custom Tom Ford caftan sleeves would get hooked into the arms of his chair, sending him stumbling across the room.

"Oh my, oh my, oh no!" Mr. Talley would exclaim during his extensive fall. Thankfully, he would land safely on his lush Hermès mohair blanket, draped perfectly over an eighteenth-century chaise lounge.

"Whew!" he would exclaim, lying down on the chaise to catch his breath. "Can you imagine if I had been carrying a tray of the most wonderful biscuits just now? Why, they would have been absolutely everywhere!" He'd pause and wave his arm to Diane. "Everywhere, Deyaan!"

I imagine this elaborate scenario because, well, do you know how impractical wide-sleeved, floor-sweeping robes are for wearing around the house? I do. I know now, because I narrowly escape death multiple times every day. No one tells you about the dangers of wearing flowing clothes. The perils of drapery. The hazards of wide-legged pants and extravagant caftans. In fact, the caftans don't even have to be that elaborate! Still, they are dangerous! It would have been nice to know about these things. It would have been very helpful to be forewarned that I was choosing a lifestyle fraught with danger at literally every turn. Every doorknob is the cause of a potential fatality. Double the chances if it has a handle. Every step on a staircase an opportunity to get my foot caught on the end of a wide pant leg and send me barreling down (or up) a flight of stairs. Every pot or pan handle a threat to an ample sleeve. Have I performed a prolonged buffoonery fall in the kitchen while preparing a meal? Yes, I have. Pots of boiling water and heavy, wide pans filled will turmeric-laden curries dashed across the walls and floors like unintentional Pollack paintings. Slips and falls that last forever. All because I desire to be comfortable and fabulous. No one fabulous will tell you that these accidents happen to them. But I promise, if they wear these kinds of clothes, they do.

The EMTs gather over my twisted and lifeless body lying at the foot of a grand staircase. My oversize kimono curled around my frame offers a glaring clue to my deadly mishap: a missing sleeve. They look up to the top of the serpentine staircase, its intricately carved wooden banister holding pieces and threads of my garment's missing, generously cut arm section. All the way down to the newel post, fabric clings to the jutting tigers and dragons that form the rails.

"Huh," one of the EMTs says. "It's hard to tell whether she fell up, or down, the stairs. That's weird."

They all nod, with confusion. One of them steps forward and waves a showcase arm over my mortal remains dramatically. "Well"—she pauses briefly—"at least she died doing what she loved." She turns to them with a wide flourish. "Being fabulous." They all nod and begin a slow clap over my corpse.

Have we all been taught to expect Drape Life at some point in the aging process? I think about the drape and caftan icons of my Gen X childhood, and immediately, Mrs. Roper from *Three's Company*° is my go-to. Helen Roper, played by Audra Lindley, with her tightly permed, auburn wig. Her extensive wardrobe consisting entirely of brightly colored, oversize caftans and robes. Her statement necklaces, earrings, and huge bangles always offering the perfect complement to each outfit. Mrs. Roper's presentation was intentional and told you so much about who she was, on sight. She was sex positive, quick witted, and always excited to learn new things about a younger generation. She dreamed of romantic getaways and far off travels. And most importantly, she was so comfortable with being herself . . . even if her husband, Stanley, was a piece of shit and always attempted to detract from her zest for life. Ugh. He'd always take digs at her appearance, her hobbies, her everything. I think it would have been a fun episode if she had strangled Stanley to death with some of her macrame. I would have much preferred the spin-off sitcom of HELEN, instead of what we got: *The Ropers*. Helen vacationing in Italy, St. Croix, Mozambique. Helen, fucking her way through France. Helen, on a yacht with her new gaggle of queer friends, dancing until sunrise. Helen, like her caftans, finally unbound and unrestricted. Helen being fabulous and doing her best to not catch the hem of her robe on a boat railing and fall overboard.

As a kid watching *Three's Company*, I viewed Helen Roper as an old lady wearing old lady clothing. But her character—get this—was only fifty-three-years old! Lord, it's so hard to revisit things from your youth and realize that it was *you* who was the baby. I've been watching a lot of old comfort movies lately, and the people who were "old" to me when those movies came out are now younger than I am now. Samuel

---

° The famed progressive sitcom from the late 1970s to 1980s. Hijinks, innuendos, brilliant slapstick, comedic genius, witty quips, and jiggle for all of us. John Ritter, Joyce DeWitt, and Suzanne Somers at the heart of the original cast, where two women and one man share an apartment in Santa Monica. But how could a man live with two attractive women and maintain purely platonic relationships with them? Impossible!

L. Goddamn Fucking Jackson was forty-motherfucking-six when he starred in *Pulp Fiction*. I am older than that! *Screams like any old transatlantic White woman who is falling onto a fainting couch or racist old asshole Katharine Hepburn: shakily*° "Noo-ooo—oooo-oo-o-o-o-o-o—."

The Ropers were middle-aged adults, and Helen was a cool-ass adult. While it could be easy to pinpoint Helen as my only adult drapery reference, she was simply a representative of an "older woman's" style. And in the 1980s and 1990s, being *an old* felt so far away. However, more than any recent previous generations, Gen X has always been well prepped in oversize and comfortable clothing.

The 1990s kept us teens in a baggy chokehold. But it wasn't drapery and light fabrics, it was all streetwear. Although now that I think about it, the iconic group TLC must have been in an incredible amount of danger while filming the "Creep" music video, what with all that silky, wide pajama material blowing all around the fucking place. That TLC moment aside and maybe the ridiculousness of JNCO jeans and rave/club kid wide-legs pants too, our baggy clothes didn't pose any threats. I've thought about how this was possible and the answer is: tapering and thicker materials.

A cuffed sleeve of a huge rugby shirt—threat averted, sleeve secured. A 2X size Polo Teddy Bear sweater—ribbed secure hem. Ribbed cuff. Heavy knit, SECURE, no threat present. Even our pants, although huge, definitely tapered. Zero dangers. When the weird business-casual style of the early aughts hit us, skinny jeans were also threat-free. Low-rise boot leg jeans with giant belts might have looked awful, but they didn't harbor any imminent danger other than exposing your thong to the world, and that was the whole point of the whale tail anyways.

As my style changed over the years I held on to a love of oversize things, but at first, they remained safely tapered at the hems. The only items that could have actually been death traps were the stilettos I wore in my twenties. To this day, I am unsure how I did not die while running around New York City in three-and-a-half and four-inch heels. Clubbing all night in strappy sandals and then somehow taking the train home? Then walking home from the train? Casually? Fuck out of here. Pleasers! Y'all, I used to be able to casually wear pleasers. Once, I wore pleasers to a bar. While we partied and drank, a snowstorm hit the city. Four hours later, I walked the eight blocks home. In the snow, in SEVEN-INCH HEELS.

Old man grumble: Back in my day, we used to party all night at Bushwick dive bars, drinking pint glasses full of Long Island iced teas with no Coke. Then, we would walk half a mile home in our pleasers, through the snow. And we were grateful! You kids don't know anything! Baaah!

If I attempted to wear a thin three-inch heel now to do anything beyond sitting, my ankles would roll right over and snap in half like dried branches. "Baaaah!" I would scream, falling to the ground on my knees, causing my kneecaps to shatter into a trillion shards. "Baaaahhh . . ." I would breathe out quietly.

"Well." The EMTs crowded around my twisted, still alive body. "You know you can't wear those thin heels at your age, ma'am." They shake their heads down at me in unison.

"Baaaah," I angrily growl at them in a shaky voice. "I'm not a ma'am and I don't care about the misgendering, but you could have at least said Miss, or Ms. I'm only in my forties goddammit, baaaahh!" I grab my splintered ankle bones and writhe in pain.

The expectation of stiletto danger makes sense, even though I never thought the fear would be my own. In my late thirties, I had completely abandoned the idea of wearing a thin high heel, but I kept *buying* them. I would continuously add to my closet of precarious designer footwear and rationalize every purchase with a thought like, "Someone needs to buy these! They can't just sit in the store!"

Every pair of shoes came with multiple-injury scenarios, most of them involving a mishap, trip, or slip walking onto a stage, to a talk show couch, or up steps to collect an award. I have had so many imaginary heels accidents, at so many imaginary press events.

I mean, have we not all seen people trip in heels? Even if a full-on injury doesn't occur, it hurts *taps heart* in here. I was finally able to purge a lot of my nonwearable shoes in 2020, talking myself into the fact that if it was indeed the apocalypse, footwear like my four-inch Louis Vuitton pony hair heels wouldn't be a wise choice. Even if the apocalypse, or the race war, had a shindig, I'd have to wear flat shoes in case we had to flee a location, or fight a zombie . . . or worse, stupid racists.

Besides the shift of the global pandemic and the political climate, something had started to shift in me before I moved out of New York for the first time. In 2016, I had ordered a bunch of clothes from a very fast fashion online Chinese store. The kind of clothes that you order and then forget that you ordered, because two months have passed before they arrive. I'd never ordered from that kind of store before and didn't again, for terrible fast fashion slave labor reasons and also—more incredibly selfishly, cancel me if you want—because the quality of items is wildly low and it's a real crapshoot on the sizing. Is a 4X going to fit like an 8X or like an extra small petite toddler's onesie? There's no way of knowing.

The haul I received included eight things that were toddler-size and immediately went in the trash because that was their home. But one item was true to its oversize nature and surprisingly was not made out of plastic and whispers. I wore that tunic into the fucking ground. I was so comfortable and got so many compliments about how I *looked* so comfortable *and* how people wished to obtain that same level of comfort. The tunic also had pockets, which yes, I did shout about and demonstrate the usage of in every conversation.

"I think this is when I start looking like a fucking art teacher," I declared to the world. My Pinterest boards and searches became filled with tunic and wide-pantsed muses. I started ordering boxes of clothes from my favorite online thrift store, mostly oversize menswear and pajama pants. My soothing trips to my local Rainbow repositioned my searches to the plus-size section, grabbing 2X shirts and sweaters that didn't scream of . . . Rainbow. In my personal references, I thought about my mom's 1980s and 1990s androgynous wardrobe, very akin to

Dorothy Zbornak's* style. Structured but loose. Shoulder pads and big outerwear. My mother leaned heavily to designers like Issey Miyake and WilliWear, but where she had always leaned to a long skirt, I leaned to a pant.

"This is it!" I'd say all the time. "I finally found my style!" I sourced so many things before the first accident happened. There were no warning signs of impending doom. There was only comfort. I had been so excited to finally be able to emotionally deal with taking my mom's boxes of clothing out of storage. Holding them and having the whole apartment fill up with her lingering scent of L'Air du Temps was both healing and intense. I sent things that needed extra care to the dry cleaners, like her now vintage Max Mara 1990s cashmere coat. Her saying, "This is the most expensive thing in this house" to anyone within earshot. The rest of her things, I washed by hand. There's something really beautiful about taking care of your things that way. I *live* for "draped over a shower rod" bras, panties, and tights dripping onto the edge of the bathtub. There's something so wonderfully feminine and old-fashioned about it that I love so much. The act of handwashing delicate items is something I value deeply. Give me jazz, a glass of wine, a bucket of silks and undies to clean on a Sunday. Put a chicken in the oven to roast, the smell mixing with the fragrance of old-school Woolite. Let me roll up sopping items in a soft towel and step on them gently to release the excess water. I don't love cleaning *everything* in a house, but I will do those particular activities with such happiness.

It was during this period of cleaning my mom's things and getting so many new delicate items of my own that I learned a lot more about fabrics, sustainability, laundry care, and the importance of storing your clothes correctly. I can wash a wool sweater like nobody's business. I love taking great and personal care of all my fineries, and if anyone wants to talk to me at length, for hours, or days, about laundering

---

* Bea Arthur's sarcastic and passionately compassionate character on the 1980s sitcom *The Golden Girls*. Dorothy served fashion, babe. Straight up high 1980s comfortable fashion.

clothes in any fashion, please, I beg of you. Invite me to a chat. We will have the best time.

The long-awaited morning had come. I was awakened by both antic-ipation and intense fragrant flashbacks of my mother. Even though I had triple handwashed all her things, her scent persisted. It was more gentle, but still present. The previous night, I'd hung one of my mom's gorgeous kimonos over our bedroom door with the plan of putting it on and wearing it around our place the whole next day.

"This is it. I have reached real kimono and robe status in my life. I am the age. I am ready."

I lay in bed and stared at the kimono on the door. I couldn't wait to float down the stairs and make some coffee. I couldn't wait to turn every corner of our house and have my kimono linger on the turns just enough to disappear a moment after I did. I got up and swished it across my shoulders, regally taking my first steps onto the stair land-ing. As I descended, the kimono caught the air behind me and floated. "Mmmm," I hummed.

There's a video game that I have played for many years called *Tek-ken.*° It's a series of fighting games whose dramatic storyline surrounds a fictional battle: the King of Iron Fist Tournament. I've been playing *Tekken* since it came out in 1994 as an arcade game, when I took great delight at beating men (in the game, I guess) in public places. When *Tekken* became available on the first PlayStation gaming system a year later, I switched to taking great delight at beating men in *private spaces*. One of the longest-running characters in the game is a ninja from space named Yoshimitsu. Yoshimitsu has a special move where he steps out of his own body and creates a clone of himself that fucks

---

° Fun Jean fact: My two giant dragon neck tattoos were inspired by a character from *Tekken*: Bryan Fury. Bryan is described on the *Tekken* Wikipedia as "a re-animated zombie cyborg with no morals and a penchant for violence." His fight style is best described as "punch opponents very fucking hard to death" and he has two very large neck tattoos. Bryan resonated with me, and I always picked him as my character when I wanted to punch my actual opponent "very fucking hard to death" IRL.

his opponent up, before he reaches out and helps his own clone up off the ground.

When, unbeknownst to me, the left sleeve of my kimono hooked itself into the top of the wooden banister at the top of the staircase and my NDE (near-death experience) began, Yoshimitsu's clone move was the first in a line of eight hundred memories that flashed through my mind. I don't know if you have ever suffered a vicious sneak attack from your own clothes. Clothes that are in cahoots with an inanimate object at a perilous height. The way that my soul was yanked forward out of my body and down the stairs as I was simultaneously yanked backward and *up* the stairs was a physics-defying event. I fell and also levitated for what seemed like twenty minutes, but was only about three seconds.

After I died, determined to keep wearing the kimono, I wrapped it around my body, gathered it up in my hands, and slowly crawled backward down the stairs to lie on the couch and regulate my heartbeat. That day, I didn't take the kimono off. I was not going to let my dream of being fabulous die! And that day, I was yanked back into four rooms by handles and doorknobs, again caught on my kimono. I tripped up the stairs three times on the hem, managed to break my coffeepot, and fling a full skillet of pasta (our dinner) across the kitchen floor. I couldn't believe that I hadn't smashed my teeth in on the steps, or suffered worse injuries than incredibly jarring heart rates and a little broken glass in my foot. I hadn't actually died, but I had added a whole new slew of daily How'mi Gonna Death Thoughts that I did not want. Like the sound that happens when a new player joins a *Tekken* battle round, a tiny jingle played to only my ears.

Over the years since The First Day of Fabulous Accidents N°1–10, I have really racked up my Fabulous Accident numbers. They're somewhere in the thousands, and they're definitely not confined to in-house occurrences. They're also not just from kimonos. Oh no, no, my friends. My everyday dress code has evolved into one I can describe as: 1980s director of clever action movies, somehow both on the set of the movie *and* snapped by the paparazzi at the airport in the 1990s. Because 1980s directors fashion is everything to me, and all celebrities snapped by paparazzi at the airport in the 1990s are also . . . everything to me. The Venn diagram between the two is almost just a circle, but this is not a full book about fashion, and I would need at least six more chapters to really even start getting into it. If anyone wants to talk to me at length, for hours, or days, about these two specific eras and situations in fashion, please, I beg of you. Invite me to a chat. We will have the best time.

Anyway, even with my new non–Helen Roper style, at least one portion of every outfit, every day, causes an accident or injury. Like tripping over my own wide pant legs while trying to put my shoes on at the end of airport security and knocking over a TSA agent. Or falling up an escalator while trying to avoid my oversize coat from being eaten by escalator teeth. Sure. Some of the mishaps are only injuries *to the clothes*. Like the time I unknowingly closed half of my mom's vintage, airy overcoat in the door of an Uber and, upon arriving at my destination, stared in shock at the five miles of New York City dirt that it had collected on its dragging limb. I have gotten the boxy sleeve of a very cool vintage T-shirt caught on, wait for it . . . a toilet paper holder. I don't really like to talk about what happened with that one. And since I started wearing baseball caps again, the amount of hair that has been ripped out of the middle back of my head by the caps strap, well, I am deeply saddened by it. And yes, like my imagined fatality, I have in real life ripped the sleeve of a kimono clean off by getting it caught, once again, on a banister.

Every time I make, or buy, a new item I think about the promised accident it will cause. I have completely written off thin heels, with the exception of changing into them onstage, like a sassy Mr. Rogers. I've bought myself a bunch of briefcases that will house the shoes and are also fashion statements by themselves. "Oh, let me put on my sitting shoes," I will say when you come to hear me talk about this book, or watch me on a late-night talk show.

Since the option of "sitting shoes" now exists, I'm pretty happy that I get to buy heels again, because I fucking love beautiful shoes. I just love my ankle bones to be intact *more*. I've made some good compromises with my past loves and my future dreams, but I make no compromises in my insistence that society has lied to us for so long. Not just about the mortality salience numbers, but also that this comfortable, relaxed, middle-aged-and-up, fabulously dressed character we've been shown has been in just as much, if not *more*, physical danger than, say, a woman wearing a form-fitted dress and stilettos in her seventies. What do you think she's going to break, a hip? Probably not. I bet that woman has perfected walking in heels and the last time she fell was 1972. I can't imagine Grace Jones falling anywhere, fucking ever. Watch your mouth, Grace Jones doesn't fall. She might bless the ground with her presence for a few moments, and if so, the ground should be so grateful.

I regularly think about Mrs. Roper and how none of the *Three's Company* jokes involved her giant sleeves getting caught on anything. How! Well, there were those steps up to Jack, Chrissy, and Janet's apartment that she would have had to navigate. But we never saw her walking up those steps. Maybe she fell all the time! I think about Dorothy Zbornak, and all that fucking tunic fabric swishing around. Dorothy never got yanked back into her bedroom by a doorknob. They were in and out of that kitchen all the time with such intention—ohhh. Swinging door! That kitchen had a swinging fucking door! How smart, very smart, to remove the threat. Maybe I should only have swinging doors in my future house(s)! But what to do with the stairs? Ranch house? Have my fashion choices locked me into a ground-floor living style? But, I love a grand, serpentine staircase! I truly do!

Die doing what you love, I guess. Die doing what you love.

In my remaining years,
there will be so much
Chaaa.

14.

The Price of Grief and Joy

In 2013, I got the phone call about my mother's very unexpected passing.

In my kitchen, I crumbled to the ground in shock. In the moment, I didn't think about the consequences of my knees hitting the floor, sans cushioning, I only thought about the news being delivered and the fact that I wished someone else, other than the shit fuck man I was seeing, had been there to comfort me. No one wants a shit fuck man as the only possible source of reprieve when you receive the worst news ever. I could see his eye roll and feel his annoyance fill the air, rife with his regret at choosing a fuck buddy who would so very inconveniently have a parent die. I too was rife with regret. Both at the news and at his general existence.

Four days after my mom's death, I would perform at Afro Punk, the annual arts festival. In Fort Greene, Brooklyn, at Commodore Barry Park, I took the stage for a performance that I can only describe as *hardcore disassociating on a metaphysical level*. For thirty minutes, I was both very present in front of an audience, performing songs, and not anywhere, in any dimension I can make sense of. There are times, prior to this performance and after, where I've disassociated casually onstage. My muscle memory keeps the show going, the audience none the wiser, as I crawl into my mind palace and think about a whole slew of other things for quite a while before rejoining my body. The process is much like Highway Hypnosis, where, during a familiar or monotonous drive, your procedural memory can take the wheel. When you snap back, you are much farther along on your journey. So, although I don't drive an actual car, I myself am the vehicle, in a far less physically dangerous way than operating steel at incredibly high speeds. But my Afro Punk performance felt . . . perilous. In the moment, I knew I was creating a long-term damaging experience, but there was nothing I could do about it.

I wanted to scream and dissolve into a million pieces before I got onstage, but I didn't know how to make that happen and still be paid for the show. If you've been thinking, "Why would you perform, Jean? Why?" you'd be asking a very valid question. The answer to the question is, of course, *money*. The answer to the question is something that I thought I could circumvent, somehow. Something I thought I could learn and correctly navigate in the future, in order to never have the experience of wanting to scream and dissolve into a million pieces in front of an audience again. Or better yet, the same act of shattering, but alone with myself. Surely, there was some way to allow my existence the right amount of time to grieve before having to work again. Surely, I was the one at fault, for not conforming to the industry and the world's standards, because if I had simply done that in the first place, I would have already had the money to pay my rent, bills, and roundtrip ticket to South Africa for my mother's funeral without having to be destroyed on all levels.

It was surely both of our faults (my mom and myself) for not conforming. Our faults. She would have lived a lot longer if we both respectively could have gotten with the program, thus enabling us to get the money. The money. The money. The money. If I couldn't travel back in time to change things, I could at least figure out, moving forward, the right amount for the price of grief. Because anyone could die, at any time. I would have to make sure that grief was a financial possibility. I would have to budget for death.

| | |

During the pandemic lockdowns, I'd somehow managed to do well for myself, monetarily. I had, for the first time in my life, not only repaired my credit, but also achieved the American Dream requirement of *excellent* credit. I would relay my score to anyone willing, or very unwilling, to hear this information. I had two seemingly stable projects and had created a production company to film my puppet show. All of the jobs were full-time jobs. My brain. Was. Melting. Every second of every day. I barely ever stood up from work, and it was destroying my body. But, I had "done it," right? For all of the past when I was wrought with grief about money. I had eliminated that problem! Did I have any enjoyment of life moments or thoughts in my brain that were not work? No! But that's what the *money was for.* It could buy me the time to be joyful and have my own thoughts again at some time *in the future*! America's slogan should be: "*Something something*, put your joy in your pocket for the future when you're too old to enjoy it! And Jesus!" Who, by the way, is also: "Joy afterward, now is only pain!"

"I am a rich adult," I pep-talked myself. "I am middle class for someone who lives in this particular neighborhood." I nodded in the mirror with tears in my eyes. "But I am only New York City poor, which is still not doing badly everywhere else." I leaned in farther. "I can afford to go to three doctors." I gripped the edge of the sink. "I could buy a house . . . kind of, maybe." My knuckles were white. "Just because I can't put anything in savings doesn't mean I am not a *real* person." Through my teeth I finally said out loud, "If my mother died *this* year, I could have gone to the funeral *and* paid rent with no problem."

As I left the pep-talk restroom, I knew that only part of that was true. How could I have left New York and gone to South Africa with the amount of work I had? I couldn't have. I have tried to imagine which situation would have been less painful. They were both equally shitty griefs in the mouth of the monster of time.

Like my excellent credit, I was finally 820 percent sure that the American Dream is killing yourself to have a few days off and be able to pay the bills, when your most loved ones die—including you.

Physical death, the actual ceasing to live, is one thing, and since my mother is already gone, I feel like I got the big scary one out of the way. But it has been over a decade now, and I am afraid that my understanding of "how to find the time to grieve" has widened so into "how to find the time for joy" and created a chasm that I will forever be trying to figure out how to traverse safely.

Into the canyon has fallen so many important things: so many parts of my personality, my optimism (even if it was cynical). I know that I'm not intrinsically an angry person, or an unhappy person; the dark humor doesn't make me "unhappy." I know that I'm not really as tired as I feel, even though the Ehlers-Danlos syndrome does come with some fatigue. I hate that my mood shifts with money. I hate that I am joyful when I am not broke. I know that it is not a real thing, this money. But they have made it real and they have made it everything.

I wonder what my marriage would have been like if we had ever, ever had the time to really get to know each other without the crushing weight of capitalism. Not the stolen moments we spent being exhausted on a couch, or in bed together repeating how we knew we were supposed to be working, but it was okay, okay, okay. Just one day, we could take . . . just one day off and then we would have to suffer the aftermath of backup work. It was okay.

I think about what beautiful thoughts my brain has in there that are simply things I want to enjoy doing or making that don't need to be monetized. Things that just want to exist. And because I don't have a human child, I think about my cat a lot. Probably more than the disappointments I am afraid of inflicting on other humans, I am most afraid of not fulfilling the promises I have made to Littles. I am afraid of not providing him with a good-enough life while constantly working, because I am trying to provide him a good-enough life. But he doesn't understand that; he only understands that I am not playing, or petting, or loving on him. I really don't fear ageism or a long career journey. I have time. But my cat and I, the time is so very limited. The time is so very fucking short.

"Littles, Mom has to finish this one more thing, okay?" I try to at least look up from my work and make eye contact with Littles, who is walking around forlorn, doing the sad "meows" I know are cries of desiring enrichment in his apartment enclosure. "Also, same. Same, my love. I would also love enrichment and playtime in the enclosure and outside of it. I'm sorry, I'm sorry."

I have tried telling Littles things like, "It's late-stage capitalism and if I don't work then we don't have treats. Or a place to live, so you just gotta let me finish this." But he doesn't understand that, and honestly, neither do I. Because I could keep working this hard and we could still end up with zero treats and no fucking place to live. There is no assurance of this not happening.

When I remember not only this important fact but also that he is already eight years old, I save my work, close my computer so he doesn't hit a random key and log onto the dark web as he inevitably will, and I play with him for at least twenty minutes. I chase him around with his favorite game, "Chaaa." This is a game where I say "Chaaa" when I peek around a corner in a high-speed, hide-and-seek extravaganza chase. He loves this game. I grab his favorite piece of long plastic and I become an Olympic ribbon dancer, until I can tell that it is more of a performance he is watching than an interactive game we are playing together. I throw him gently from the coffee table to the couch—this is a game that goes for three rounds of throwing and then one round of heavy butt pats—listen, it's just what he's into. And sometimes he just wants to crawl up into my lap and cuddle with me until he decides that I am a stranger who is holding him against his will.

During my excellent credit phase, I was not as good at stopping work to play. And I suppose that's how my credit got excellent, but I also missed a good chunk of Littles's life. I would get frustrated with his clinginess. I considered very seriously that he might need a home with someone who could spend more time with him. I considered it very, very seriously. And yes, there are times now when I don't stop work to play enough. He doesn't really meow too much, but he looks sad, and it breaks my heart. I pour too much food and too many treats in a bowl, because that only takes a few moments, but it feels like I am doing *something*.

I know it's not a good replacement. *"Presence over presents."* Leave me alone. I will make sure there is always a throw, sheet, or hastily formed blanket fort on the couch next to me, because he likes to be close when I'm working. I stop to rub his ears, do a round of "kesses," or unwisely rub his belly, which he shouldn't be showin' all cloudlike and floofy to me if he doesn't want it touched. And the middle ground between long play and no play has become "Tube." Where I hope to be having a bonding moment by spending five minutes feeding him a weird tube of cat food that he loves so much and consumes in adorable licks. His eyes closed in Tube ecstasy. But it doesn't feel like enough in comparison to the lofty promises I have made him, year after year. The lofty promises of continuous joyful moments that I have still failed to provide as our time gets shorter with each passing day. My guilt mounts.

"And we're gonna go on outside adventures all the time. And when I get my next place, it's gonna have a *biiiig* outside that you can go to all by yourself, with flowers and sun . . . and butterflies and plants that are safe for you to chew . . ." I pause before adding the realistic safety measures. "And big huge brick walls with no spaces to escape under, or climb on, and you'll probably have to wear one of those hawk vests, because you are a fluffy white cloud with no survival instincts."

Littles slow-blinks at this story, and at this point in our lives together, I don't know if he believes me anymore or is just humoring both of us. Does he, like me, need to believe the fantasy to go on? For him, am I like the dream, the myth of a NYC rent-stabilized apartment? Are my stories the hope of closets in said apartment? I have told Littles of this "outside place" for six years and I really thought I'd have it by now.

I grieve my own ideas.

As a shared custody child, Littles has many of the "child of divorce" features, like alternate stay weeks. When he came for his stay at my tragic NYC loft, he asked for a tour. I happily obliged, knowing it wasn't what I had promised. I nervously followed and talked him through every space in the apartment. He would sniff, touch a wall, and then look up at me for the next move. I could feel the "yeah it's . . . real nice" reluctant vibe as he headbutted me and kissed me on the forehead when it was done. I could see the disappointment as he walked away and still looked around for more floors of the house, like back in Baltimore. For the garden with the flowers and chewable plants that I had said would be there. I tried to say, "Look, central air! In New York! I'm kind of winning, right?"

"It's nice, Dad, no. Really. You did a good job" is what his looks felt like. This "divorced dad, trying to make his bachelor pad nice for the kids' visit, who feeds them hot dogs for dinner" trope is not how I had planned this to be at all. I was supposed to be the rich mother with the garden! I had done everything I could to be the rich fucking mother with the garden and the joy. I had looked for a New York place that would have a little yard like the one I promised, but even with my "stable" jobs, my bathroom pep talk had been right. I was still NYC-poor, and those things were, still, unattainable.

And, by the time Littles had visited, I had gotten fired from one of those "very stable jobs." I was barely eating, and although the work-load of the now-gone job had been a thirty-two-hour-workday, big-corporation nightmare, I was back in nonstop creative hustle "make a thing, anything, and sell it" mode. That job has never-ending hours. In between panic attacks and monetizing my soul, I watched Littles look out the window onto the parking lot below and wondered if he was imagining playing outside like I used to do when I was little. Only, my mom had known better than to promise me some sort of garden. Maybe I shouldn't have mentioned a garden, but is that not what we're supposed to be doing? Especially at this age?

Providing things for our kids that our parents couldn't give us? Or providing things as adults for our older parents? I think about me promising my mom a garden for her later years, which she did want, and she wanted one in New York. I thought I could pull that shit off too! Nope. I know where all these failed, guilt, grieving, joy promises converge, and it doesn't make me want to fulfill them any less. I am combining the time I didn't have surrounding my mother's death and the time I do not have with Littles in the future. With human kids, there is a time restraint on childhood promises, but usually, you at least get a chance to attempt to make up for that later in life. I'm not saying it works, but the time exists, even if the children don't want the acts. Littles and I . . . we don't have that.

| | |

At my new Downtown Baltimore place, with its *almost* "city I know" sounds, I look around and see the best I could do at fulfilling some kind of life dream that brings me enough joy—no—a big enough shower to cry in. Maybe a place where I can spend time getting to know myself again.

I can take walks to the art museum and panic among the exhibits about the potential of pests, since I now have pest PTSD from my New York loft. That's a level of disappointment as well. I'm still not making enough money to not think about pests. The price of renting great houses has gone up in this city in the last four years, and I'm not sold on owning in America, nor am I interested in going through the process of the American Dream ever again. I am once more on the fringe of what is considered being "a real person" here. And I don't *want* to be a real person here, if that's what it all means, but I would like the option to refuse it instead of it being stamped upon me.

I don't know how many capitalisms I have to do to leave all of this behind. But I will do them. Because there is no outside, big walled garden for Littles yet. But I have a little bit of new hope—not hope for the terrible system—but for a medical advancement. There is a new shot for cats called the AIM injection. It prevents kidney disease and potentially can extend their life span by double. This is amazing news, but I am not using it as a crutch for certain joy. I haven't done enough research into the effects of this injection to selfishly want to keep my baby along for longer than he wants to be. I will keep working hard, but still take all the breaks I want to run around with him. Finding the time inside of no time and finding the joy that we have together in the now. And I do my best to reframe the reason for enduring, to be about that future garden. Even if it is, in truth, about the money. The money. The money.

In my remaining years,
I will NOT become the
thing I hate most.

15.

Old Baby

W e laughed about the fact that you looked like an adult baby." My husband chuckled to my frowned face. I did not return the chuckle. I'd just asked him what he and his friends had said about me when we first met. I sighed hard.

"No, not in a bad way!" He was trying to save it, but it was too late. "Your face—"

"No. No. I know. I get it. I look like an old baby." I stuck my lower lip out slightly and rolled over on the pillow, so he didn't see me look more like an old baby, by doing a thing a baby would do.

"No, no. A *big* baby. Not old . . . and, and cute! A pretty ba—none of this is going to sound good for either of us." He sighed, maybe crossed his arms and maybe made a face. Even if I couldn't see him, I knew his face would not look like an upset baby. He probably looked like a regular upset adult. That made me more upset. I wanted to look like that.

"All my life I've had to fight *and also look like a fucking baby!*"*

---

* In the movie *The Color Purple*, the character Miss Sofia delivers the line "All my life I had to fight" as part of an incredibly intense and complicated scene that

That is not a phrase that garners much sympathy, and it's also a weird way to finish the iconic fighting cry at the beginning of that sentence. Nonetheless, it is true. People tell you how cool it is to look so young, for so long, but it's not all cool. It's *weird* in so many ways. For one, it's hard to be sexy when you look like a baby. And if you do feel like you look sexy, you still look like a baby. Which makes it weird when someone thinks you look sexy. Now you know that they like a Sexy Baby. See?

Looking like a baby has never been cool for, say, putting on makeup and makeup-adjacent things in a manner prescribed for a non–baby face, and I'm not talking about R&B longtime impresario Baby Face. I have always wanted to look *not baby*, but it took a long time to figure out that I couldn't, say, contour my face in the same way that popular makeup tutorials suggest. For Baby Face reasons and for Round Face reasons. At first, I assumed that makeup artists would have far better skills than I, to successfully not have me out in the television or publication streets looking like a child beauty pageant star. But that turned out to be a terrible assumption.

"Whoa! What the fuck!"

A tour mate recoiled in abject horror as I entered the tour bus. I had tried to make it back on board earlier than everyone else, on account of my new face. I had planned to hide and attempt to rectify things. I had failed to do so.

I was returning from a daytime photo shoot for a popular magazine (from the time of physical magazines) in which the MUA had leaned *so* far into not understanding my baby face, that even she joined me in the performance of "Smilemmm"[*] upon completion of her horrors.

Given that I had performed a fifteen-minute Smilemmm at the photo shoot, I understood the reaction I was receiving on the bus. I looked like

---

is in no way about having a baby face. But it is a common and brilliant line to riff off when discussing far less important topics.

[*] **Smilemmm:** A smiling, nodding, and low "mmmm" offered as a response to someone's terrible execution of a paid service. People who regularly embrace confrontation may also perform Smilemmm, depending on the circumstances. Length of a Smilemmm performance is situational and may last anywhere from three seconds to twenty minutes

a contestant for Frankenstein's Child Beauty Pageant. There was the glitter lipstick and the circles of rouge, but it was the handfuls of individual eyelashes glued to my lids that made it all so bad. My small eyes felt so heavy. The weight of the burlesque-fan-size lashes felt maddening. I had cried hard on the way back from the photo shoot to the bus, making the lashes even heavier. By the time I'd arrived, I'd started thinking that maybe my face didn't look so bad after all, just different. I—

"That's. . . . whoa!"

My tour mate backed up, hands in the air as I stormed past him, trying not to blink back tears furiously. This caused the ginormous eyelashes to flutter so hard, it felt as if I would take flight right through the roof of the bus. "Squaaaaw," I would screech as my cry-blinking lifted me higher and higher into the sun until like Icarus's wings, the lashes would melt off and my lifeless body would plummet back down to Earth, smashing into the roof of the tour bus and crushing a bunch of people, which, take your wins where you can get 'em, I suppose.

That night, after the show, I climbed into my tiny top bunk and spent hours ripping each individual lash off my eyelids, with limited mobility, no mirror, and no assisting soothing products. Yes, it would have been nice to not do it this way, but this was an underground rap tour. There were no stops for products for the face. No makeup assistance. Of course there were stops for weed and white T-shirts, both of which I had no need for. Honestly, I would have accepted an old-school makeup remover like Albolene, or even Pond's! But there were no comforts for me. It was either face ripping or Child Pageanting it up for the rest of the tour run.

This incident was nineteen years ago and I remember thinking, "I won't always have this stupid baby face. Once I reach my thirties, I'll be able to wear adult makeup things. This will all go away," while squinting my aching eyes at the rising sun, peeping through my tiny bunk window. I wanted to look beautiful like other adult women. When would my adult face come? Is there a Disney song for this?

My thirties arrived and everyone else achieved Adult Face but me. Digital publications, until very recently, kept using pictures of me from twenty years prior. People in general assumed that I had not started my rap career in the mid-1990s and kept putting me on "up and coming" lists for a very long time. This was also the result of a wild number of other kinds of disrespect, but my baby face didn't help.

Baby Face gangs interactions with the world are different. People treat you like you don't know things or are always surprised when you *do* know things. Service in the world is different, because people act as if young people don't expect anything, so they don't have to treat you like—anything. When I have expected, or requested, a certain level of service, even if that service has been the most mediocre level of service, I have always received pushback, attitude, and rudeness. I have definitely had verbal battles and, at the worst times, physical altercations. Let's add my Blackness, combined with "questionable Black" to some people. It hasn't really been a fun ride. Speaking of rides: cab drivers. Cab drivers and ride share drivers have been the people I had physical altercations with. And it was always African men, or South Asian men, which makes me so sad and mad.

I don't know what having a Man Baby Face is like, but for those of us who are not men, y'all . . . men will talk to you crazier than their normal crazy. When it comes to men hitting on you, the fact that they think they are talking to someone much younger is immediately so gross, gross, gross. Now. I can see it as gross, NOW. I think about the fact that I "dated" men who were in THEIR THIRTIES when I was in my teens. AND I looked like the youngest of the damn teens. What the fuck?

Upsides to having a baby face? Well, the world values youth, so people being shocked at your age feels like a compliment sometimes. No one ever stops exclaiming, "*[Insert age here]!* Stop playing around! No, you're not!"

"Yeah. Yeah I am. I have ID." I was very used to whipping out ID and holding it in front of people's shocked faces. "See. I am old."

"Why do you have a passport?" they would ask, after their shock wore off.

"Oh, I'm not from here . . . but I am . . . but I'm . . . I don't drive. I'm from New York." I would choose the shortest way to end the conversation and toss New York in as a warning shot.

But sometimes I would forget my passport, or would have lost it somewhere in the world on tour. I have been denied entry to nightclubs, shows, bars, events in general. Once, I got denied from entering a Dave & Buster's. I was sad about that, since I had never even heard of Dave & Buster's, and playing games while getting drunk and eating a burger sounded fantastic. Hundreds of times at restaurants I have been considered underage and unable to order a drink. I've had to ask someone in my party to order alcohol for me and sneak-drink the drinks when the staff wasn't looking. I have been denied purchasing cigarettes, which is always frustrating, because what adult wants to stand outside a bodega, or anywhere cigarettes are sold, and ask another adult to buy cigarettes for them? No adult, that's who.

When I reached my early forties and Baby Face persisted, I began accepting that I was going to look like a baby forever. There I'd be, when they discovered my spectacular cadaver, facedown on the imported Moroccan tiles of my bathroom. My silk robe, pulled back to reveal one shoulder, ever so delicately. My hair fanned out, like heatwaving patterns over the cool floor. My half-finished martini, perched on the elaborately detailed double sink vanity. A scattering of pills falling out of my well-manicured hand. They would turn my dazzling corpse over and gasp, "But she looks so young! Like—like a *baby!*"

Confused and in awe, the EMT in the doorway would point to a small blue rectangular object, falling out of my pocket. "Wait. What's that? Check it out, Jerry."

Jerry would grab the object, my passport, already open to my picture page with my date of birth right there. "Stop playing around! No she's not *[insert age of death here]*!" He'd pause. "Oh, and isn't it nice that this fabulous robe has pockets? Sleeve's a little ripped, but look at those pockets!"

Sometime in early 2021, I had woken up and plodded down the hallway to the bathroom, ready to perform my morning face staring, as we were in The Great Face Staring Era of COVID lockdowns and quarantines.

What. Who. Who the fuck was that?

There I was, but there I wasn't. My face . . . it was lower, somehow. Heavier? My lips had a downturn that I hadn't seen before and . . .

what the . . . was that a jowl? Did I have a singular jowl? I'd never even thought the word *jowl* in reference to myself. What the hell was going on?

Right away, I thought that maybe I'd suffered a stroke during the night and not noticed, which is a thing that can happen. After a couple minutes of pushing and pulling my face around, a stroke felt like an unreasonable option for my facial tragedy. But where the fuck was my baby face? I kept staring, turning, and touching my loose skin. I remembered reading about "The Drop." "For sure," I thought as I pushed the bottom of my face back up where it used to be, "for sure this drop couldn't have happened to *me.*" As it's been described to me, The Drop is when you look in the mirror one day and your face . . . has fallen . . . down. Fallen down, as if you had slept standing up with a kettlebell attached to your cheeks. Agh!

I've always had pronounced nasolabial folds, but they were now seemingly eight hundred inches longer than they had been when I'd gone to sleep just hours ago. Why was my philtrum so much longer? This was absolutely not the adult face I had been wishing for. How did I just get here without getting angles and things . . . that old faces— *gaunt!* How had I skipped Mid-Tier-Age Gaunt Face! I was mad.

I was so mad, but I was also kind of prepared. I was just kind of prepared for the wrong parts of my face doing old things. I was prepared for the chance of being Old Baby Face. Crow's feet and eleven wrinkles. But no, I had gone straight to Old Baby Motherfucking Dad Face, and that was the worst possible scenario. To have to look at the face of my mortal enemy in the mirror every single day? To have that fuckin' Old Terrible Man's Face now be MY FACE? I thought briefly about punching the mirror, but it felt too much like what a man, *that man*, with this face would do, and I didn't want to encourage it.

"Fuck that!" I yelled as I jetted to the internet to compare pictures of my father's face and my new face to make sure I wasn't tripping. After an hour of comparisons and a lot of yelled obscenities, I confirmed that my The Drop had, indeed, created Old Baby *Dad* Face. "Well, fuck," I said to myself as I exited the bathroom. "That's not what we're not going to do. No thank you and put that shit in the trash. Put this face in the motherfucking trash!"

So in October 2021, I came to New York City for my first-ever round of facial fillers. I'd chosen a medical spa and had done months of research to find it, which I combined with my previous long-term research on "keeping up with surgical face and body technological advances." Again, I like knowledge.

When I walked in, I didn't know what to expect. Maybe older people, in reference to both the employees and the customers. Maybe they *were* old and the injections were just doing an amazing job? I couldn't tell. It just wasn't the vibe I had envisioned. It felt very . . . casual. A little too casual for my taste. I had talked and re-talked myself into what I knew at that point was the truth: people get this sort of thing done all the fucking time. It's casual. I mean, Botox parties have been a thing for decades. Fillers and injectables of all sorts are far more an everyday part of life than a huge population of the world wants to admit. I assure you, a large percentage of people you know and/or come in contact with every day are employing cosmetic injectable maintenance as part of their skin care.

You just think that they look "rested" or are (hate this one) "aging gracefully." What the fuck does that mean anyway, and why is that the aspiration? Not having any procedures done doesn't make you "graceful." I'll take this whole body off and put a whole new one on, if I need to, like a pod person. Mind your own business and wear your sunscreen, Susan.

I had decided on treating my nasolabial folds. They had always bothered me, even before The Drop, and my under-eye "tear trough" area, which had also been a long-standing concern. Both had increased and contributed immensely to Dad Look, along with the lengthening of my philtrum, a thing that happens with age, but not a thing that was treatable (well) with injectables. While lip filler could minimize my philtrum, I was leaning toward a very slight lip lift instead, and that's a whole other procedure that I decided to save for a few years down the line. I wanted to know how a nonpermanent procedure would feel first.

As I sat back in my chair and waited for my consultation to begin, my excitement mounted. I touched my under-eye hollows and wondered how I would feel tomorrow when they were gone. I had been imagining that feeling since I was a kid and other kids used to tell me I looked "tired."

"Tired of *you*," I had always thought about cleverly responding, but never did.

I'd been increasingly imagining the feeling of a face with untired eyes since The Drop. I could finally stop trying to cover them with concealer, because that shit had never worked, not ever. The additional joy that I held around imagining a far shorter makeup routine was so unbelievably freeing. I smiled at myself with happiness about being so close to a dream and then immediately stopped smiling, because smiling activated my jowls, and I could see them real fucking good under that medical spa upsell lighting. Fucking trash jowls.

I left the consultation feeling like it needed to be the next day, as fast as possible, or frankly, the day prior. I booked an appointment for both fillers *and* Botox. I had not even considered Botox! Other than my nasolabial folds, I had no lines or wrinkles at all. I do have my platysmal neck bands° that have always been there. I had asked my cosmetic injector if we could shoot those up, but she seemed against the idea, which was fine. First time caller, I'd be back. But the Botox wasn't a thing I had thought she would bring up.

"Well, you don't have any lines or crow's feet," she said, leaning into my face.

"Nope," I said.

"How about we take care of this orange peel texture on your chin." She titled her head and poked my chin with a soft finger. But her words, they were sharp.

"The what?" I responded with a hard *h*, offended.

She stared in the mirror in front of both of us to show me my "orange peel" chin, by asking me to purse my lips. My chin skin puckered into tiny holes, indeed creating what looked like the texture of the surface of an orange. Oh my god, what the fuck was that? How long had I been walking around with a citrus fruit on my face?

° Those fucking dark horizontal neck lines. Sometimes caused by age, or just genetics. Mine are genetic and have deepened with age. I detest them. *Je déteste!*

"Yes, get that out of there!" I said loudly.

"Okay." She nodded. "We're just going to use a small amount of Boto—"

"Yah, put it!" She didn't need to finish her sentence. Put it.

Besides the Botox, my injector advised that to get the results I wanted for both my tear trough area and my nasolabial fold area, cheek filler was the way to go. This was not my original request of putting filler directly into the areas I had named. I should have whipped out both pictures of childhood me with the same "problem areas" and then googled pictures of my father, pointing at his face and saying, "Do not want! Turn car around! Rerouting! Rerouting!"

My issue wasn't the vast loss of volume in my face she was assuming, but . . . I was kind of whatever'd at this point. I just wanted her to do *something*. I didn't feel like explaining that perhaps she was following a general treatment for a specific type of aging and beauty standard that was rooted in Eurocentricity. Besides, if this didn't work out, then worst-case scenario was that I would look weird for nine months. What was nine months in the grand scheme of things anyway, like three days? The pandemic had really fucked up my concept of time.

When I returned the next day, the procedures were quick, and honestly, I looked good. I looked "rested." I looked like me, a younger me . . . maybe a younger me from an evil dimension that only I would be able to discern as not me? I looked a lot less like my father, so . . . huzzah. I stared in the mirror when it was all done and low-level Smilemmm'd. I mean, it was *something*. And I couldn't really trust the instant results; I would have to wait for the fillers to settle.

After a couple of months, the fillers settled, sort of. I looked less like evil younger me. Much less emphasis on the Dad side of things, still huzzah. However, a singular jowl had kind of started to resurface, and I wanted to kill it. Since I had received only filler, not directly in my "problems" (minus the orange peel), it seemed reasonable to go *really* target the areas I had wanted to in the first place. But I didn't want to return to the young, trendy medical spa. I wanted one of those Upper East Side doctors' offices. I wanted a real doctor's office where the whole waiting room smelled like Xanax, barely used Birkins, and old women who wore Elizabeth Taylor's White Diamonds and might still say things like "that nice colored fellow" from time to time. And I don't mean "Coloured" like me.

In December 2021, I arrived back in NYC for my appointment with a pricey UES non-White doctor with thousands of glowing reviews on Google from women named things like "Margorie" and "Irma." He also had a ton of glowing reviews from non-White patients, which was more of a sell than the Birkin scent. Excitement. I wasn't concerned with being overfilled—a pillow-faced, fluffy appearance that could happen, especially going back-to-back with injectables—since I was requesting help in spots that hadn't been touched in the first round. This time, I decided I could just do a quick consultation and then go right into a same-day procedure. I was a real casual user of syringes now. Hmm, that doesn't sound right. Once in the chair, I told the doctor all of my spot requests and he said, "Yeah, we can do that."

"Oh!" I exclaimed at every affirmation, still unsure, so I pointed them out.

I pointed to my alar creases. They're the kind of "problem area" you can show to people and they will definitely say, "What are you talking about? Everyone has those." But when people draw me (I have seen many drawings of me) they always include super-deep alar creases, so I *know* it's a distinguishing feature. My dad has very notable alar creases. Also, when people draw witches, they always draw them with deep alar creases. Does this depiction always feel super racist? Yes, yes it does. I wasn't craving ethnicity-erasing procedures, just DAD ones. If my father had no alar creases, I'd probably ask a doctor to sketch some in. I poked one side of my nose hard and leaned in, asking again, "We fill these creases in?"

He shrugged. "Sure."

I sat up straight. "Oh!" I said again. "Okay, yeah let's do this!"

That day I got my tear troughs and my nasolabial folds filled. I got my alar creases filled. I went back to my hotel and stared at my face. I was very impressed. This was not like the results from before. I absolutely loved it. Ooh, that one jowl had disappeared! Gotcha bitch! When I got back to Baltimore, I stared at my face a lot, a lot, a lot. With happiness. Three weeks later, I frowned at my face in the mirror. I went downstairs to ask the man.

"Do I look crazy? Like, does my face look puffy and weird? 'Cause I *feel* like I look puffy and weird."

He assured me that I didn't look *that* puffy. Which I took to mean: "You look somewhat puffy."

I poked my face. "I think the new fillers are making the cheek fillers really pronounced. I knew I didn't need cheek fillers!" I felt like a moon drawing from the 1800s. So very round. He assured me once again that I didn't look *that* round. Which I took to mean: "You look somewhat rounder than usual, Moonie." Being upset about looking so round wouldn't last past January of 2022 though.

I stared at my face for the billionth time. "Where . . . where did it go?" I was looking for the fillers that I was very certain had been in my face and were supposed to be there for at *least* another six months. It had only been three months. What was going on? I had the insane thought that maybe I'd woken up in another timeline where I had never gotten any work done. I shook my head and leaned into the mirror, poking my face with confusion. Where . . . how . . . Much like the sudden appearance of The Drop, a sudden disappearance had taken place.

I called my UES doctor's office and left a very concerned message with the front desk. My doctor called me back shortly after and suggested that I come into the office, but taking another trip to New York wasn't something I really wanted to do. I was tired of going back and forth for apartment hunting, and my wallet was also very tired. He did offer me the fun factoid that sometimes, if a person's metabolism is too fast, their face . . . can eat . . . the fillers.

"Sorry, their face can what?" I breathed heavily into the phone. "Did you say . . . *eat* . . . the fillers?"

He had, in fact, said "eat the fillers."

While he could have used the word *absorb*, instead of *eat*, to make the situation less creepy, the bottom line was, yes, it was possible for people with higher metabolisms to have short filler-lasting times, as their bodies can break down the compounds in the injectables much faster. So, if a filler injection were to last, say, six to nine months for someone with an average metabolism, someone with a higher metabolism might be in the position of having to "get topped up" every three months.

Looks at you and Smilemmms.

Every three. Months.

Every three months, my body would nom nom nom any injectables right up. Every three months, if I wanted to stay Better Jean Baby Face and not be Old Baby Dad Face, I would have to pay thousands of dollars. I thought about the money. I thought about not wanting to put so much shit in my face. I thought about how jealous I was of everyone who uses cosmetic injectable maintenance regularly. My mind raced through acknowledgments of all the overrecommended dosing of medications I regularly had taken my whole life. I thought about generally processing everything really, really fast, and then I thought about the broken cocaine. These all had to be related somehow!

I have not returned to get fillers. Not because I don't want them, because I do. But it is, for me, an unsustainable option. A month ago, I brushed my hand past my chin, and instead of my fingers having a smooth journey, they got stuck on my jowl fold. I'm doing it right now. My hand is in the fold. It's in there real good.

You guys, as soon as my bank account involves face-lift money? I'm face-lifting so fucking hard. I'm face-lifting until my whole body is hovering two inches off the ground. Okay, I don't mean to stitch my ears together at the back of my head so you can bounce a quarter off of my newly tightened skin, I just mean to face-lift me *immediately*. Has the check not even clear—FACE-LIFT! It will clear when they have finished the procedure, and if it hasn't, good luck finding me. They'll be out there looking for a much older person who looks exactly like my father anyway. Ooh, maybe they'll try to make him pay for it. What a splendid and modern revenge that would be!

Anyway, I'm at a great age to get a face-lift. It's right around the time when *everyone* gets a face-lift. My lift of choice will be a mini face/neck jam. The whole lower half of Old Baby Dad Face and my neck? Snatch that shit right on up. Change my future, so I do not continue to be visually berated by my remaining shitty parent. Because the surgery goal is not to simply look young again. It's to be able to age into myself without the constant painful reference of a person I have never wanted to be associated with.

So while we're on the table, I'll also take a conservative lip lift—which does sound like a right-wing torture activity, but it's just a small lip lift to minimize the Father Philtrum. Phather Philtrum? What a lovely procedure. Give it to me! Render me an indistinguishable orphan!

Even all the men have been getting face-lifts, but probably not to look less like their fathers. Men usually lean into a softer more feminine visage as they age. Isn't that wild? We're all out here Uno reversing faces as the days grow long. Have I shared enough information with you about why I don't want this Old Dad Face? I don't believe I have. I will share with you now:

pulls my face skin open like curtains, but in a Terry Gilliam way, so it's not too creepy

Come on in!

He's a terrible person.

Seeing an aging terrible person's face on your own face, living your life every day, can truly suck. If my face became Charles Manson's face, it would be very distracting and I would not like it. But I have never met Charles Manson, and we share zero DNA. You may say, "Jean, that's a weird example. Charles Manson was a murderous maniac, with a lot of dangerous rhetoric. Your father can't be that terrible." And I will blankly stare at you for five minutes in silence, before saying, "There are some similarities."

I have come to terms with not having, or wanting, a relationship with That Man. As much as he may keep trying, my healthy boundaries were drawn a long time ago. Way before I was a teenager he shouted "I'm not your father" at me. To which I shouted back, "That's such a stupid thing to say! You don't think I also don't want that to be true? But look at my face!" I think that threw him off. I honestly think I've been throwing him off the whole time I've been alive. I don't fuck with That Man. Never have, never will. And by the way, as a teen my face wasn't as Dad Face as it is now, but there were warnings it would escalate.

I think that I have been very kind, overly kind, in my public non-mentioning of him. It took a lot of thinking and decision-making, waffling and some long cries, before I decided I was ready to share any of it with the world. Honestly, I thought he would have been dead years ago and had assumed that in my life plan of "memoir release timing" I'd be free to do this with no probsies. But, evil lives long for no reason. The good mostly die young, so here we are. I still have to see people posting photos of his new tours, and sometimes people put his face next to my aging face, and now it is also glaringly obvious to other people that we look so much alike. This is not a normal situation. We both have a sort of celebrity status, so consider that all of this isn't just happening in a normal "I hate my dad" personal vacuum. It is an international problem, as well as an internal problem. I do not want to hate my own reflection, because I am not a terrible person.

And not all gender nonconforming people want to look masc in the face-ies, or even necessarily androgynous. Just because my clothes might be gender neutral doesn't mean I want Old Man Face. And definitely not That Old Man's Face. Why is that face on my face? Get it off!

It's a funny thing about most daughters though. I recognize that I spent a lot of time as a daughter, and I need to explain this point in that way. We truly, truly tend to look exactly like our fathers. Somehow, in the cruel joke of the universe, we especially tend to look like the fathers who are terrible people. Triple that happenstance if you are a child who decided to rock with only your maternal side of the family.

Listen, I don't make the face rules. Thems are just the rules we all have to . . . face.

This past year, at my big age of almost forty-seven, my friend Jonathan Coulton had to buy cigarettes for me at a gas station after I was denied. The cashier asked to see my identification, and I was absolutely gobsmacked. It had been so long since anyone had asked for being-old proof. I had left my passport in the car and assumed I was long past that type of interaction.

"Sorry and thanks, man," I said as he handed me my illegal cigarettes. I threw my hands up in annoyance. But quietly, inside, I was elated. "Still got it," I said to myself as I lit my cigarette in the gas station. "Old Baby Dad Face still got it."

In my remaining years,
I have
SO MUCH FREE TIME
for SO MANY
REVENGE FANTASIES

16.

An Artist Creating Harmonious Balance

I am sitting in a thin gray robe, perched on the edge of a (very nice) surgery consultation room chair. I squint at myself in the large mirror directly across from me. Dammit. I have shaved my legs incredibly haphazardly. Again.

The lighting in this room really brings out the large patches of black hair on my legs. The lighting in this room really brings out everything I have never wanted to see on my entire body. It's actually the perfect lighting for a cosmetic surgery consultation room. I bet this lighting upsells so many surgeries people weren't even thinking about before they sat in here. I'm not here for a full head-and-face transplant, but I would now like to ask if that's a thing they can do. I swivel my legs around, shit. How do I have *more* hair than before I shaved? I had been as thorough as possible with the razor this morning. But I *do* have to take off my glasses in the shower, as the steam makes it impossible to see anything, so that's part of the problem. Why don't we have no-fog shower eyewear? Contact lenses? Is that what I'm supposed to wear during a shower shave? We need to talk about this as a community. I sigh and mourn my original Young Eyes yet again.

Oh god, it's really a lot of fucking hair. I lean forward farther in the chair and feel my boobs stickily detach from my chest. Oh, *right*. That's also definitely why I have leg hair patches. If you know how hard it is to shave in the shower while managing your jangly, dangling participles tits, then you feel me. Frustrating pendulums, swingin' around with wild abandon. They shamble about in the steam like giant leeches that have leaped out from a jungle mist and latched onto my torso. Darting every which way, purposefully obstructing my already shitty view as I attempt to hack through the thicket below. The steam is punctured with my sharp obscenities as I perform this amateur contortionist act on the worst stage imaginable. The swinging tits. The zero visibility. The search for an inch of space on the bathtub rim so that I might perch a leg and get at the right angles with the razor. A terrible performance of femininity for the world.

For what?

"Pete Davidson was invited to go to fucking *space* and, still, bathtubs don't have a leg shaving perch," I say out loud and wonder what would happen if my doctor walked in the room at that moment. "Stop letting men build and design things. Can we stop, please? As an Earth?"

Actually, it's an apropos thing to say to a plastic surgeon who specializes in breast reductions and augmentations. Very apropos. Did you know that many people awaken from breast reduction surgeries to find that they do not have the smaller-size breasts they very clearly requested and had agreed upon with their surgeons? This happens because some doctors decide *during* the procedure what size suits their patients best. They ignore their patients wishes, saying that they are not only doctors but also "artists creating a harmonious balance." The fuck? Balance for whom exactly? Whose song? As a person who has been researching breast reductions for decades, I had only discovered this fact within the month of my initial consultation. First, through reading online reviews of doctors and then when my own doctor said this to me. The fear of potentially waking up after surgery and still failing to match my physical body to the one in my mind after a damn near lifetime of visualizations and clearly communicated wishes? The fear was all-consuming.

Still alone in the room, I began to dig into some dazzling self-reproach. Annoyance at my own decision to play into the stupid fucking patriarchy yet again by having shaved my legs for a doctor's appointment. Why do I continue to do this? Why do I care? I reached under my armpit and touched my soft hair gently. A tiny nonpartici-pation trophy in the patriarchy games. I'm proud of myself for leaving it, but hate myself for even thinking that it is some sort of win. It's all so much to take off. I mean, the hair and the boobs, but also the systems. The colonialism. The White supremacy. The hygiene Olympics. The constructs and the expectations. I take a deep breath and remind myself that this is not an overnight journey and I am taking a very big step by being here. A very big fucking step. And that I have nothing against Pete Davidson. I've never met him. He seems fine. I hope that statement doesn't age badly.

| | |

Curaçao, January 2020.
I wore boob tape for the first time. If you're not familiar, boob tape is what it sounds like, special tape made to hold up your boobs so you don't have to wear a bra. I had bought two rolls of boob tape and spent a full hour trying to apply it correctly, wrangling all of my loose boobs together in a hot room.

I had nailed it, kinda. Well enough that the boobs were secured (huzzah!), and I was excited to put on my silk shirt, undone down to my belly button. The moment I walked outside into the night air, the breeze from the ocean passed all over my body. It swept up into my shirt and caressed my freed back. "Uhh," I whimpered in unexpected ecstasy, stopped in the middle of the road, and burst into tears. I must have felt that breeze on my back many times when I was a small child but I couldn't recall any of those memories. This state of being was so new. What was it? It took a second, and then I knew.

I cried out, "Is this what *freedom* feels like? There are people who feel like this all the time?" I whipped around to address my husband.

"Is this what you feel like all the time?" Astounded, I threw my arms wide. "Then what the fuck are men so angry about?"

That night for a few hours out at a small casino and around our vacation neighborhood, I walked taller than my normal walk. I laughed lighter and louder. I moved differently. I felt like the real me. If it had been daytime, I would have frolicked somewhere in some grass. I've never "frolicked" before. It has always been more of a "gliding scramble." By the time we returned to the house, the other vacationers were packing it up for the night. I forced myself to stay up longer in my freedom clothes, to enjoy my freedom feelings and so many thoughts I was having that were usually taken up by breast thoughts. When it was time for sleep, I discovered the price of my freedoms.

Per instructions for boob tape removal, I had soaked all of the tape (and my entire chest for good measure) with oil. I even left it on longer than the recommended time. But two hours later, in the middle of the night, I lay sobbing in the bed as most of the tape still clung to my skin. I was tired and frustrated with the tape. With the feelings. With my body.

For months, I had struggled to decide which tape to purchase, and now it seemed as if all that time researching had been spent in vain. Wasted time because of my body, yet again. Wasted thoughts, energy, and wasted optimism. I had taken my cup size, breast shape, tissue density, and weight into consideration before buying. There were brands I wanted to try, but none of them went above a DDD cup as a recommended workable size. Silicone adhesives only work well up to C cups. There was a new plunge, wired strapless contraption that looked painful, especially if you decided to bend over, or sit down, which were two things I was sure I'd be doing. There was waterproof wear and coloring to worry about. By the end, I had spent two months researching and run out of time. I purchased the tape that would arrive early enough for the trip *and* had no reviews of skin ripping (most tapes had skin-ripping one-star reviews). I was sure that I'd made the right decision.

During my attempts to remove the tape that night, I considered how many things I could have thought about instead of breasts. I could have written a half-hour sitcom pilot. I could have slept. Shit, I really wanted to go to sleep right then! Four hours later the tape was off, leaving huge welts and blisters, and taking with it a fair amount of flesh. I'd cried through the hours and then cried myself to sleep. It felt like an inordinate punishment for just a few, brief moments of freedom. I want to tell you that it wasn't worth it, but it was, it was, it *was*. It was worth every blister and every drop of blood. It was worth every piece of skin. Of course I would do it again, y'all. I did do it again. But *why* did I have to? Why do so many of us have to? Perhaps you've also let the tears fall as you begged the question: What have I done to be cursed with my body? I hated that I could only have fleeting freedoms, always followed by physical pain. Not just with the breasts, but also with so many things in my life. I was always so jealous of anyone with small breasts. I was even more annoyed with men. Why should they get *all* the freedoms? That wind I'd felt on my back, I needed it all the time. I couldn't ever go back. But man, oh man, I wanted the freedom of my thoughts even more. We should be able to have the freedom of our thoughts far more frequently than we do.

Before surgery, I was never not thinking about my breasts. Never not feeling the weight of them. Always having to choose what I wore every single day, what I could buy, with them at the helm of my decisions. All year-round clothes were bad, but the search for summer or vacation wear—a sundress, a top, a bikini—took more planning and research than any trip. I have cried in many a hotel bathroom, getting ready to sun or swim, and having to wear ill-fitting items, or be in pain trying to make myself look presentable. I had always dreamed about walking into a little tourist shop and being able to buy a bikini that would fit me. They don't sell those. They sell the ones for "acceptable-size women." The ones I would have to pull so tight around my neck until they cut through my skin and I had to pop painkillers for days after from the strain. What would it feel like to just breeze into those stores and grab one off the rack without a care? I had always wished to walk into a regular store and buy any dress or tank top that I wanted. What would it feel like to look at a spaghetti-strapped item and decide that I didn't want it, simply because I didn't like it?

I have always enviously (not creepily) watched small-breasted women in stores, flippantly handling clothes. Knowing they're not thinking: "What kind of bra do I have to wear under this? Where am I going to buy *that* and for *how much*? Ugh. I *can't* because there's not enough time to order one now." I have watched them and wondered if they knew they were so lucky in this respect. What would I do if I too could just casually BE? Without all the extra planning. What would it feel like if we all had that kind of freedom and access? How many of us cry in dressing rooms? See our reflections in those nightmare overhead lights and—boom—any confidence we had when we were pulling things off the racks shifts to self-hatred. In that little room, I'd wonder why I couldn't just look like *me*. Not the person I saw in the mirror. The *me* that only I could see.

For years, I very seriously thought about ditching my eight hundred other dreams and instead, making affordable, accessible bras and swimsuits that would fit all people in all situations. Because the people who are making bras and swimsuits fucking suck at their jobs. I still see *supermodels* in campaigns, or on the runway, wearing the wrong-size bra. Again, Pete Davidson, space invitation. Yet, ill-fitting bras? To take the onus off the wearers of bras, no one is telling y'all how to really size yourself correctly; every bra company is different, and all breasts are different. It would be awesome to know your size, shape, and then buy a bra that would correspond to those measurements at *any* store. AWESOME.

You wouldn't have to research the company or the reviews. You wouldn't have to try eighty bras, hating yourself and the world. You could do something else with your free time and your thoughts, like plot an elaborate, long-term revenge fantasy. Or, whatever.

Most people who wear bras don't even know that the gore on a bra is supposed to tack. That means, the entire middle of your bra (the gore) should lay flat (tacked) against the middle of your chest and your cups should have no spillage. If this is not happening, you are wearing the *wrong size bra*. You shouldn't have quad boob. They should be separate—and not equal—segregated boobs. That is a good joke, because if you know boobs, you know asymmetry. If you are a wearer of bras, I want you to go try on your favorite bra when you can with the information I have just told you. I guarantee that 98 percent of bra wearers reading this are wearing the wrong size. I was forty-one years old when I finally learned that our concept of how bra sizes work is all wrong and is—surprise!—the work of the fucking patriarchy.

"Whoa, lookit those big ole double Ds!" said a stupid man, and we listened.

Double D cups can be small, medium, and are not very large. They are far smaller than we've been led to believe. All breasts are different, depending on their shape, tissue, positioning, weight, frame, genetics, hormonal changes, band measurement, and *more.* Right now, at least five of my friends are wearing the wrong size bras. They are sticking to the DD cups they've donned since high school, and they were probably not DDs then either. We don't know these things, because women's breasts are only sexualized and not thought of as "regular things on your body that everyone should have the correct information about." It's not your fault, and also, who has the fucking time? Not me, but I spent time in order to make time.

"A G CUP? Who the fuck wears a fucking G cup?"

I stood with my tape measure in hand, yelling at my hundredth YouTube breast measurement instructional video. What the fuck. I had been wearing a 34DDD for decades, and here I was discovering that my real size was 32G, and a 32FF in UK sizing. Guess what? A G is a standard-size cup that many people SHOULD be wearing. And I won't start with the sister sizes, that's a whole other scam. Okay, great! I had solved a big part of the problem and could get to the solution by going to the store and—haha—do you know how hard it is to buy a smaller band/larger cup bra at a department store? It's impossible. None at plus-size stores either. You have to order specialty bras from specialty sites and specialty brands. These bras are expensive. They don't have to be, but they are. A week later, I knelt on the couch, looking out the front window of our apartment, eagerly awaiting the delivery of my G bra haul. Looking around like I was Pearl on the 1980s television sitcom *227.*

Whoa. I didn't even know bras could fit like that! Over the next few months, I bought *more* bras in my right size. I told strangers about the fantastic bra time I was having. But I still wanted those boobs gone.

The new bras were a temporary solution to not feeling fully insane, but I was still in pain. Still sad. Still thinking about my chest every second of every day. Still not free, or . . . me.

| | |

I am nine years old, shopping at Alice Underground, a "vintage" store, with my mother. We are looking for a dress for my school dance. I'm filled with excitement and nervous energy, nine-year-old shit. We sift through large bins of clothes and my hand falls on a bone-colored piece of tulle. I grab it and pull out the most perfect dress my nine-year-old eyes have ever seen. "It's perfect!" I gasp.

I hold it up to show my mom, victoriously grinning, and she smiles. I can't wait to get home and try it on. I can't wait! At home in my bathroom, with its vintage pink chipping tiles, I stare at the dress, hanging on the back of the door. It takes up so much space, and I like that about it. It's puffy, pretty, and perfect. I reach out and touch it gently, thinking, "I'm gonna look like Cyndi Lauper or Jody Watley. This is my dream dress!" So cool. I look at the strapless top above the tight satin waistband and I have concerns about putting my body into this dress. When I put on my leotard for dance classes, my chest doesn't look like any of my classmates' chests in their leotards. I don't understand why I look different, I just know that I hate it. I love dance, but I dread getting into my leotard and tights all the time. I focus on how I look compared to everyone else in all my classes more than I focus on the choreography. My stupid body. My pooch stomach, which none of the other girls have. So I have concerns about this dress, but I bite my lip and think, "It's so puffy. It will cover everything!" I'm excited to hide myself in this outfit.

I whip off my clothes, yank the dress off the hanger, and shimmy into it. My long bendy arms reach back to zip myself up. I stare at myself in the mirror, and tears form right away. The dress does not hide everything. It, in fact, accentuates all the things I hate the most about myself. My armpit fat folds and spills over the sides of the dress. The same fat that none of my friends have. The fat that my mom doesn't have. The fat I've never seen in magazines or on television. I am different and weird and I hate it so much. I can see the creases of my chest above the top, which make the dress look "bad." Why does my chest look droopy? Why! I try pulling it up, but there's no more extra room to do that. The waistband pulls in my tiny waist, but my pooch forms a roll that pushes the tulle out in a way that makes me so mad. Why do I have these things? Why can't I just be a normal girl! I am devastated and don't stay in the dress a minute longer. I rip it off, tears spilling down my face, and then, I quickly break the zipper on purpose.

"It's broken, I can't wear it. I guess I have to get another dress."

I'm standing in the living room and holding the stupid dress out at arm's length toward my mother. I don't want to be near it anymore, but it takes up so much space and seems to be everywhere. I wish it would just go away. My mother takes the dress from me and inspects the zipper. "Oh," she says softly. "I thought we checked this before we left the store."

"Yeah, but I guess we didn't or maybe we did and plus it's an old dress, so it could've just ripped in the bag on the way home, you know." I am rambling and doing badly at hiding the fact that I've been crying.

"I wish I could have seen you in it," she says, smiling gently. This statement prompts my tears, which I fight back as she looks at me. "It would have been so beautiful on you."

"Yeah." I am really holding the tears in tight now. "Yeah, well I guess that's too bad."

My new dress for the dance had a black top with a sweetheart neckline and puffy sleeves, a too-tight drop waist and a black-and-white polka-dot skirt. It didn't make me feel like Cyndi Lauper or Jody Watley. I don't know why I picked it. I must have just run out of steam. I was mean to myself when I wore it. I carried a small purse and held it in front of my stomach most of the night, but I forgot to when I was dancing and laughing with my friends. There were brief moments of freedom where I was just being a kid having a good time at a dance. I remember other moments where I stared at all the girls, wondering what it was like for them to not be thinking about their chests and stomachs and only having a good time. I wish I could go back and hug nine-year-old me. I would say, "Hey. Mostly everyone here is also thinking bad things about their bodies. So just be free now. You're gonna hate so many things about yourself well on into your forties, so don't waste it here."

I am in my forties, in my bathroom, holding my boobs up under my sleep tank top.

"Ugh." I turn to the side and sigh. "Ughhhh." If they could just . . . just sit up *here*.

I look at my reflection, my hiked tits in my hands. *And here.* I apply pressure and they flatten against my chest. "Ohhh." I sigh longingly. I look so much younger when they're up and small.

What a fantasy. I let go of them, and both my tits and face drop into utter disappointment. My reality body is fucking depressing. I lean forward until my head hits the medicine cabinet and I stay there for a while. I have been doing variations of this routine, multiple times a day, for over thirty years. Wishing. Dreaming.

I straighten up. I would have stayed in that position, but the weight of my chest is too much. I wonder if in the future, I could be sad and lean against a medicine cabinet boob-free. That would be so nice. I've also always dreamed of being sad in a tank top, sitting up in bed. My tank top would be so thin and have a really low scoop neck and very open armholes. I'd serve casual side boob. Ugh, under boob, side boob: forever dreams. I wouldn't have a pillow on my lap and jammed up against my torso to support my fucking chest, or anything! I'd just sit there, do no continuous readjusting and be . . . sad. Sad, small, and tight.

During my first visit and consultation with my plastic surgeon, my reasons for wanting a reduction came out like projectile word vomit. "For freedom and fashion," I'd said excitedly. "I wanna wear shirts with my whole sternum out. Shirts unbuttoned to my belly button and no bra! I wanna wear tuxedos with no shirt! And spaghetti straps! And camisoles and tube tops! If I ever wear a bra, I want it to be a choice. I want my back to feel the wind. Oh! Jump. I wanna jump. Oh, oh! Lean over, I wanna lean over . . . oh! When I lie down I don't want them to move. Yes. That's a big one. I wanna wear a tank top to bed and I want them to stay in the tank top the *whole time*. Oh and . . . I would really like it if while I was just sitting still, a thin strap could gently fall off my shoulder, you know what I mean? A top, or slip dress, or nightgown—any one of those straps. And I don't want it to fall off because I've *moved*, I want it to fall from *lack of movement* because nothing has to be strained. And then . . . and then . . ." I was breathing really hard, but this was important.

"And then . . . I'll gently scoop the strap back onto my shoulder and brush a tendril of hair behind my ear, but the hair and the strap will fall again and then I'll smile. You know that °*I make the motion*° you know that move? That's my dream. Yeah."

"Okay," my doctor said. "Okay?" I tilted my head and raised my eyebrows, skeptical. He then said the thing about him being "an artist and creating harmonious balance," and my heart dropped even lower than my boobs, which were currently just out in the open during this consultation. I looked past him and the nurse at the mirror. At my hated reflection, hair patches, and chest of sadness under those glaring lights, and swallowed hard to fight back the tears I could feel making their way out. "I really want to be a B cup so much. A small B, not a full B. Please."

"We'll do our best," he said, and I nodded. I didn't want to find a new doctor. It had taken so long to find this one. I knew that he could do what I wanted him to do, but I needed to make him understand the severity of my needs before I might wake up after all of this, still in a body that wasn't ever mine. "Please. I just wanna be free," I said, knowing that I needed to find better words to make this clear before it was too late.

The morning of my surgery, I stood, disrobed in front of my doctor, and he started to mark up my torso. The cold tip of the marker dragged against my skin as he composed his surgical road map. If I didn't say what I needed to say right now, this architect would continue drawing his blueprint for a slight revamp and not the gut renovation of the structure that I so desperately desired. If I wasn't brave enough to speak up, I would regret it forever. My heart was racing. I was nervous about the surgery in general, but I was more nervous about how my doctor would react to the new information I wanted to share. The information that was new to me as well. I thought about how this was Maryland and not fucking New York City, which, listen . . . I rightfully get more concerned about people's reactions to me the farther south in America I go. But then I thought, "I make pretty good decisions about reading people and I chose this guy partially because of that." BUT STILL . . . YOU NEVER KNOW. Fuck it. Fuck it. Fuck it. I took a short breath before saying what needed to be said.

"So. Umm. I know that I have said many times, about the fashion and freedom and wanting a more radical reduction, but I wanted to tell you another pretty big factor in this . . ."

||||

"You know," I paused. "If I were part of a younger generation, I would probably choose . . ." I paused again and looked out of the window. "No . . . I would say . . . that I was nonbinary. I would have said that." A lightbulb went off in the back of my head. I didn't even know that sentence could exist in me. I wasn't done.

I frowned. "I guess, no. I guess I don't have to be part of a younger generation to say that. I dunno why I would . . . I guess I could say that I might be nonbinary. That would be the closest thing." I couldn't fully claim it in the moment, or understand the right words for myself just yet. But I had said . . . a word.

I was at dinner with a friend in NYC and we had gotten past the obligatory What Is This Show: the pointing at, grabbing of loose skin, and yelling at our surprise new body droopings, like old people do when they hang out. Discussing our love of Margiela Tabi shoes before they became popular with the normies led us to talking about unconventional fashion and our own gender presentation. And that is when I had my lil' breakthrough. After I'd said those words, we talked about what it meant to finally have the right language for ourselves in our middle-aged years. Because even as New York City kids growing up in possibly the most gay, queer, trans, hippy-dippy ass environments in the *world* around us, some descriptors and self-identifications had just taken longer. Longer to be commonplace in the outside world and, for me, longer to take the other part of the world off my shoulders.

I had known I was bisexual since I was very young—four, or five—

which I have come to see better as probably pansexual? Honestly, who knows, and it's not of grave importance for me to put a name to it either. I grew up having friends who had same-sex parents. Two dads, two moms, a collage of partnerships, and again, I grew up in the notoriously gay neighborhood of Chelsea. In the Chelsea Hotel. I went to school in the West Village in the 1980s, down the block from the fucking Stonewall Inn. What I'm saying is, pursuing heteronormativity should not have been as pervasive an activity as it was for me. But I suppose it was all part of having immigrant parents of a certain age. Of assimilation with acceptable behavior in Black American culture. Definitely part of having a father who wanted his household to be Muslim. And my mother absolutely had gay friends, nonbinary friends, but still, *still*, I could not find the language for myself. I only knew that I did not fit in with groups of girls. Or boys. Or women. Or men. I chalked that up to a lot of things, none of which ever involved questioning my gender.

When I returned to Baltimore, I had the conversation with my husband, who was supportive and thought my new self-identification made sense. It was a very easy conversation. Even though at this point we were separated, we had come to a civil place. I told friends but kept adding the "that's what feels closest as a descriptor" part after saying "nonbinary." I went back to looking at pictures of child me. Oh. Oh my.

"That's a lot of button-down shirts." I stared at little me. "A laaaht of button-down shirts, with the sweaters." I know it's not just about the clothes we choose to wear, but it *was* a *lot* of button-down shirts with a *lot* of the sweaters. It was either that or big puffy dresses that took up so much space. Yep. Checks out. Like all the other parts of me, it made so much sense that gender-wise, I wouldn't be one thing. If every other aspect of my existence contained multitudes, why would I think that this would have been any different? It all felt very easy, right, and like the satisfaction many of us get when watching objects "just fit" into each other on social media clips.

| | |

I was only about thirty seconds into my nervous "nonbinary" speech when I noticed that my doctor was drawing far more marks and making adjustments. "We're gonna run out of markers at this point," he joked. I did not laugh. Not because it wasn't funny, but because he had responded so quickly, nonverbally, and I physically felt when it happened. It was wonderful, to establish safety in such a beautiful way. He did stop marking up to tell me that he was glad I had said something and that he understood.

He would absolutely take what I said into account, and while he wasn't yet well-versed in dealing with a lot of nonbinary people, he recently had one nonbinary patient and felt as if he would probably be seeing a lot more radical breast reductions in general. Did I know that this year a B cup was the most requested size from women? I did not, but I have watched the world change, and it made sense. He expressed his interest in learning more about people desiring different things and being open about themselves. Then we started talking about which chain restaurants had the best large salads as he continued his body drawings. This was the best possible scenario. Say a thing, have it understood, adjusted, and then some light casual banter about kale.

It was the first moment I had been calm in the year-plus preceding the surgery. That should be how everyone feels when getting care, but especially when getting gender-affirming care, which I had finally figured out is what I'd been trying to do all along. Without a doubt, I know that I would have gotten some "artist who creates harmonious balance for women" results if I hadn't said anything. I had wanted a reduction all my life, but if I'd scheduled one even a year prior, I wouldn't have known exactly *why* I had to have one. It wouldn't have been correct. And that shit right there is a fantastic explanation of what the whole of reaching middle age—as a Gen Xer with a very specific past and human form—has been like for me so far. Wondering why things took so long and then realizing that I didn't have the language, the framework, to comprehend it all until right now.

I'm witnessing this sort of epiphany happen for many of Xers. It's beautiful to both watch and be a part of. What an unexpected twist. A new kind of midlife crisis! Our parents gave us their hot metal playgrounds, with melting tar to land on, and told us to walk it off. And we did. That's probably the thing that not only scarred us the most but also made us resent authority so much. It absolutely thrills me to see so many people my age rediscover themselves several times. To open up and reject so many societal standards of the generations before us—not just in teenage rebellion, because we did that—but in being a different kind of "adult" in the here and now. Probably in being the adults we wished many of our parents could have been, for our sakes and theirs. Or even our grandparents.

I can't say with certainty that my grandmother desired to be anything other than her AFAB° identity—that would be wrong for me to do, and I can already imagine the protests of some family members, just bringing it up. I'm just saying that she wore a lot of button-down shirts. And pants. And smoked cigarettes in the streets, which was not acceptable for a woman in the 1930s. I'm just saying, my mom always said "you remind me so much of your grandmother," and now I raise my eyebrows and tilt my head at that memory. I'm just saying, I know it's not just about the clothes we choose to wear, but my grandmother did wear a *lot* of button-down shirts . . . in the face of danger. She stayed in them shirts and pants, boy. And I'm just saying that many of our ancestors might not have had the language, framework, or the freedom to even have a moment to begin comprehending it all. But we do. And it's a big fucking deal to not only have the access to the moment, but also to seize it. To find the joy in revealing ourselves.

The joy that I am finding in revealing more of myself *to myself*, like endless personal magic, it is *addictive*. What a fucking rush! What a fucking continuous high I am experiencing, all the time. Even better than my recovery morphine, which I had to take more of than other people . . . because I am me.

| | |

° Assigned female at birth.

I am in bed high as a kite on morphine. It is my second day postsurgery and my friend Nandi lies on the covers of my bed next to me, listening intently as I drug-cry out my feelings. Nandi is the first of four friends who would travel to Baltimore to help during my recovery. She got me to and from surgery, as I repeatedly said "make sure I don't die," which she absolutely did, for five days. That may sound dramatic, but this was my first major surgical procedure, and taking care of people post-surg is a lot of business. She was so on point with food, care, checking in, hanging out, and administering drugs correctly.

"Her body processes things very fast," she says, standing by my bedside, shaking the bottle of morphine at my friend Marianne, who has arrived to relieve Nandi of her duties. "So you have to make sure to give her the painkillers." She picks up another bottle. "An hour before it says to."

"Please." I am nodding, lying on my seventy-two pillows. "If I'm starting to feel anything, it's too late."

"And she likes to eat the pills like a horse," Nandi continues, and Marianne laughs. "What?"

"If you hold out your palm"—I am demonstrating—"I don't have to sit all the way up, so I can just kind of turn and"—I mash my lips around—"eat it out of your hand, like a horse."

Over the next two weeks, my friends came, stayed, and helped. We laughed, ate, and slept. They cleaned, took the trash out, and took me to my checkups. I did my absolute best not to lift or push anything over ten pounds (you're not supposed to), and this was difficult for me, the general not-doing of things. I was, at times, unsuccessful at "not doing things." This was most evident when my friends would say "stop doing things!" There were difficulties, unexpected issues, and a whole other book I could write about what people don't tell you involving getting a reduction. Including the roller coaster of feelings you'll have about your own body and the health care system. And I focused on all of that for a long time, but now I don't.

Now, I focus on how I would not have gotten through the whole process without community. A community that was so generous with their time and energy. They were open to hearing my many morphine rants about "finally being in the right body." I focus on the surgery being a brave thing to do amid so many other tumultuous life upheavals and that I didn't put it off until later. When things feel shitty, day to day—and of course they sometimes do—I remember that I am experiencing moments that were once only fantasies. I still get overwhelmed at all the access I have to clothes in stores. I'm not used to it yet, and sometimes I have to walk out, take some deep breaths, and circle back. I only recently bought and wore my first tube tops and bikinis that I only thought hard about, because I didn't believe they would ever fit me. They did. The shirts have been unbuttoned all the way down to my belly button. I have jumped and leaned and sat up in bed in a thin tank top, serving side boob, and been sad. And so many times, one thin strap has fallen off my shoulder from lack of movement. I have brushed a tendril of my hair back, only to have it fall again. I have placed my strap back on my shoulder, only to have it fall again and then I have smiled to myself softly. I have considered reaching out to my surgeon and thanking him for his work, not just the scalpel stuff—although that was great. I'm referring more to the balance I have felt in my body and mind since the surgery. One might describe it as being in harmony with your own being and—ohhhh. I see now. Well then. I guess he is truly an artist after all. But, ultimately the artist was me. A person finally ready to be brave out loud, in order to design their own life and create their own harmonious balance.

In my remaining years,
I will continue to search
for them
in all of the places.

17.

Janet, In My Remaining Years

He's thinking . . . this rich bitch!"

Janet leans into me and softly says this as the ticket agent who's been harassing me on our Northeast Regional Amtrak train stomps away down the aisle, again. I clutch my invisible pearls, lean into Janet, and we both giggle loudly. "He's got it out for you!" my new friend and seatmate says, touching my arm gently. "I know," I reply. "And every time he walks by I'm gonna hold up my phone to his fucking face." We both laugh as Janet says, "You're trouble, in a good way." I laugh haughtily, closemouthed, and we continue chatting away, our new bond only made stronger by the repeated interruptions of the agent.

On my Uber ride to Baltimore's Penn Station, about an hour prior to having this conversation, I had decided, in a very last-minute move, to switch my assigned seat on my train to New York City. No real reason, just a feeling. I'd opened my Amtrak app and chosen to move my seat one row back and to the right. My new seat didn't give me any more leg room, and I remained on the aisle. Truly, there was no apparent difference in my changed seating. I almost stopped myself from doing it, questioning myself briefly about what difference it could possibly make. But I decided to trust my feelings, however odd they felt in the moment, and clicked on 7a. If I hadn't chosen to move, I would never have had to argue with the ticket agent about their system not recognizing my seat shift, even if it said so on my phone. If I hadn't chosen to move, I wouldn't have had to repeatedly say that I was indeed where I was supposed to be. If I hadn't chosen to move, I would have never met Janet.

We were instant friends. I'd stood at my newly chosen seat just a short moment before Janet glanced up and our smiles met. She moved her bag off the seat, apologizing for taking up the space. Our conversation started so quickly and naturally, it felt like we had somehow been in the exchange for hours. Have you ever met someone like that? Where your banter flows so effortlessly, even in the silent moments? Janet and I talked from our first glance to my disembarking in New York, as I shouted back to her over my shoulder, on my way down the aisle, "We'll see each other again!" I have met people who I've connected with before, in the right places and at the right times, but none more serendipitous than Janet.

Janet was an adept conversationalist, and as we unraveled more of ourselves to each other, I found myself marveling at both her shared experiences and her deft communication maneuvers. "Shit," I thought to myself, after she would pose a question that opened another door for us to walk though. "Shit, I was talking about myself for too long and didn't return the volley." But I was able to slam the brakes on myself purging and express more curiosity about her life. And I was genuinely interested and fascinated. Because Janet is a fascinating woman. It was nice that I could feel the same sense of genuine fascination coming from her.

"You have some of the best original sentences I've ever heard," I told her, with excitement.

I could have said that in response to anything she said—but at the moment, she was describing living in a former Saudi diplomat's penthouse apartment in London in the 1980s. Janet had worked for Reuters for many years and lived in many places around the world. She had just finished telling me how they "removed" her car from the street, outside her fabulous apartment, along with all the other cars, when the diplomats came to town. "And the next morning they returned all the cars, like nothing had ever happened," she said. I was rapt.

It wasn't just the travel tales we shared. I was equally invested in talking about family and friends. Janet was on a long train trip back from a family funeral. By the time I had boarded the train, she was seven hours into her journey. When I would get off in New York City, she would continue on for several more hours to her destination. After her train trip, she would then ride another hour until she was home. "Sheesh, that's a long ride after something so emotional," I said. "I've never been on a train for that long." I thought about all the train jaunts I held in my future and immediately hoped I might find a fascinating person on those rides, but was sure that no one would be able to defeat Janet's intrinsic sparkle.

I told her about my impending divorce and that I was returning to New York City to finalize giving up my nightmare of an apartment. I told her about my past careers, current book writing, and future plans. We talked about my search for community and yearning for hosting night-long salons. I told her about my short- and long-term goal of moving to Paris, and we shared stories of times in both Paris and other loved regions of France. "I think you would do very well there. Really well. You can find what you're looking for," she said as I nodded.

She relayed stories of her experiences living in France and not only told me about her friends who had a wonderful place in the South of France but also that she would absolutely put me in touch with them. Our talk became more giggly and loose as we peeled back our layers and started tossing in more curse words. I asked about her family and the funeral, we began joking about what time in an event the drinkers turn to hard liquor and begin looking for a second location to go to. We talked and laughed and continued to ask each other questions as the hours passed.

About two hours in, I had been asking myself if I should address the fact that we'd been calling each other "women." I didn't know if that would disrupt our groove and change the connection of experiences, but I decided that if Janet and I were to continue being real, I'd have to be real. Expressing my identity to her was a wonderful moment, and it's something I had, at that point, not yet figured out how to do. I have since become far more comfortable with conveying my identity without so much fear, and Janet had a lot to do with that. This part of our dialogue opened up race, and I immediately unlocked my phone and handed Janet my 23andMe ancestry.

"Mmm, they must have given you a really hard time," Janet said, scrolling slowly through my list of Me and speaking softly to the screen without looking up. "Oh, they didn't like this, huh."

I wanted to cry, but instead just said, "Yeah. They didn't like it at all." She handed my phone back to me and we didn't need to have that conversation any longer, but she did regale me with a very old story about some ancestors and a boat with a shortage of alcohol that needed to make an emergency stop in Cape Town. I had wanted to hug Janet at least thirty times during our ride and I got the feeling that she had too, but we just kept expressing that we were so glad we had been seated next to each other and how dare the ticket agent try to keep us apart!

Janet and I never spoke of men, other than my one short sentence: "I'm in the middle of getting a divorce." We never spoke of children. We spoke of adventure and loss. Of joys and work and beautiful destinations. Of rainy days and learning new languages. And we never spoke of being parts of different generations, only stating our ages once. "I'm forty-six," I had said, in a portion of the conversation that didn't surround age. "I'm eighty," she had said, casually tossed into some surrounding fabulous account, also, not about age. We never focused on anything other than similar experiences and . . . well, my taunting of the ticket agent, because I kept my promise and held up my digital ticket every time he passed. She was getting a real kick out of that.

I reached out to Janet later that evening as I was making a very quick pit stop in my "fuck you" apartment before turning right back around and heading out of town the same day. As the heavy rain came down in sheets on the windows of the bus to Baltimore, making it almost impossible for us to see the highway, I texted her. Of course we had exchanged numbers. I told her how wonderful it had been to make her acquaintance, and that I hoped she had gotten home all right because the weather had turned so vicious.

She responded, and we talked briefly. I considered, in that moment, that the storm could lead to a horrible accident and, see, this is why I hated taking the bus, besides it being "the bus." I considered that I could die that evening on the highway, and truly, for the first time, I understood what it was like to have mortality salience with absolute peace.

| | |

My desire to control the narrative is also something I am finding (some, LOL) laxity and peace in. Not with people who desire to use a form of revisionist history on my or others' experiences and accomplishments, in attempts to free themselves from the accountability of their actions. Or, to diminish anyone's greatness. But in a more communal way, where I am learning to relinquish control over the narrative of how a day can operate in an intimate or platonic relationship. Or at a friendship gathering. Unless I'm hosting it myself, then leave me alone and let me give you a masterly time!

Beginning to release control in a community setting has been a fucking rough thing to do and I'm at the starting line, but I already feel a lot better. A lot of the journey has involved *screams* asking for help. I know . . . I know that many of us have been burned, stung, and let down when we have asked for any form of help in the past, and that can give us a damaging level of hyperindependence. That damage takes a very long time to work through—if you even get to the stage of acknowledging it and then being willing to do the work. Trust me, if just two years ago, Hyperindependence, The Company, had needed a brand ambassador, I would have been the best candidate on EARTH. At this time, I might still be in the top three choices of candidates, but I'm trying my best to not get hired. I'm showing up at the interview in a bathrobe and hoping the higher-ups don't view that as a positive trait.

Because here's the deal, we don't—we *can't* build real community only by helping others and not accepting any help ourselves. You're gonna need to ask for some—I'm throwing up in my mouth, it's still so hard to say—you're gonna have to ask for some help. *screams louder* Try again. Try asking better people. Don't give up. Don't give up on yourselves, and don't give up on who we could all be—together.

It can all be so exciting if we let it. The aging. The being in connection fully with the unknown. Being in connection with each other. Getting to have all these learned new thoughts. Just the other day I was wondering why I felt I was at the end of my rope when it came to renting apartments. Older, wiser inner me said, "It's because you don't want to live in anyone else's dream anymore." If I could have high-fived my inner monologue, I would have. I'm so tired of literally living in someone else's plans and dreams and then having to consult them about what I can do. And I'm not thinking about this in a way that I'm placing importance on "ownership." Or being all alone. Okay, like maybe a little Colonizers Reparations ownership would be fun, but that's a very specific thing.

I'm thinking about it in the way that I hear all my friends discussing that—maybe the dream is to collectively buy a plot of land for all of us. I don't think that has to be such a pipe dream. We should stop placing that desire in the land of imaginary futures. It can be real. I mean, I personally might want my lil' house to be a tad bit farther away from everyone else's—but yeah, I still wanna be down!

I'm unsure of how getting to this point exactly plays out, but I know what the first and potentially *first-and-a-half* steps are. I have some umbrella guidelines of an outline with possibilities. But I have no absolute plan, because that is impossible and unhealthy.

Whew, the importance of healthy community has by far been the most surprising revelation I have had in my middle-aged years. And maybe that sounds crazy to you, that I would only figure this out now, but I have been in fucked-up isolation all my life and looking in all the wrong places to find my people.

Locating your community is not about finding people who look like you. Or people who are the same age. You may not have had the same life experiences; it's actually so much better when you haven't. It's not about your church folk, or gender, or race. It's not about the foods you enjoy, or if you have five children. Your real communities don't just form because you live next door to each other, or went to elementary school together. It's not about your career path. It might not involve the person you're married to, or the friends you have from work. Because you can be in all of these groups that you are "supposed to" fit into, feel whole with, but instead, feel completely fucking alone. I thought of myself as a lone wolf who was not a team player for over forty years. And it is only since my midforties that I have come to terms with the fact that I was just a part of the wrong teams. The wrong communities, for so many reasons. I was in them because of things people assumed about me and things that I assumed about myself based on *motions wildly to the world* all this shit.

I struggled. I struggled to make myself fit where I should not have. I struggled in caring about doing said fitting. I stayed because people like to hold on to things even when they hate them. Worse, because they hate them. I knew I wasn't liked and stayed because that's where I had to be for some kind of survival, or for work. And sometimes I stayed because I thought I could push through their hatred of me and reach them? Or I convinced myself that it was my own self-doubt and irrationality creating false narratives of their hatred for me. No, y'all. Sometimes people just fucking hate you and they stick around for reasons that don't have to be your problem. You can leave. And again, not live in someone else's dream, or nightmare.

I really thought that I also did not fucking like people in general. Okay, hold on. I'm not saying that I now like *all* people. But I do like people who also know that *they* don't like *all* people and can say that shit out loud. Not in a "fuck the gays" kind of way. Not in a gossipy way. Not in an irrational or fear-based way. Not in a projecting-one's-inner-self-hatred-onto-others way. Not in a way that avoids confronting and owning one's own accountability in all situations. I like people who can critically think about why it is they hate people and, if needed, present a compelling PowerPoint on the subject with well-researched, completely fact-checked resources and generally with facts at the core of their hatred. I don't fuck with feelings based in hatred, but I do also fuck with intuitional slash pure fact (not rumor) based hatred real hard. Unbiased hatred for terrible people community, I am a part of you guys. Please call me. I'll tell you where the monsters live, and after that, it's up to you to decide if you want to join their communities in any way.

I am a unique entity in that I am able to be a part of so many communities and friendships that I enjoy so much. People from the outside looking at these friendships might consider some of them to be "weird" or "random." I and John Hodgman, my very good friend for over a decade, developed a friendship that some in the outside world, using their limited brains, might see as: "Look, how weird! Like Snoop Dogg and Martha Stewart, yuk yuk how weird." People who know us well know that our friendship makes so much fucking sense. And I know that we will be friends until the perishing time. John officiated my wedding. If John outlives me, he will be the person to read my eulogy. I have a top-three list of people for this job ('cause we're all old), but he's number one. I trust him with my life, and I know that if I asked why he hates someone, there is an incredibly valid reason for the hatred. One that he would happily demonstrate in a lengthy and overly well-prepared PowerPoint presentation, and with the addition of a live unbiased professional, to back up his reasonings.

We talk about things including our new, uncomfortable normals. About the fact that we cannot have ten martinis at a dinner the way we used to. We tried that, and it took four days for everyone to re-cover. But we are also just regular old friends who can make each other laugh, cry, and make nonhurtful snide comments in corners of rooms. Besides that, John and I have very easily opened the doors for each other and strolled over into new communities where we have both been so dearly seen, welcomed, accepted, and celebrated. Places we wouldn't have been, portions of life we wouldn't have lived, had we existed as people who were unwilling to be all of who they are, with accountability, and to ignore what the world says your community experience should be for the body you exist in.

And that is the only way that I would like to continue moving forward. Now if you'll excuse me, I have to go find one of my cheap-ass Amazon pairs of readers, because I have broken all of my expensive progressives glasses in various ways, which is fine, because I need a new prescription anyway. And if constantly having to update your eye-glass prescription every year so you can see things clearly is not the best metaphor to end this chapter with, I don't know what the fuck is. Today I'm trying to find Janet's old business card that she gave to me with her new number written in pen. I want to give her a call and just see what she's up to. I hope she hasn't died, I mean . . . she was eighty. Either way, I'm grateful that I met her and hope that it wasn't a one-way exchange of a community gift and only I gained something. But I don't think that's the truth. And I'm 100 percent sure that she would laugh at my "perhaps she has done a death joke." That's my kind of people.

After my remaining years,
I will still not trust
YOU
MOTHERFUCKERS.

18.

Don't Fuck Up My Funeral

And a good early evening to you all.

extended hand flourish

My wrists. Are very tight. And may sublux if not stretched and turned. That was not a benevolent gesture. Today's gathering will function as a test run for my services and life celebration, in the event of my passing. Perhaps some of you might say that my passing is indeed, inevitable; to you I say, "Oh?"

pause for staring at attendees until a relative level of discomfort is achieved

Over the years, technology will advance in many forms, and although you should already be aware that I do not wish for immortality, I am open to living on in some variation of a physical form, if and only if I have acquired an enemy that my continued existence would provide a great deal of uninterrupted discomfort to. I understand that from this present time, I will gather many more enemies along the road of life, but for my proposed Spite Living to achieve its highest spite, the enemy must be most formidable. So, we shall see if one is formed. In time. Moving on.

Many of you will not be in attendance at my actual services, and to that, I say *fabulous*.

pause for laughter

The reason for your absence may be the same as mine, that we are both dead. Many of you will be very dead, long before my services. In case you have not perished yet, your absence will be due to you being on a no-admittance list. A list that, I assure you, will be strictly enforced. I do urge that it would be extremely unwise to attempt any circumvention of my reasonable ordinance. While I would like to avoid any unnecessary violence at such a joyful commemoration, if needed, blood of the nonbelievers of the ordinance will, and must, be spilled.

pause for nervous laughter from crowd

Upon entrance, you've each received a memorial bulletin and have been asked to not open it as of yet. In case you've already begun disregarding my requests and breached the seal, your actions have been noted and the proper measures have been put in place to handle your inability to follow instructions. You will also not be receiving the gift I am so generously providing. But, for all others, please open your bulletins now—when you are supposed to—and enjoy the perk of your mindful behavior—

pause slightly

A brand-new car! *release of a single handheld confetti cannon*

pause

Kidding.

Your reward is simply this: GOOD JOB.

Moving on.

If you'll please read page one along with me.

That is the page aptly titled: "The Reason We Are Having This Gathering."

The Reason We Are Having This Gathering

1. Trust

Although there is only one item in this section, it is broken up into subsections. This has been done to avoid any misunderstandings, assumptions, or insertions of inaccurate emotional projections onto and surrounding my decisions and desires. You do not need to guess, ponder, pontificate, mull over, or suggest any other reasons as to why we are gathering, other than the ones I am painstakingly providing for you. This may seem to some a superfluous amount of information. I assure you, after extensive, exhausting dissections of my experience on this Earth, it is very much not. Very annoyingly and unfortunately, it is the exact and correct amount of information.

1A. There Will Be No Celebration of Theoretical Jean

Without the existence of this gathering, I hold no doubt that although someone would be celebrated at my final services, the person celebrated would not be me. I am not referring to some sort of 1980s switcheroo-corpse, hijinks movie plot, perhaps starring Jamie Lee Curtis as a hot dead mom, when I say this.

My life experience thus far has shown me that although I have been extremely diligent and open about my presentation to the outside world at all moments of existence and growth, this presentation has been completely disregarded, ignored, and abandoned. Instead, a celebration of a person who does not exist has been foisted upon my being. A more palatable and conforming sheath of an imaginary individual, constructed from the bowels of the patriarchy, colorism, and internalized misogyny, has been placed over my actual existence. Confusing, frustrating, annoying, and suffocating, it has been a great disappointment to both endure and to engage in. If indeed any celebration of theoretical Jean is detected at my grand finale, it will be seen that great harm is brought to the perpetrators who have chosen to do so.

I generously bestow upon you the gift of time between now and then, to be used for self-reflection and self-inquiry, on why it is you may have chosen to do this. To use an incredibly distinct human being as a base to create an individual who you can relate to. I am not indeed the being you have invented and never have been. I have never ever been the droid that you are looking for.

Side note: ten bonus points for identifying that reference, and points are redeemable at the bar for one cocktail!

1B. Religion Trumping Your Ability to Respect My Beliefs/Wishes

I did not realize that this would need to be stated until I experienced my mother's funeral services.

"Do not put me on display when I die," she said to me all her life. "I don't want anyone staring at me like that, I'm not even in there anymore. Just have some wine and play some music, some Stevie Wonder. Don't put me in a box where people stare at me. It doesn't have to be in a church or anything, I would just like a celebration. Put my ashes in the places I wanted to go and the places I love."

I stress that she voiced these requests many, many times. Somehow and beyond my control, there I was, standing outside of the space where my mother's body lay in an open casket. I did not enter the building and did my best to not catch a glimpse of her in that state. I smoked cigarettes feverishly outside and paced. But I did catch a glimpse. And that was the visual that both she and I never wanted. That visual has stayed with me.

Exactly what she requested *not* to happen in her services is what took place. I am aware that some members of my family are, indeed, reading this and present today. I remain vigilant in my feelings of being forever disappointed that no one respected her wishes. Her passing was sudden and without warning. Which shouldn't have any bearing on whether or not her wishes and requests were honored. She was not a Christian, she belonged to no organized religion, and would always state: "We are all stardust." Or, another personal favorite that she began to voice in her late fifties: "Fuck. I can fucking curse, because I'm spiritual."

My services are not about you. Not your beliefs. Not your ideas. Put them away, deep in your pockets, and do not reach for them. Respecting anyone else's life does not detract from your beliefs at all. If you indeed feel differently and know that you will not be able to control yourself, or your need to mention perhaps, Jesus, on the day of my great celebration, it would behoove you to alert one of the staff positioned around the event today, so that you may be removed from the memorial invitation list ahead of time and avoid any bodily harm that will most certainly be inflicted upon you on the day of the event.

Please, accept this not as a threat, but as a pledge to my commitment of values. My methodology may seem unscrupulous to you, and let me tell you right now, as I may only be able to tell you in whatever form of haunting is available to me in the future, I do not fucking care. Most people will refer to their wedding day as their "most important and special day," but I have had two weddings and can tell you, that statement is untrue. I have had and will have many more "most important and special days," including the day of my death jam, which out of all the special and important days, is the one that should be:

MOST ABOUT ME. All other ideas and suggestions may fuck off. *pause for another discomfort stare*

Fabulous! If you'll turn to the next page, we'll get started on the specific DO'S and DO FUCKING NOT'S of the event. I've positioned the DO FUCKING NOT'S first, in order for us to leave this space today with a positive outlook on the future. You may turn now.

Do Fucking Not

Under no circumstances will any of these activities listed in the following section be tolerated at my services. If a request for an exception, or substitution, is made, don't. If you are feeling unsure about whether or not my stance on these things will change, due to your limited understanding of the construct of time, I assure you, it will not.

1. No Beatboxing

No beatboxing will be allowed in any form, medium, or format. No live performances, recordings, holograms, thoughts of, or mentions of beatboxing will be tolerated or permitted. In death, as in life, I would not desire, or enjoy, beatboxing being enacted anywhere in my circumference of perception. The act of beatboxing has only been forced upon my being, on innumerable occasions. My trepidation around this rule being ignored necessitates the mandatory and immediate execution of anyone choosing to disregard its actuality. Security's response will be swift and fatal. It is for that reason that number two on this list is in place.

2. No Gum Chewing

Potentially indistinguishable from beatboxing, please refrain from utilizing gum, for your own safety.

3. Any Reference to My Existence as "FEMALE [insert anything here]"

As my request in life, for decades, to not be referred to in this manner continues to be disrespected, I have no faith in the ability of people to not extend this as a postmortem act of contempt. On chance that you may, at some point during the services, lose all sense of common decency and decorum due to consumption of alcohol and misgender me, do not worry, you will be less aware of your death in this state. Everyone wins!

4. No Children

This is an 18+ event only. Do not attempt to bring "babies," "infants," or "toddlers" thinking you have found a loophole. You have been made aware of the ramifications.

5. No Rap Music

No Other Songs of Any Genre Than Those That Have Been Selected By Me Shall Be Played/Sung/Performed/Re-created As Spoken Word/Presented In Disguise As Any Other Art Form (including interpretive dance)/Played On An Instrument/Performed Or Presented By A Robot/Projected Onto A Flat Surface In The Form Of Sheet Music/Handled In The Form Of Sheet Music/Mentioned In Passing, Or Mentioned As A Focused Point/Hummed/Shown As Picture/Translated To Binary Code, Wav Forms And Read By A Personal Or Otherwise Acquired Robot/Whispered/Tapped On A Surface/Worn On Clothing/Pinned On The Collar Of A Pet/Graffitied/No Requests/I Have It Covered Already I Promise You

This includes all songs performed, written, composed by me, which also includes any guest appearances I have made, composed for, written—nothing. Absolutely no rap music I have ever been involved with in any way, shape, or form. I do not care how much you wish to do this. You may feel free to listen to whatever you wish outside of my services. I do not mean "outside of my actual services on any sort of device that plays sounds." I do mean at another point in time. I expect that this section has somehow not been comprehensive enough. Somehow.

6. NO PHOTOS / SHARING OF PHOTOS OR CAPTURED MIND LINK MEMORIES / NO RECORDING OF ANY SORT / MIND LINK INCLUDED

Do not attempt to bring any technology, advanced, current, or past analog devices to the services to record your memories, or anyone else's memories of my services. Any device and person with said device will be detected and destroyed. Do not be concerned as of yet with the Mind Link, although you can postulate how the Mind Link operates.

7. NO PLUS ONES

YOU are on the list. All other beings, entities, and structures will be refused admittance.

All right! I trust at least a third of you have understood so far. Not a number I love, but one I expected. Moving on.

cue Walter Wanderly's "Summer Samba"

DO'S

1. HAVE A GOOD TIME! HARK BACK

I want you to have a good time! It is a memories celebration! It's right there in the name! Memorial!

Une célébration des souvenirs! For all of my French friends.

Remember all the shenanigans we shenanid once and shenanigand. Recall the adventures! *Rappelez-vous les aventures!* Hark back. Hark hard upon the *jouissance* we experienced when I was not a *carcasse*. Recollect the joie de vivre that I so many times probably screamed at you was of the "utmost importance!" Think of how much radiance and euphoria I exuded every time someone systemically problematic died. Reminisce on the text messages we shared around those passings. The many times when you asked me, "Did you talk about *[insert terrible dead person's name here]* yesterday, because they are dead." Killing people with my mind! The good times! *Les bons moments!*

2. DANCE!

Don't dance small and don't think about the cyborg security sharpshooters when you're dancing. They absolutely, probably will not recognize your dance movements as threats. So be free. Use the space.

3. CRY

I do not trust people who do not cry. A "reality housewife dry cry" will not be tolerated either. Dry cry exceptions are only granted to Mumm-ra. I will be very dead. *Je serai très mort.* I expect tears.

4. LOOK FABULOUS

I cannot stress the—

stop music

I cannot stress. The importance . . .

pause again for discomfort staring

It was of incredible consternation to me that at André Leon Talley's services—THE André Leon Talley—*everyone* in attendance did not show out. OUT. HARD. FIERCE. Everyone was not impossibly fashioned down to the fashion britches, and every single morsel of style that could be styled, was not styled. I thought I would tearfully watch attendees be ten feet tall, in unimaginably decadent caftans, draperies, hats, and gloves. In dresses, capes, and satin-bowed Blahniks. In trailing sheaths and billowing gowns. In the most dramatic homages and intentional, dazzling tributes, fit for such an icon's honoring. However, I am merely an outsider and had to consider that I was projecting my own desires and lack of trust onto someone else's experience and wishes.

As an André Leon Talley stan, I know how incredibly important details were to him. All of the details, right down to the very last bit. I understand this way of existing. I am also aware that he had spoken before about the gravity of making comprehensive notes for your own services. He spoke of handling his father's service and taking great care to ensure that he was buried in the finest of wears. Fabrics, styling, truly thoughtful and meticulous choices. But it wasn't just about the impeccable detail in choosing the clothing, down to the literal socks. It was the additional things, like choosing the right scent to fill the coffin and an additional new "fresh scent" that his father might enjoy on his journey. I felt extremely validated in reading and hearing about someone else's conscientious planning for a very special day.

I am today and will continue to be a very particular motherfucker. I like very particular things. I am a stickler for detail, subtlety, nuance, and can see both the large picture and the pieces that make it so. The many parts that make a whole. What I have found in fashion, style, in presentation, is the ability to present visions wholly. In it I am free. Expansive, immersive, full reference, and new ideas. These are the things I want you to think about when choosing the correct garb to wear to my victory service. I do understand that is mainly a term employed in the Christian church, but it will and must be, victorious.

It is mandatory that you wear things from the depths of your wildest imagination. Do not think about practicality. Do not stop yourself from being a fantastical being, even if it would sadly be for this one night only. Dreamgirls.

pause for acknowledgment of reference

You must feel like the most you that you have ever felt yourself you-ing, as long as you have been you, in your outfit for my services. If your outfit requires that you must be lowered from wires in the venue—the fashion commission will work with you to make that happen. Push. It. Further. Hats, eight feet tall. Capes and trains, two city blocks long. Four tuxedos as sleeves on a Victorian wedding gown that levitates in front of you. Burn it. Embellish it. Lights, motors. When you have done all those things, stop and think how can I be MORE ME. Think about the details. The fabric, the layering, the origin of the textiles. The patterns. Seams. Stitching. Hems, buttons, and lack thereof. What story are you telling the world? If you do not feel as if you have the ability to do any of these things, please let security know before you leave the space today. Superhero costumes are welcomed.

I will probably not bite the dead bullet for a long time. That means, you should begin thinking about your outfit . . . *now*. As mentioned before, there will be a fashion commission in place ready to approve all outfits before you are allowed to attend the glorious event. You will have one chance to readjust your choices and one week in which to fix your horrible mistake, before resubmitting to the commission. At that time, you will either be approved or denied entry as a final decision. One chance is very reasonable of me.

pause for unraveling of a second large white banner over the existing banner with VERY REASONABLE in black, bold font and an arrow that points down at my body

Very. Reasonable.

pause for a very deep centering breath with closed eyes

Calm. All right! Moving on to number five! Love this one!

5. Wear a Fabulous Scent

There will be Scent Sections at the service. But it is also mandatory that you choose something signature, or a new scent to wear. It is up to you what properties the scent holds. Whether a whisper, a shout, sex, or platonic understanding is what emanates. Bring it all. A sillage that creates a trail that brings all the boys to your yard and then kills them. A projection that turns every head when you enter the room, or one that patiently waits for the right person to desperately search for your bouquet. "Who is that? Who is wearing that?" is what I expect to hear from beyond the grave if that is how that works.

One of my favorite recurring living moments is always hearing, "Who is that? Who is wearing that?" I always know that the answer is: "me. It's me." Once, someone tried to say that it was them who was bewitching the space, to which I quickly laughed and said, "No it's not." It wasn't. Of course it wasn't.

You may also want to begin working on this scent plan . . . *now*. If you think that scent is not of the utmost importance, please raise your hand and I will strangle you directly after we are done reviewing the bulletin.

waits for hand raising

I will be creating a memory on all sensory levels in honor of *me*. Fragrant flashbacks are part of the fabric of life, as is death. I would be doing a great disservice to the . . . service, to not present a full, gorgeous tapestry. Perhaps, in whatever realm I have journeyed to, I will be able to create a new memory as well. Perhaps the sillage and projection of my being will contain the multitudes of you all from that day, for eternity. Or, perhaps it will just smell really good in the locale. Either of those things are

puts both thumbs up

All right.

That does it for the DO'S! Good times! Please turn the page.

This will be a curated speakers event, with preapproved speeches only. The speakers will be selected to the absolute best of my ability, by using my knowledge of their capacity to follow instructions. These selected speakers will be people who have demonstrated to me over time that they do not place their feelings before facts. However, I understand that we must always plan for worst-case scenarios. Not with dread and fear in our hearts, but rather with the comprehension of a vast array of possibilities that may occur. There is the possibility that the night prior to the event, a speaker may decide that their preapproved speech would be better cast aside and in its place, a collection of stanzas, pauses, an echoing of a last phrase. In that event, they will be killed.

And . . . please close your pages for now.

The Eulogy

One speaker will be chosen to read my eulogy. A eulogy that is written by me. There will be no changes made to this most wonderful of speeches. To maximize the accuracy of my eulogy, I have decided to make it available to you now. By the time my ever so rigorously mortised frame is laid to the first real rest I will have ever had, you will know this speech well. I give you full permission to enact violence on the speaker of this speech if they have malfunctioned and gone off script. What happens at my service stays at my service, and snitches will indeed receive many stitches.

I begin.

Jean was everything. I do not mean that in the sense that she was everything to me, whoever me is. Only, that both ancestrally in her literal DNA and through her infinitely curious and passionate journey through life, she truly became, everything. In the first half of her life, oh. It says to just put up on-screen, too much to read, very well. Show the screen! I will remain silent while you read.

Dancer. DJ. Rapper. Producer. Singer. Composer. Arranger. Audio engineer. Writer. Visual editor. Director. Cinematographer. Director. Lecturer. Teacher. Actor. Voice actor. Hair stylist. Minister. Wedding officiant. Puppeteer. Comedian. Pianist. Visual artist. Clothes designer. Stylist.

Is that . . . all right, retract the screen!

After all those things, Jean was far from done. She was . . . un . . . done. The second half of this glorious entity's life had so many more things in store for us all. Global adventurer. The greatest perfumer the world has ever known. Fifty-six star Michelin Chef Restauranteur, reminder that the fifty-six stars were all for the one and only year her restaurant was open. Famed hotelier and owner of the highest-rated and honored luxury hotels in the world. And all of those things were only in the year 2032. Amazing.

After her wildly successful interior design company, Evelyn Henry, had donated all of its earnings to ending world hunger—and succeeded—Jean took a ten-year sabbatical in which she did . . . nothing. Later on, Jean would describe this time of her life as "The Fuck Off" years. She called them her tenth coming-of-age, and it was during this era that she finally learned how to drive a car, since no one was driving cars on roads anymore, only using hovercrafts and teleportation devices. "Finally," she is famously quoted as saying, "no fucking people down here. Now can we work on getting rid of the men?"

In her later years, Jean's visionary films and hologram content broke not only human boundaries but also AI and specifically cyborg ones. As we all know, before becoming the first human to include cyborg actors in her works, Jean was the first human to join the ranks of the Cyborg Revolution. One will never forget her historic speech at the Grace Jones Memorial and ObSERVEatory Center, when Jean stepped out of her twenty-foot-tall mech suit and shouted to the gathered cyborgs, "I stand with you! They never thought I deserved rights either! We fight together!"

It would, of course, be silly to talk about Jean without mentioning her scientific work in the Cat Immortality Program. Yes, she was a psychologist, but her doctorate in Catiatry is what truly revolutionized the way that so many of us today have unlimited time with our healthy pets. "Let them make the choice when they wish to no longer be here," Jean said of immortal cats. "They are emotionally intelligent, even though they eat plastic. Are we not intelligent beings who eat McDonald's sometimes? When our small companions would like to leave this Earth, we honor their decisions." Her companion, Littles, chose to leave this mortal coil one hour after Jean. And today we shall honor him as well. There is small plastic to be had for everyone. Many people assumed that Jean would desire a human companion, a romantic counterpart to live out her fabulous years with. But she found her companion in all of us, in her passions, and also in one and a half martinis every day.

Jean lived a life based on intentionality. She danced all over life's face, and she didn't do it like no one was watching. She did it like everyone was watching and everyone "didn't get it." She said, "Do everything despite everything. Not for awards or accolades. Not for praise, or credit, or clout. Do it because there is life to be lived. Dances to be danced. Clothes to be fabulous in. Trains to travel on. Fabrics to touch. Wines to drink. Songs to be sung. Water to float in. Cats to be immortalized. Food to be savored. Robot wars and revolutions to fight."

She never feared death, but in her early years she did fear not being able to live enough life. Not in the Sylvia Plath way; she hated

Sylvia Plath, as we all should. Jean let go of all the expectations. She took all of the outside noise off and was finally free. She removed time. Space. And other people's fear. So know that when the transition revealed itself, she was not sad. She was excited for a new beginning. Another dance. Another chapter to add to her story. Before I step away, I must let you know that as per her request, Jean's remains were crushed into a fine powder and served to you in the canapés you enjoyed at the earlier brunch.

I leave you with Jean's last words for you all: "Being buried in a coffin doesn't make any sense. Where is my body supposed to go? Into the satin? Why? That's stupid. Make them eat me instead. Now I am inside of you. I am inside all of you."

Thank you.

cue Walter Wanderly's "Summer Samba"

Okay!

I feel as if we've covered a lot of very important ground. Do I feel as if I have provided the substantial documentation that would, without a single doubt, guarantee a triumphant occasion?

No! Of course not!

I would love to say that it has been a great pleasure to see you all today. I would love to.

But the truth is, I would rather be lying facedown, in a bikini, on a small boat bobbing in the waters off the Amalfi Coast. Filling out the squares of an Italian crossword puzzle in ink with random letters, because my Italian is not good. Villeggiatura. I would rather be doing that.

By the time of my demise, I will not have to do things like this gathering. I will have reclaimed my time. My time spent explaining myself to the outside world. Explaining ourselves robs us of greatness. It robs us of creativity. It robs us of fresh fish, wine, and large sun hats enjoyed at a small beach café.

It pilfers from us pieces of joy, of flesh, of existence and demands that we feed ourselves, bit by bit, to the ravenous monsters at the gates of fear. It robs us . . . of life.

I would hope that for all your sakes, you might take today as the moment to actually pay attention, when people tell you who they are. When they tell you who they aspire to be. And when they don't and are simply existing. It is a skill to understand people. To pick up on subtlety and nuances. It is a skill to not require teachable moments and explanations. You are a human being who can work on that skill, and it is actually not done by learning, but by unlearning. You are not monsters, or at least you do not have to be. You do not have to be shot by my cyborg sharpshooting friends, *smiles* but you can be. You definitely can and will be.

pause for silent thirty-second-long stare at audience

Okay! The king crab leg and one-and-a-half filthy martini reception will be in the TALK ABOUT IT space just adjacent to us. It has truly been an absolute fucking annoyance to have to do this.

Let's go, Death!

Roll Acknowledgments

Please imagine a credits crawl epic tune from a movie of your choice playing in the background for this portion of writing—feel free to play it for maximum pleasure and effect. Thanks so much.

The word "acknowledgment" has shitty letter structure, and the process of attempting to spell it is an adventure in self-doubt. All of the letters feel wrong when placed next to each other. Over and over, the red "error" lines appear on my screen as I repeatedly try to produce the word. Each time I get it wrong, a morsel of my self-confidence plummets off a cliff. "Why can't I do this? I'm great at spelling! How many letters are in this word, why am I still typing, it's been ten minutes! Did they change the spelling? I've been trying to do this all my life! ARRRRRGH!" The yelling doesn't make it better.

The process of spelling *that word* is kind of what making art is like. Not all the time, and not all art, but enough to make the correlation. I could say the same for all of us trying to "do a life," as well. And I could apply it to writing this book. Not all of it, but enough to, again, draw the comparison. And I am incredibly proud of myself for the red errors. In art, in doing a life, in this book. So—

HUGE congrats to me for being so fucking spectacular. For remaining living, vulnerable, kind, and curious. For not committing homicides. For choosing to be brave, while being scared. For dying a million deaths and living a million lives. For still loving my creativity and believing in myself, even if the world has not. For my boundaries and self-advocacy. For telling motherfuckers off and leaving dangerous places with no support. For pushing back against being called "crazy." For reclaiming my narrative. For never going quietly into the night. I cannot be stopped. Many have tried. All have failed.

All except my editor, the person who bravely has brought you this book—Nadxi. She succeeded in stopping this book from having so much shit in it. Listen, when you've had minimal large-scale opportunities that value your being, you try so hard to smash everything into the single chance available. To be finally seen, understood, and realized. Oh, the trauma. Nadxi gently (as gentle as a Gen X New Yorker can) reminded me that I didn't have to do that. She slapped the essays away while holding my intentionality high. I trusted her. I always will. She probably has a box cutter blade concealed under her tongue, so we should all trust her.

Thank you, Nadxi (Jelli) for coming to get me. Maybe this was the plan when we met at four years old, those nine thousand years ago. I know that Sathima is ecstatic about what we've made. She loved you, Dxiña, and Sylvia *so much*, and so do I. Thank you for your understanding, passionate advocacy, and fight. Your willingness to break in shoes, steam clothes, and open your home. Your many lives, skills, and similar anger about inefficiency. Understanding how design influences our lives and choices. I love Lu with all my heart. I am a better person as we are once again in each other's orbit. Thank you for making it safe to ask for help. Glubgrafutz.

To everyone at Flatiron and Macmillan, thank y'all so much. The genuine excitement from every team and the support employed in a joyous way are rare things for me to encounter in a business model. Most people in the "bringing dreams and imaginations to life" sectors of work should not be there. You're not those people, and that gives me hope.

Thank you to my agents, Kirby Kim and Hafizah Geter, at Janklow & Nesbit. Both brilliant, kind, and amazing. You made this first-time author feel as if I wasn't wearing an ill-fitting author costume. Thank you for being open to questions, ideas, and my meltdowns about taking "too long to write a book"; your continued ideas and apocalypse hypothetical chats. Big thanks to the whole Janklow & Nesbit team for their work, sincerity, and efficient communication.

Mindy Tucker—every time we work together is incredible, but this was an awakening. Thank you for always seeing me and allowing me to visually see myself. For your art, organization, and intentional flexibility. Again! Again! Again!

For my small circle of friends, thank you, I love you but—I tell y'all this *every day*, so get out of here. You are talented, generous, nerdy, and empathetic humans. For my frenemies, I am aware. *finger guns* Full enemies, I shall drink your milkshake eventually. I'm willing to Count of Monte Cristo this out. Thank you for all of the long-term revenge fantasies that provide me so much joy.

Reader, thank you for spending this time with me. Your time is a big deal! And I hope to see you and chat about so many passions. I hope to *see* you in general and I hope you see me too. That's all we really got. That's how we make this life great. And snacks, that is also how.

My monkey, my baba, libblelegs. Littles. Thank you for teaching me patience and love on a deeper level. And you also can't read this, so . . . I'll stop and say: it's you and me and CHAAAA. Forever.

Sathima. A genius. A supernova. You did so good, you did it, you know? I hope you know. I miss you more than words can contain. Thank you for sending all the songs and signs. The unexpected digital communications. This doesn't have to be long, because like you keep saying: I'll be seeing you. I'll be seeing you. I'll be seeing you.

All right. That's all of the acknowledgment- aknowled- acknolege- men *throws table*

Encore

Very Parisian accordion music plays in the background.
It has no determinable source.

"Quand j'étais jeune, j'étais pauvre. Maintenant, j'suis beaucoup moins pauvre—mais j'suis toujours pauvre à New York! Qu'est ce que la vie? Quoi?"° I said this to no one in particular while being proud of myself for employing the more fluent French speaker contraction of *"je suis"* and the even more Frenchy little filler of *"quoi"* in my sentences. I know I don't sound like a native French person, and I'm not trying to. Attempting to assimilate and blend in is now in my past-actions bag. And I use that bag for laundry on Friday evenings because it is very big and can fit both my clothes and Littles, who rides on the top of said bag, ruining all the work of doing laundry. Besides, trying to sound like a native speaker here is a futile effort. Since arriving in Paris a few months ago, I've done my best to not only speak French, but also to

---

° "When I was young, I was poor. Now, I am a lot less poor—but I am still New York poor. What is life?"

use the Verlan slang that is so popular here. Verlan involves inverting the existing syllables in a word to create a new word.

"*Cimer!*" I said, giving Verlan "thanks" to the Senegalese gentleman who lives in the apartment below mine. I'd just traded a carton of my (not sold in France) Parliament cigarettes for a thirty-pound jar of his homemade hazelnut spread. "Verlan is not for you, Jean," he had said with a sigh and the utter disappointment the French will use to destroy every ounce of confidence you have ever had. "You are too old. Even though . . ." His fingers, holding three cigarettes, drew a smoke ring around my face like a Disney channel intro from back in the day. "Even though the face is *vieux bébé* . . . old baby. Don't speak these young things." I nodded as I dug a whole bare palmful of delicious spread out of the large jar and jammed it in my mouth. "Wowwrewwd." I should have waited to deliver my old New York response of "word" before eating, but those hazelnuts are so damn good. I needed to figure out how to make my own hazelnut spread so I wouldn't get berated anymore! And maybe I needed to force people harder to keep speaking French with me instead of letting them win by switching to English. But that one waitress at the good steak frites place did try to call the police after I grabbed her mouth and tried to puppeteer her lips to form French words back to me. There had to be another way! Duolingo has zero advice for this dilemma.

Shaking my head and taking a sip of both my coffee and wine simultaneously, I mumbled, "*Ce foutu hibou. Bof.*"° I'm still mad that Duolingo owl keeps telling people on that cursed app that he "bought a bridge in Brooklyn for a thousand dollars." And I'm very unclear on whether he is a *hibou* or a *chouette*. A *hibou* is a male owl with egrets. A *chouette*, a female owl sans egrets. On the app, he claims to be male, but calls himself a *choue*. "Oh . . ." I stop my anger and smile. Okay, Duo. We're all on a lil' gender journey. Get it in. But that bridge story is still absolutely fucking ridiculous.

"Duo set *en voyage intérieur!*"

I yelled to the one sun ray piercing the everlasting French clouds,

---

° That damn owl!

as many bits of croissant sprayed from my mouth and fell onto the black, small gift-like box I held on my lap. The box's large, velvet fuchsia bow retained as much of the buttery flakes as my lightly dabbed in Perfect Red Parisian–style lipstick did. I could brush the pastry morsels away from both places, but that's something the old me would have done. The old me, with my less-Parisian mouth. The old me, who wouldn't have enjoyed being so carefree in this moment. The old me, who would have accidentally smeared this Perfect Daytime Red lipstick all over my hands. Then, inevitably, all over every single thing I touched for the rest of the day. New me would rather keep the mosaic of crumbs as a *souvenir*. The crumbs themselves, not the important kept things, but instead the memory created by my choice to keep them—the treasured item. The moment. In French, *se souvenir* is "to remember." It seems far more special and lovely to think that we move through our lives collecting nonphysical souvenirs, rather than using this beautiful word to describe a cheap trinket. Perhaps one that was bought in an overpriced store and kept on a key chain.

Well . . . I looked down at my key chain with all of its new foreign keys. With its little blue and white NYC coffee cup trinket that reads THANK YOU. The corner of the tiny replica cup is slightly chipped from the bus accident a week ago. I gently touched the corner of the chipped cup with my finger, noticing my equally as chipped oxblood nail polish, both things a nod to today's planned activities. Maybe some physical trinkets are lovely too. I had risked yet another daily chance of death by wandering back into the street to retrieve said trinket, which had unhooked from its clasp and fallen into the gutter. The gutter, filled with a thousand regretfully discarded polyester tourist berets, had cushioned its fall. Dashing to retrieve my souvenir, I narrowly avoided getting hit by an excessively "Paris" level of speeding bus. If you don't know, Parisians drive like they're Matt Damon being chased by high-level government operatives in any Matt Damon action movie. "*Merde*, Matt Damon!" My heart pounding, I screamed at the large vehicle that continued barreling down the street. The driver repeatedly honking the horn, which was, of course, the sound of a hundred Parisians saying "ouf."

As the "oufs" faded into the distance, I remained at the edge of the curb clasping my tiny piece of New York to my heart. My mother's dark words echoed in my head: "You could step out into the street and just . . . get hit by a bus . . . bus . . . bus." I only tempted the wheels of bus fate because I knew that it was not my time to die yet. My story could not possibly end with any involvement of bad fabrics, so I thanked the berets without using Verlan and trucked back up the hilly blocks of Montmartre to my eightieth-floor walk-up apartment. Yes, I tripped down (and up) the steps of my apartment building every single day, but my neighbors had begun tossing their cheese scraps into the hallways to cushion the blow. Like my trinket and nails, my knees were also now a little chipped . . . but in a cool French way, so I wasn't complaining.

"Peux-tu s'il te plâit éteindre la musique de l'accordéon!" I think these words are what the woman sitting at the next table over from me is screaming in my direction. I can hardly hear her over the smell of the trash cans we are sitting in, at this new conceptual sidewalk cafe. Café Poubelle translates to Trash Coffee. When I had asked the café owners why the need to clarify from every other sidewalk café—"They are all in the trash, no?"—they had gotten a little perturbed. Long story short, I'm not allowed to sit inside anymore. Ugh, this lady was still yelling. *"Quoi?"* I screamed back at the woman.

"La musique! La musique!" She was pretty angry. If the accordion music weren't so loud, I'd be able to hear her. I sighed and turned slightly to the cat backpack I was wearing. "Littles. *Arrêtez de jouer de l'accordéon une seconde, s'il vous plâit."* I couldn't see him, but I heard a small "maaah" of cat sadness after I said this. The accordion stopped. I hated asking him to stop playing, because it had taken months to order a custom-made, tiny accordion that could be managed by paws. And he really loved playing that thing!

"Quoi?" I turned back to the woman, who just shook her head at me and finished eating her three-foot-tall brioche. Well, I guess I'd never know what she'd been going on about. I continued to feel terrible about asking Littles to stop playing, so I climbed out of my trash can seat and geared up for our walk with its accompanying soundtrack, as we had planned it. "Here we go," I whispered to the small box as I tucked it under my arm. "Littles, play 'Someone to Watch over

Me,'" I said, slightly turning. A small "mow" of happiness and two minutes of trudging through the café's refuse and we were happily on our slapstick-esque downhill-ass way to the water.

During the walk, the air was warm and the pervasive smells continued to not make up what many people would describe as "a wonderful-smelling city." But that was kind of what felt like home to me, among some other things like "don't make eye contact on the metro." Pissy, trash-strewn streets. Diverse food smells wafting out from everywhere. The sweat of millions of people doing their best to live out their dreams. The electric energy of that combined life force definitely has a scent, and I don't love the smell it produces everywhere, in every town where it can happen. But I had visited Paris many times when I was younger—enough to know that it was New York's smelly sibling city.

"Don't romanticize Paris," people said to me. "Shut up. Everything comes with something," I'd said back. There are not many romanticized cities on the scale of the ones I adore and am very familiar with. I know what it means to embrace all the bullshit that is just out of frame in every pretty still photo, or edited video clip set to beautiful music featuring these cities. I know that everything cannot be "houh houh houh" while twirling a stranger's mustache and sipping wine atop the Eiffel Tower. The same way I know "concrete jungle wet dream to-mato," as a misheard Alicia Keys–sung lyric in the song "Empire State of Mind," is more realistic a description of my city than the actual lyrics. It is a concrete jungle. It is even more, a wet dream tomato. I still fucking love it. And I still fucking love Paris. And there is a sense of romance there that isn't the way people tend to think of "romance." I love the kind of love you can have for something, or someone, with-out having to falsely see everything as perfect. And I love being able to love something that I worked very hard to get to. It doesn't have to be everything I expected it to be. It can't. That shit is a losing game. Don't play it.

I'm very proud of the things I got through to make sure that I got here. To experience all of this. For myself emotionally and for the general global adventure I'm having as the sentient exclamation point of my lineage. Because what a fucking cool person, in a cool position, to end up being! For all the women I have come from who couldn't freely do all of these things. I don't feel beholden to live all of my life out so hard because of some responsibility that I have to right wrongs—but it would just be such a waste to not go all out at the end. Wouldn't it? It's me and then . . . nothing. So how could I possibly not live so big?

How could I possibly not embrace all of the—everything there is to offer. That is my form of romance.

Oh! I'm also very proud of Littles's ability to play jazz standards on his custom mini accordion—and he learns by ear! I also know that he and I both have to pee and we're not gonna pee on the sidewalk, even if this town's surrounding air does make you think that it's an acceptable activity. I walk a little faster and slightly slide down some more hills, keeping both Littles and the gift box from harm.

Standing at the edge of the water, Littles has switched his deft paws to playing "Lush Life." A song that we both agreed would be fitting for this moment. "Lush Life" is not a song that a small child would usually say is "their favorite." But I did. My mother's version of the song is the one I knew before hearing the iconic Johnny Hartman version. I love both of them, but my mother's holds a different kind of weight for me.

"You need to live some life in order to know how to sing it right and even then . . . might not be the right time yet," my mother had rightfully taught me about the tune when I was younger. This is not just a way she felt about singing it—every singer who tries to tackle it (if they're worth anything, and self-aware) knows that it's a fucking doozy. I performed it only once, in my midforties, when I had thought it was time. When I had thought I'd lived enough life to understand. As the songs says, "But ahh. I was wrong." Sometime into my fifties perhaps.

It's such a mind fuck that Billy Strayhorn began writing that song when he was just sixteen. Sixteen! It became a very predictive time machine for him, and it can have that time machine quality (forward or back) for anyone who takes on the task of performing it. It means something different for everyone, but I had always especially clung to that "a week in Paris would ease the bite of it" line. My mother had too. And then we had actually spent our respective weeks/months living it out in person and found it to be true in very different ways. I had thought my real adult feelings about Paris would be the same as hers when I grew older. And maybe they would have been, had I not been willing to be self-aware and accountable. If I had not been willing to let go and sing the song my own way. I am not a romantic in the same vein as my mother, and for a long time, I thought I needed to fix all of her unrequited hurts by attempting to relive them "correctly." But Paris, albeit the same goal city, does not hold the same goals for me as it did for her. The song I sing is my own, but I still honor my mother's love and brand of romance for it. And today, I also honor her wishes of being a part of this place in a different way. I honor letting her go.

I unwrap the ribbon from the box and I let the hot pink bow slip into the small breeze. I watch it sail away slowly, down the Seine. My mother loved fuchsia, and although it's not a color I wear myself, it was striking on her. Today especially, seeing this material swim through the waters—a bright spot in a dark place—feels so right for Sathima. As I take out but pause to open the smaller box inside, I think about this moment being one of a few stops in the letting-go process, and I am slightly scared about how I will feel in each of the locations. Paris. Cape Town. Santa Fe. Saint Helena. I will let go of her where she felt connected and where she held ties. Each time, will I feel more or less whole? There is only one way to find out what the hard thing feels like, and that's doing the hard thing.

I take a deep breath and open the small jewelry box that contains her remains and tilt it toward the water, just as a gust of wind from out of nowhere blows my mother mostly back into my very damp and sticky face. Some of her makes it into the Seine. Some. Standing very still, I think about every scene from a comedic movie or television show where this happens. I also hear Littles cough a tiny cough as he stops playing the song. I assume that my mother has gotten into his mouth as well. And I start laughing, thinking about how hilarious and dark my mother continues to be. "*Merde*," I say quietly, with her ashes stuck to my Perfect Red lipstick. "*Merde*, Mom," I whisper, giggling as I am finally realizing how to both let it all go and to hold myself together.

Appendix—Yes, Please. Thank You.

- Good combs: ethical bone/wood/cellulose acetate.
- Fancy international toothpastes. Who knew? Fancy toothbrushes.
- Old, sustainable goods: heavy utensils, heavy furniture, iron, wood, rugs, lighting, tiles, paint, fabrics.
- Build empire NBD.
- Well-worn-in leather bags / Note: add to ridiculous check-in names.
- Great travel luggage for international shit.
- Vintage shirts, loafers, reconstructing menswear, coats, sew more— build empire NBD.
- Studying scents/making my own scents/packaging-perfumer-build empire NBD.
- Great bars of soap. Great lotions and pure oils.
- Really good boxers (not the fighters, the briefs). Really good socks and hats.
- Doctor's appointments when nothing is wrong. TEETH WILL FALL OUT? How do I get a new back?
- Friend sleepovers/long friend time/dinners. FRIENDS IN GENERAL that I will not overthink my time and what I said around them/questioning confidentiality after a hang.
- Paying professionals to do things: my hair, cleaning, massages, Littles's grooming.

- Long periods off from whatever I am working on: balance, balance.
- Beach/ocean: without water and sun I am sad, sad, sad.
- Get on more boats. How do I find someone to sell me a secondhand Italian speedboat?
- Learn to drive an Italian speedboat. Okay, sigh. Maybe learn to drive a car MAYBE.
- Buy property somewhere foreign that makes me feel like I am LIVING.
- Second reduction down to A cup/lift more weights—these go together somehow.
- Sweaty dancing, classes/parties/whatever, this makes me feel alive.
- More research on face and neck snatching that celebrities won't tell us about. Can I make a new celebrity friend who will tell me??? Do I have a celebrity friend already who will tell me?
- Rest and laughter.
- Get Littles to stop flopping over in harness/he needs to learn! We have adventures to do!
- Continue to decolonize mind.
- Make more things without the pressure to monetize/pitch/rejection. Write shows again.
- Remember that I now have a one-and-a-half-drink maximum.
- Congratulate myself. Compliment myself. Continue to ask for help not just help others.
- Spread Mom's ashes, start in Paris.
- Find custom tricycle company.

Appendix—No Thank You

- Productivity guilt.
- Questioning/ignoring my intuition because it seems "unreasonable" to others.
- Being overly nice/positive when it is damaging to my own spirit and not saying "who the fuck are you talking to" or "NO" or "is there a reason you are doing this right now?"
- Caring if I am liked/relatable/making something beautiful to others/ if people "get it."
- Life lessons, fuck off, experiences fine. "Lessons" can suck my dick.
- Anxiety about unreasonable futures; reasonable ones that have been fact-checked are allowed but no anxiety surrounding them, only calm solution-based approaches.
- Trusting everything Duolingo says to do will make me sound like a fucking fool.
- STRUGGLE ANYTHING, taking a stand for others' struggles is good, you know what I mean.
- Staying in anything a second longer than I should
- Doubting my reasons for existing because of outside noise, ignorance.
- ALLOWING MY TRAUMA TO BE ANYONE ELSE'S PROGRESS.

- Taking my time to teach men how to be functioning/caring/responsible adult humans.
- Worrying if I'm "ugly."
- America.
- Being quiet about spending money on expensive things.
- Accepting less than what I say I deserve. THE STANDARD IS THE STANDARD like "the price is the price." Nothing more, nothing less. I dictate and set my own standards.
- Letting my feelings about my cellulite/body stop me from wearing shit.
- Calling my EDs "diets" or "detoxes." This is serious work, gotta start/stop somewhere.
- Smoking cigarettes, LOL just kidding. I can't raw dog the world without any vices shut up.
- America.
- Pretending I like and want to be around children (very few exceptions).
- Being silent about being seated in a shitty part of a restaurant.
- Chipotle online orders.
- If people have distanced themselves from me, obsessively wondering what I have done wrong.
- Spending time with people who enjoy gossip.
- Allowing misgendering, especially when it is being done on purpose.
- Letting Littles go longer than a month without getting a fucking haircut.
- Allowing weaponized incompetence to go unchecked/not called out.
- Stop opening things with teeth. Teeth will fall out!

About the Author

Jean Grae is a multidisciplinary artist, humorist, and former rapper with more than twenty-five years of experience in the entertainment industry. She's collaborated with influential musicians, including the Roots and Robert Glasper, and a selection of her musical work is featured at the National Museum of African American History and Culture. In 2019, the Public Theater commissioned her one-person show, *Jeanius*, which played for a limited time to sold-out audiences in New York City. She currently resides in Baltimore with her shared-custody cat, Littles. *In My Remaining Years* is her first book.